THE RIGHTS OF WAR AND PEACE

THE RIGHTS OF WAR AND PEACE

Political Thought and the International Order From Grotius to Kant

RICHARD TUCK

OXFORD
UNIVERSITY PRESS

OXFORD
UNIVERSITY PRESS

Great Clarendon Street, Oxford OX2 6DP

Oxford University Press is a department of the University of Oxford.
It furthers the University's objective of excellence in research, scholarship,
and education by publishing worldwide in

Oxford New York

Auckland Cape Town Dar es Salaam Hong Kong Karachi
Kuala Lumpur Madrid Melbourne Mexico City Nairobi
New Delhi Shanghai Taipei Toronto
With offices in
Argentina Austria Brazil Chile Czech Republic France Greece
Guatemala Hungary Italy Japan South Korea Poland Portugal
Singapore Switzerland Thailand Turkey Ukraine Vietnam

Published in the United States
by Oxford University Press Inc., New York

Reprinted 2009

ISBN 978-0-19-924814-8

Printed in the United Kingdom by
Lightning Source UK Ltd., Milton Keynes

PREFACE

This book is based on the Carlyle Lectures delivered at Oxford University in the Hilary Term 1991. I would like first of all to thank the Committee in charge of the Lectureship for conferring on me the great honour of an invitation to deliver the lectures, and individual members of the Committee—Larry Siedentop, William Thomas, and David Miller—for their hospitality and advice during my stay in Oxford. I would also like to thank the Warden and Fellows of Nuffield College for welcoming me into their society for the period of the lectures. While at Oxford I benefited immeasurably from associating with the wide range of people there who are interested in these topics, including Gerry Cohen, Adam Roberts, John Elliott, Geoffrey Holmes, Mark Philp, Oliver O'Donovan, the late Angus Macintyre, Andrew Hurrell, and the students who came to the seminar I gave after each lecture. Many other people, both in Cambridge and further afield, have given me help with drafting and rewriting the lectures: I should single out Jim Tully (who inspired a great deal of it), Istvan Hont, John Dunn, Emma Rothschild, Gareth Stedman Jones, Anthony Pagden, Pasquale Pasquino, Daniele Archibugi, Tim Hochstrasser, Peter Borschberg, Sir Robert Jennings, and James Crawford. There were six original lectures, and broadly speaking this book follows their structure, though I have split the introductory lecture into three parts—the Introduction and two long chapters dealing respectively with humanist and scholastic theories about war. I have also, of course, greatly enlarged each chapter, but I hope those readers who were present at the lectures will still recognize their general shape in this new guise.

I mounted the podium to give the first lecture in the Examination Schools on 15 January, the afternoon of the day that war was declared against Saddam Hussein for an act of aggression against Kuwait. This was the kind of war with which the writers covered in the lectures were eminently familiar, and its presence throughout the lecture course acted as a constant reminder that in this area, perhaps above all, the history of political thought is unfinished.

Richard Tuck
Cambridge, Mass.

CONTENTS

INTRODUCTION

As I said in the Preface, this book is based on the Carlyle Lectures which I delivered at Oxford University in the Hilary Term 1991. At the time I was also working on a book, published in 1993, in which I tried to set out a general account of the relationship between the modern, liberal political theories of the seventeenth century—the theories which rested on the concept of *natural rights*—and the humanist political theories of the previous century;[1] the Carlyle Lectures were another attempt to understand and characterize this relationship.

In one form or another, this question has played a central part in political philosophy and the history of political thought since at least the eighteenth century, for it is of course another aspect of the celebrated contrast, drawn most plainly by Constant, between the 'liberty of the ancients' and the 'liberty of the moderns'. It was obvious to many eighteenth- and nineteenth-century observers that there was a major difference between modern political thought and the political thought of the ancient city states. Modern politics rested on a notion of individual autonomy, and treated political and social relationships as the self-interested constructions of autonomous agents; their individuality was expressed in the language of rights, and the most characteristic modern regime (though not the only possible one) would be a broadly liberal arrangement, permitting the continued exercise of as extensive a set of individual rights as possible. Ancient politics lacked the idea of rights,[2] insisting instead on the power of the citizen body, acting collectively, to determine all aspects of people's lives. 'If this is what the ancients called liberty, they admitted as compatible with this collective

[1] This was *Philosophy and Government 1572–1651* (Cambridge University Press, 1993).

[2] An observation first made explicitly by Condorcet (*Oeuvres* VII (Paris 1847) pp 202–203), but implicit in the account of their own history offered by the modern natural lawyers—see my 'The "Modern" Theory of Natural Law', in *The Languages of Political Theory in Early-Modern Europe*, ed. Anthony Pagden (Cambridge University Press, 1987), 99–119.

freedom the complete subjection of the individual to the authority of the collectivity.'[3]

Eighteenth- or early nineteenth-century discussions of this contrast, on the whole, supposed that modernity in this sense is coterminous with modern commercial society, and was therefore a product of the seventeenth or eighteenth centuries; in this respect they followed the history of their own origins which was manufactured by the great natural rights theorists of the late seventeenth century, in which the entirety of human history before the early seventeenth century was seen as a kind of Dark Ages.[4] But by the end of the nineteenth century it had become commonplace for historians to insert into this story a theory about the medieval origins of modernity: the opposition to ancient values found (it was supposed) in both Christianity and Germanic tribal life was now seen as the basis for the later flowering of rights theories and of the rule of law in modern societies. At its subtlest, as for example in the hands of Gierke, this idea could accommodate an account of the Middle Ages as both the nursery of individuality *and* the bulwark of communities.

Political Thought when it is genuinely medieval starts from the Whole, but ascribes an intrinsic value to every Partial Whole down to and including the Individual. If it holds out one hand to Antique Thought when it sets the Whole before the Parts, and the other hand to the Modern Theories of Natural Law when it proclaims the intrinsic and aboriginal rights of the Individual, its peculiar characteristic is that it sees the Universe as one articulated Whole and every Being—whether a Joint-Being (Community) or a Single-Being—as both a Part and a Whole: a Part determined by the final cause of the Universe, and a Whole with a final cause of its own.[5]

A corollary of this view was that (as Constant may also have supposed) the Renaissance was seen as in some crucial respects *anti-modern*. As Gierke (again) said.

in the fifteenth century Humanism broke with even the forms of the Middle Age and in its desire to restore the purely classical, seemed for a while to be threatening those medieval elements without the retention of which the Modern World could not have been what it is. The drift towards Antiquity

[3] Benjamin Constant, *Political Writings* ed. Biancamaria Fontana (Cambridge University Press, 1988) 311.

[4] See my 'The "Modern" Theory of Natural Law'.

[5] Otto Gierke, *Political Theories of the Middle Age*, trans. F. W. Maitland (Cambridge University Press, 1900), 7.

pure and undefiled, whether it takes with Aeneas Sylvius the turn to absolutism or with Patricius of Siena the turn to republicanism, did as a matter of fact wholly repulse for a season the Germanic notions of State and Law.[6]

Something like the same thought is found in Friedrich Meinecke's famous book on the idea of reason of state.[7] For Meinecke, Machiavelli was the key Renaissance figure, for he developed an ancient notion of reason of state, putting it into a modern and ambiguous garb. This anti-legalist and anti-moralist view of politics was then sharply contrasted with the modern natural law tradition which (like Gierke) Meinecke saw as continuing an essentially medieval outlook. Writing about the seventeenth-century rights theorists, Meinecke observed that

> The remarkable fact is that only one of them, the German Pufendorf, directly accepted the doctrines of *raison d'état* and State interest[8] . . . Grotius, Hobbes and Spinoza on the other hand did not make a direct use of the doctrines, but rather built their theories of the State on the traditional foundation of Natural Law, which they developed along their own lines.[9]

And Meinecke elaborated a general account of Western history in which natural law and reason of state had been in constant tension with one another, sometimes (as in the early seventeenth century) reason of state dominating, sometimes (as in the eighteenth century) natural law.[10] The Terror represented the victory of naked reason of state, and in reaction to it (this being a familiar piece of historiography) Hegel constructed a synthesis of the two principles. This synthesis itself fell apart in the twentieth century, leaving naked reason of state once again triumphant; though Meinecke conjectured—naively, given the moment at which he was writing—that some new kind of synthesis was imminent.[11]

This late nineteenth-century model, in which the profound antagonism in Western history is between antiquity and natural law, and in

[6] Ibid. 5–6.

[7] *Die Idee der Staatsräson in der neueren Geschicte* (1924), trans. Douglas Scott as *Machiavellism*, ed. W. Stark (London, 1957).

[8] Meinecke had in mind, as his ch. 9 makes clear, Pufendorf in his capacity as author of historical and polemical works, not as author of the *De Iure Naturae et Gentium*. 'His great *Jus naturae et gentium* of 1672 remained firmly fixed within the bounds of the method of natural law, and was incapable of using the insights into the individual interests of States (possessed by Pufendorf in his role of politician) in order to attain a broader insight into the individual and historically peculiar aspect of the separate State-forms' (p. 230).

[9] *Machiavellism*, p. 208.

[10] See his remarks on p. 346.

[11] See the last three pages of the book.

which the Renaissance is seen as the moment in which the antagonism was opened up in its starkest form, has (in one form or another) found its way into many works on the history of political thought produced in the twentieth century. It is there in Ernest Barker's use of Gierke; it is hinted at in various passages in Quentin Skinner's *The Foundations of Modern Political Thought*,[12] and I myself produced a book twenty years ago in which I set out a similar story.[13] There have been few writers in our century who have not presupposed a model of broadly this kind; among those who have not, the most interesting, it should be said, was Leo Strauss.

In his *Natural Right and History* (1953), Strauss (in his chapter on 'Modern Natural Right') told a very different story, in which the modern natural law writers such as Hobbes and Locke in fact subverted the old tradition of natural law: Hobbes 'transplanted natural law on the plane of Machiavelli' and the modern school of natural law was profoundly opposed to the moral vision of politics found in the original school of natural law.[14] Strauss even recognized that Rousseau and Kant, who might seem to be the great critics of a Machiavellian or Hobbesian attitude to politics, were at best highly ambiguous in their criticism.[15] This historical insight must have appeared very disturbing to Strauss himself, for it must have seemed to undermine what had

[12] See, e.g., the discussion of the concept of the state in the Conclusion (II. 349–58), in which it is seen as broadly the product of a kind of late medieval 'humanism'—the ultimate consequence of the repudiation of (among other things) Augustinian theology by thirteenth- and fourteenth-century writers. The heroes of this story are a rather different set from the heroes of the story of 'modern natural-law theory', which Skinner ties explicitly to the revival of Thomism in the sixteenth century (II, 135), and which includes the principal anti-Machiavellians of the period. Of course, it is a subtle and complex narrative, and (as was also recognized by the nineteenth-century writers) it appreciates that the coming of humanism changed natural law theory for ever; but something of the familiar dichotomy remains under the surface of Skinner's account. It also comes out more plainly in his later works on republicanism, in which a humanist republicanism is sharply contrasted with modern liberalism, to the latter's discredit: 'To insist on rights as trumps . . . is simply to proclaim our corruption as citizens. It is also to embrace a self- destructive form of irrationality. Rather we must take our duties seriously, and instead of trying to evade anything more than "the minimum demands of social life" we must seek to discharge our public obligations as wholeheartedly as possible . . .' ('The Republican Ideal of Political Liberty', in *Machiavelli and Republicanism*, ed. Gisela Bock, Quentin Skinner, and Maurizio Viroli (Cambridge University Press, 1990), 308).

[13] *Natural Rights Theories: Their Origin and Development* (Cambridge University Press, 1979). What I argued there was that rights theories are a product of the very late Middle Ages, and particularly of the anti-Thomist writers such as Ockham and Gerson; they fell out of use in the Renaissance, but were recovered in a fairly pure form by the seventeenth-century authors from Grotius onwards.

[14] *Natural Right and History* (University of Chicago Press, 1953), 182.

[15] See e.g. his remarks on p. 279.

been seen traditionally as the principal modern defence against reason of state (and Strauss had particular reasons for being alarmed by this possibility, faced as he was in his youth by the naked immoralism of the Nazis and the equally naked advocacy of a politics of struggle and domination in the writings of Carl Schmitt). It was no doubt because he felt that he could not appeal to the conventional representatives of modern moral politics such as Locke or Kant that Strauss's own moral prescriptions came to put on their notoriously strange character, and he came to put his faith in a covert and highly implausible history of natural right doctrine from antiquity to the present day. His views on ancient political thought have rightly received a great deal of criticism;[16] but I am bound to say that his views on early modern political thought seem to me to have been extremely penetrating.

Indeed, it was a rather similar idea which I began to explore during my work on *Philosophy and Government*. I began to think that the argument of *Natural Rights Theories* was wrong, and that in fact the 'modern' school of natural law arose not out of a critique or repudiation of the Renaissance, but out of a profound sympathy with some of the fundamental themes of Renaissance political and moral thought. In particular, I came to believe that the most striking and obvious feature of the modern school, its drive for a radically simplified and 'minimalist' universal morality, was derived from the humanist scepticism of the late sixteenth century. Sceptics such as Montaigne or Charron were not simply putting forward an epistemological argument; like their predecessors in antiquity, their scepticism was part of a *moral* argument. What they believed was that the 'wise man' (a constant point of reference in their writings) would preserve himself best from the dangers of life by cultivating a sceptical detachment from all contestable beliefs; by doing so, he would avoid the hazards of a commitment to such things as patriotism or sectarian loyalty. They thus associated scepticism with the principle of self-preservation, and it is clear that the seventeenth-century theorists did likewise. For Grotius, Hobbes, and their followers, self-preservation was a paramount principle, and the basis for whatever universal morality there was—for, they believed, no society could be found or imagined in which people were denied the moral right to preserve themselves. Compared with this principle, all other

[16] See Myles Burnyeat, review of Strauss, *Studies in Platonic Political Philosophy*, in *New York Review of Books*, 30 May 1985. But see also Catharine Zuckert, *Postmodern Platos* (University of Chicago Press, 1996) for a more sympathetic account.

traditional moral principles were plainly local and contentious, and were fit targets for scepticism.

But a commitment to the paramountcy of self-preservation also underpinned the doctrines of *raison d'état*, promulgated (often) by the same people who expressed sympathy with the programme of the sceptics, such as Justus Lipsius. *Raison d'état* codified the techniques by which a prince (usually, though there are republican versions of it) could preserve his state, dismissing all other moral and constitutional considerations. By preserving his state, the prince preserved himself; but (seen as an agent or representative of his citizens) he was also the means to the preservation of the citizens from the dangers of civil war, foreign defeat, or even economic collapse. If this is correct, then the old dichotomy between *raison d'état* and modern natural law was more or less the reverse of the truth: the natural lawyers saw that the ideas of the sceptics and *raison d'état* theorists could be put into a juridical or ethical form simply by construing self-preservation as a universal right. Furthermore, this allowed them to construct moral systems which were immune to this kind of scepticism, for the assumptions of the Renaissance sceptic had already been built into their theories.

I have spoken of the 'minimalism' of the modern natural lawyers, and their sympathy with scepticism was clearly an essential part of their minimalist approach, for they were concerned with the residue left by the sceptical challenge. But even as I was writing *Philosophy and Government*, I began to think that there was more to be said about this issue. The most characteristic feature of the seventeenth- and eighteenth-century writers on natural law and natural rights is their use of the idea of a *state of nature*, in which agents defined in minimal terms—that is, possessing an extremely narrow set of rights and duties—engage in dealings with one another which lead to the creation of a civil society. There is no doubt that the idea of a state of nature, playing this kind of pivotal role in a moral theory, was a creation of the seventeenth century, despite the various earlier accounts of the 'natural' life of man; the term seems to be an invention of Hobbes, who remains the most clear-cut example of a state-of-nature theorist, but the idea seems to be present already in effect in the works of Hugo Grotius, the founder of the modern natural law school. One might suppose that the idea of a state of nature is simply a rather dramatic fictional device for making a point about the minimal character of the law of nature: strip away from agents all that is culturally specific, and one is left with merely the bare natural rights and duties which seem to be universal. The notion that the state of nature is an heuristic device or a 'thought experiment', like a frictionless body in theoretical physics, is very widespread; it is assumed, for example, by John Rawls in *A Theory of Justice*.

In justice as fairness the original position of equality corresponds to the state of nature in the traditional theory of the social contract. This original position is not, of course, thought of as an actual historical state of affairs, much less as a primitive condition of culture. It is understood as a purely hypothetical situation characterized so as to lead to a certain conception of justice.[17]

But it is not clear that any of the social contractarians, even Kant (who is the only one whom Rawls actually cites in this context) had quite this view of the state of nature. It is true that they did not think that it had to be historically proved—that would have been an impossible task, and would have made their whole argument easy prey to their opponents. But they did think it was a *possible* state of affairs, and indeed Kant, in one of his principal discussions of the issue, makes its possibility a touchstone for its application to actual politics.

If the law is such that a whole people could not *possibly* agree to it (for example, if it stated that a certain class of *subjects* must be privileged as a hereditary *ruling class*), it is unjust; but if it is at least *possible* that a people could agree to it, it is our duty to consider the law as just, even if the people is at present in such a position or attitude of mind that it would probably refuse its consent if it were consulted.[18]

The 'possibility' which Kant had in mind here was not what we would call *logical* possibility; on the whole, he was rather critical of an undisciplined discussion of logical possibilities, in the *Critique* describing such things as telepathy as the 'fancies' of 'playful inventiveness'.[19] For something to be relevant to philosophical discussion, he believed, it had to be possible in a stronger sense, and to agree in some way with experience; it is probable that he would have been very critical of Rawls's original position, for, as is well known, the men in the original position are required to have no knowledge of their own future selves and of their distinctive tastes and preferences—something which many readers of Rawls have regarded as beyond believable experience.

[17] John Rawls, *A Theory of Justice* (Oxford University Press, 1972), 12.

[18] *Political Writings*, ed. Hans Reiss (Cambridge University Press, 1991), 79.

[19] *Critique of Pure Reason*, trans. Norman Kemp Smith (Macmillan, 1933), 241 (see B266/A219–B274/A266).

Whether or not Kant took this view, there is no doubt that his predecessors did, and that the empirical possibility of a state of nature defined in their terms was an important part of their argument. For Hobbes, indeed, one might say it was the *most* important part, for it enabled him to use the threat of the state of nature's appearance or reappearance as a major incentive for his agents to continue in political submission to their sovereign. All of the writers in this tradition, including Kant,[20] were prepared to give actual examples of the state of nature, something which would have been ridiculous had they genuinely believed in its purely heuristic character.

In part, their confidence that a state of nature is possible came (I conjectured in *Philosophy and Government*) from their relationship to the ancient and Renaissance traditions of moral philosophy, and in particular to the sceptical (and, I argued there, also in a way Stoic) idea that the 'wise man' will eliminate from his personality many of the features which we regard as familiar—such things as passions, desires, and intellectual commitments. The liberal agent with his stripped-down psyche was a genuine goal for this tradition of moral psychology: it *wanted* its adherents to have lost the affective qualities which, for the critics of liberalism, are the very features which possess value. But as I came to realize, this was only part of the story, for this had always been an unattainable goal, and the idea that one could have a community of such wise men interacting to form civil societies was tremendously vulnerable to the crude response made (for example) to Hobbes by one of the early readers of *De Cive*:

> *Since we see that men have in fact formed societies, that no one lives outside society, and that all men seek to meet and talk with each other, it may seem a piece of weird foolishness to set a stumbling-block in front of the reader on the very threshold of civil doctrine, by insisting that* man is not born fit for society.[21]

So one needed to understand why all these writers felt such confidence in using this mechanism as a principal part of their expositions.

The most persuasive answer to this question, I think, is that one should take very seriously an answer which the writers themselves all gave, namely that there is a real and imaginatively vivid example of just such agents interacting with each other in the domain of international

[20] See e.g. *The Metaphysics of Morals* trans. Mary Gregor (Cambridge University Press, 1991), 150 (*Doctrine of Right*, ch. 53).

[21] *De Cive*, trans. Michael Silverthorne, ed. Richard Tuck (Cambridge University Press, 1997) (I.2).

relations. We can conceive of ourselves as natural individuals behaving like sovereign states, and a conception of this kind is a very powerful way of getting a sense of what it might feel like to be a liberal agent. The idea of 'sovereignty' as a way of explicating our natural rights has never in fact vanished: thus H. L. A. Hart in a famous article of 1955, 'Are There Any Natural Rights?', could talk about natural rights as constituting a kind of sovereignty for the individual over parts of his life.[22] The sovereign state, on this account of international relations, is on the one hand an autonomous agent without any affective relationships; on the other hand, it is not entitled to treat other agents as moral nullities, but has to recognize some general principles governing its conduct towards them, albeit of a much thinner kind than would be the case in a developed civil society. Its own preservation is, however, a critical matter which trumps almost all other considerations. The international arena, seen in this light, is thus a near-perfect example of the operation of the fundamental principles of the natural rights theorists, and this book is an attempt to explore in detail the historical implications of this fact.

Though this is a powerful picture, and one which is immediately familiar to us, it must be recognized that at the moment at which it was utilized by the natural rights theorists, it was not uncontentious. Once again, we can see that it was their relationship to Renaissance political and moral thinking which was important in the formation of the rights theorists' ideas, for this picture of liberal agency was derived from what we can broadly term the humanist view of international relations, and stood in some contrast to what we can equally broadly term the scholastic view. The liberal picture was in effect the idea of *raison d'état* seen from the perspective of the relationship between states, rather than from the perspective of their internal arrangements. In the first two chapters of this book, I try to explain what I understand by the 'humanist' and the 'scholastic' views, and to show how each of them has extremely deep roots in the philosophical schools of the ancient world. The chapters are based on a contrast between two writers at the end of the sixteenth century: one is a major late scholastic, the Portuguese Luis de Molina; while the other is his humanist contemporary Alberico Gentili, the Professor of Civil Law at Oxford, and one of the most important and interesting figures ever to teach at that university.

[22] H. L. A. Hart, 'Are There Any Natural Rights?', *Philosophical Review*, 64 (1955), 184.

In the process of thinking about these issues, I began to qualify the argument which I had put forward in *Philosophy and Government*. There, I claimed that the culture of scepticism and *raison d'état* was a product of the later sixteenth century, and was associated with a turning away from the moralistic humanism of the early Renaissance. The outward sign of this turn, I thought, was the stylistic shift from Cicero to Tacitus as the model for prose, for Tacitus was pre-eminently the paradigm for *raison d'état*—indeed, many of the most important works in the genre were written as commentaries on Tacitus. Correspondingly, I saw Guicciardini rather than Machiavelli as the modern model: Machiavelli, even in *The Prince*, remained substantially a Ciceronian, with a commitment to republican liberty and the moral value of patriotism which was absent from his younger contemporary. Partly, I claimed this because I accepted the conventional account of the moralism of the early Renaissance;[23] the only contentious aspect of the interpretation would be a reading of Machiavelli as belonging fundamentally to this moralistic tradition, rather than subverting it.

But once one begins to think about humanist discussions of war and international relations, the break in the late sixteenth century becomes less striking. Although the best representative of humanist jurisprudence in this area, Alberico Gentili, was a contemporary of Tacitists such as Justus Lipsius, he drew on a clear tradition of humanist thinking about war which went back to the fifteenth century, and in many ways even further back than that. This should not surprise us, for the essential move which the Tacitists made can be seen as the importation of ideas about war into *civil* life: all politics was now seen as at least potentially civil war, and our fellow citizens were no different from enemies with whom we lived in uneasy peace. *This* was the difference between Cicero and Tacitus. Cicero in his *De Officiis* distinguished between enemies and rivals in the following way:

We contend with a fellow-citizen in one way, if he is a personal enemy, in another, if he is a rival: with the rival it is a struggle for office and position, with the enemy for life and honour. So with the Celtiberians and the Cimbrians we fought as with deadly enemies, not to determine which should be supreme, but

[23] A particularly clear and succinct statement of this is to be found in Quentin Skinner's Pastmaster on Machiavelli (*Machiavelli* (Oxford University Press, 1981), 25–6 and 35–6). See also Robert P. Adams, *The Better Part of Valor: More, Erasmus, Colet, and Vives, on Humanism, War, and Peace, 1496–1535* (Seattle, 1962); Arthur B. Ferguson, *The Articulate Citizen and the English Renaissance* (Durham, NC, 1965).

which should survive; but with the Latins, Sabines, Samnites, Carthaginians, and Pyrrhus we fought for supremacy. (I. 38)

This was a distinction which Tacitus would never have made. Tacitus's state had been founded upon civil wars (see *Annals*, I, 1) and it treated its citizens as defeated combatants. As an acute observer remarked in the early seventeenth century, the very sound of the Tacitists' prose differed from that of Cicero's: 'like heavily armoured soldiers . . . they set no store by the fragrant scents or sweetly flowing smoothness of cultivated language.'[24]

When Cicero wrote in praise of republican liberty and of the self-sacrifice of the republican heroes, he was assuming that men could subordinate their own interests to that of their republic; but he nowhere assumed that the republic *itself* should ever subordinate its interests to those of a wider community. As a consequence, as we shall see, Roman and later humanist writing about war is very close in spirit to the *raison d'état* theories of the late sixteenth and seventeenth centuries. In particular, one theme is strikingly common to all this literature, namely an acceptance of the need sometimes to make a *pre-emptive* strike against an adversary, and to act on the basis not of justice but of fear (I trace this theme in the Second Section of Chapter 1).

We can make an additional point. On this account, what the Tacitists did is, once again, remarkably similar to what the natural rights theorists did in the next generation. They took a view of war between states derived from humanist historians and political writers, and inserted it into their view of domestic politics, presenting civil life as a matter of quasi-military tactics. The natural rights theorists then simply took the *jurisprudence* of war which had developed among humanist lawyers, and derived a theory of individual rights from it. As I show in Chapters 1 and 2, this humanist jurisprudence of war has often been misunderstood. The generation of scholars who first looked at most of this material in a systematic manner—the scholars funded by the Carnegie Endowment from the time of the First World War onwards, working under the influence of James Brown Scott—left us with a very misleading picture of the pre-Grotian ideas about the laws of war and peace. Like many older historians of a particular 'discipline', they assumed that the subject of 'international law' was gradually uncovered and understood in

[24] Richard Tuck, *Philosophy and Government 1572–1651* (Cambridge University Press, 1993), 133.

increasingly less primitive terms by writers from the Middle Ages onwards, in a manner analogous to pre-Kuhnian ideas about the history of physics; so that (to cite some of the pre-Grotian writers whom they translated and reprinted) Vitoria, Ayala, Belli, and Gentili were all trying to 'clarify' some inchoate principles of international law.

Although no one today, I think, believes that these writers were trying to uncover some primitively understood science of international law, there are still plenty of historians who assume that there was a well-defined subject, the law of war, which these writers were all seeking to discuss.[25] As a result, they are still treated as if they had a common aim, of some kind; whereas what I want to argue is that there were radical differences between them, as radical as the differences between Machiavelli and Aquinas. Indeed, my principal claim in the first chapter is that the ideas of Machiavelli about the relationships between cities were not very different from those of many apparently more orthodox humanists, and that many humanist jurists followed their lead. As we shall see, a sharp division between humanists and jurists (of the kind John Pocock has drawn)[26] is very unconvincing, and may be positively misleading.

The story which I have to tell in this book, like the story in *Philosophy and Government*, has Hobbes as its central character; it was Hobbes above all who made clear the relationship between humanism and natural rights, and who demonstrated the link between the older jurisprudence of war and the new political theory. But for many historians of this subject, Hobbes has seemed to be anomalous—a critic of mainstream rights theories rather than their best exponent. This view was held already in the eighteenth century, when it was not uncommon (though by no means universal) to contrast Hobbes's 'unsociable' theory of human nature with the 'sociability' of Grotius, Pufendorf, and their successors (including Locke and Vattel). By the end of the eighteenth century, the most interesting theorists were rejecting the naive sociability of the allegedly Grotian tradition, and were praising Hobbes for his honesty and perceptiveness—thus it was Grotius, Pufendorf, and Vattel whom Kant denounced in a famous passage as 'sorry comforters' whose works 'are still dutifully quoted in *justification*

[25] See, e.g., Peter Haggenmacher, *Grotius et la doctrine de la guerre juste* (Paris: PUF, 1983).

[26] See his remarks in 'Virtues, Rights, and Manners: A Model for Historians of Political Thought', *Political Theory*, 9 (1981), 353–68, repr. in *Virtue, Commerce and History* (Cambridge University Press, 1985), particularly p. 39.

of military aggression, although their philosophically or diplomatically formulated codes do not and cannot have the slightest *legal* force, since states as such are not subject to a common external constraint.'[27] The same express distaste for the tradition of 'sociability' is found in Rousseau, again alongside an open respect for Hobbes (despite many qualifications).[28]

But these same writers could be aware that the distinction between Grotius and Hobbes was harder to draw than was often supposed. Rousseau put it with his usual energy in *Emile*.

> True political theory [*Le droit politique*] is yet to appear, and it is to be presumed that it never will. Grotius, the master of all the *savants* in this subject, is but a child; and, what is worse, a dishonest child [*enfant de mauvaise foi*]. When I hear Grotius praised to the skies and Hobbes covered with execration I see how far sensible men read or understand these two authors. The truth is that their principles are exactly the same: they only differ in their expression. They also differ in their method. Hobbes relies on sophisms, and Grotius on the poets; all the rest is the same.[29]

This was a thought which other, lesser figures had also had and, as I show in Chapter 3, it is a reasonable observation once Grotius is detached from the Pufendorfian tradition in which he had often been read. Pufendorf, as I suggest in Chapter 5, is the real anomaly in the modern natural rights tradition, for he is the only writer generally associated with the tradition who asserts anything like a rich theory of human natural sociability. Even Locke and Vattel (as I show in Chapter 6) are more like Grotius and, we can say, Hobbes in the extent to which they minimize natural sociability.

Thus Rousseau and Kant, when they turned openly against the naive and vulgar idea of sociability current in their own time, were opposed more to Pufendorf and his minor *epigoni* than they were to their major predecessors in the natural rights tradition; to a surprising extent, as I argue in Chapter 7, they concurred with the essential ideas of the earlier liberal theorists. This has a major bearing on the question of what we

[27] Immanuel Kant, *Political Writings*, ed. Hans Reiss, trans. H. B. Nisbet (2nd edn., Cambridge University Press, 1991), 103.

[28] See his remarks on sociability in the *Discourse on the Origin of Inequality*, *Oeuvres politiques*, ed. Jean Roussel (Paris: Classiques Garnier, 1989), 20; *The Social Contract and Discourses*, trans. and ed. G. D. H. Cole, rev. J. H. Brumfitt and John C. Hall (London: Everyman's Library, 1973), 41; and his remarks on Hobbes, ibid. 42 and 65.

[29] Rousseau, *Political Writings*, ed. C. E. Vaughan (Cambridge University Press, 1915), II, 147.

can learn from this piece of history, for if it is correct, there is no powerful theorist of a rights-based liberalism who has not subscribed to the basic account of the liberal agent which appeared in the early seventeenth century. If, furthermore, that account of liberal agency is indeed bound up with a particular and contentious view of international relations—a view which has often governed the actual dealings of modern states—then liberal theory in our own time is faced with an unexpected dilemma.

As I have suggested, liberals have usually prized a distinction between two kinds of principle governing our conduct. The first, represented usually by a civil law code but possibly also by social conventions of various kinds, are principles to which we have assented in some fashion and whose force over us derives from that assent. The second are the principles which are not self-imposed in the same way, and which do not require this kind of assent in order to govern our conduct. These second principles, for the characteristic liberal, are very few in number, forming the 'thin' account of morality familiar in social contract theory. However, a great deal of writing and talking about international affairs in our time supposes that there is an international community which polices its members and enforces quite a complex and contentious set of values upon them, and many people who are 'liberal' in domestic politics often favour such an idea. If what used to be the paradigm case of the liberal agent, the independent state, is now seen as inevitably enmeshed in complicated social settings; if sovereignty is widely treated (as it is in Europe, if not in North America) as an outdated and uninformative category for states; then that traditional cousin of the sovereign state, the sovereign individual, is going to be hard to conceptualize with the old vividness.

This thought is related to one which Weber had, about the historical connection between liberalism and European expansionism. It is impossible to deny that the vividness of this picture of moral agents owed a great deal to the astonishing vividness of the picture of international action in the so-called age of European expansion. It cannot be a coincidence, seen from this perspective, that the modern idea of natural rights arose in the period in which the European nations were engaged in their dramatic competition for the domination of the world, and in which there were urgent questions about how both states and individuals adrift in a stateless world behave to one another and to newly encountered peoples. The historical conjunction between liberal politics at home and the 'expansion of Europe' overseas was captured by Weber when he wrote these prophetic and moving words in 1906:

> The question is: how are freedom and democracy in the long run at all possible under the domination of highly developed capitalism? . . . The historical origin of modern freedom has had certain unique preconditions which will never repeat themselves. Let us enumerate the most important of these: First, the overseas expansions. In the armies of Cromwell, in the French constituent assembly, in our whole economic life even today this breeze from across the ocean is felt . . . but there is no new continent at our disposal.[30]

But if I am correct in what I am arguing, this conjunction runs even deeper than Weber imagined, and infects the very way in which we think about our moral behaviour.

[30] *From Max Weber*, trans. and ed. H. H. Gerth and C. Wright Mills (London: Routledge, 1948), 71–2.

1

HUMANISM

Alberico Gentili

As I said in the Introduction, the ideas about war and peace which were current in late sixteenth-century Europe fell into two quite sharply differentiated traditions. They have usually been termed for convenience the 'humanist' and the 'scholastic' traditions, though it might be better to call them the 'oratorical' and the 'theological' traditions, since the first drew most extensively on the literary and rhetorical writings of the ancient world (above all, of course, the works of the Roman orators who were openly sceptical of much philosophy), while the second equally drew its inspiration largely from the literature of early Christianity, combined with the writings of the Greek philosophers and the systematic jurists of Rome.[1] The differing views about violence to which these two inheritances led people at the end of the sixteenth century are very vividly illustrated by two works published in the 1590s, based on two lecture series delivered at opposite ends of the continent, in two countries which were in fact at war with one another at the time. One was by Alberico Gentili, the Professor of Civil Law at Oxford, and the other was by Juan Luis de Molina, Professor of Philosophy and Theology at Evora in Portugal. Each of these books can stand as a kind of *summa* of the whole literature which formed its tradition, and on which the seventeenth-century rights theorists drew. In this chapter, I propose to describe the (often extraordinarily brutal) ideas about war which are to be found in Gentili's *De Iure Belli*, and to show how they corresponded to the views of the Roman writers

[1] Examples of this distinction being drawn by contemporaries include Paolo Sarpi's description of the Jesuit Mariana as 'more rhetorician than schoolman' (*Lettere ai Gallicani* ed. Boris Ulianich (Wiesbaden, 1961) 88); and Johannes Felden's complaint that Grotius's idea of the primacy of self-interest was 'more oratorical than philosophical' (*Annotata in Hug. Grotium De Iure Belli et Pacis* (Amsterdam, 1653) 24). The distinction goes back to the beginning of the Renaissance—see J. Seigel, *Rhetoric and Philosophy in Renaissance Humanism* (Princeton University Press, 1968).

about warfare. In the next chapter, I shall deal with Molina, and trace the roots of his ideas among the jurists and theologians of the Middle Ages.

Gentili was born and brought up in the March of Ancona, but was driven from Italy by his family's Protestantism. He eventually settled in England, and from 1581 taught at Oxford, where he became Regius Professor of Civil Law in 1587 (he described the university as *proculdubio augustissima in toto orbe*). Both the young Selden and the young Hobbes may have heard him lecture at Oxford in his old age, since he did not give up his university duties until 1605 (Hobbes came into residence in 1603 and Selden in 1600).[2] He was quite open about his intention to incorporate into the teaching of law an entirely humanist viewpoint: thus in the 1590s he lectured at Oxford on the injustice of Roman imperial expansion, arguing the case against Rome in one lecture and for it in another. The lectures were published in 1599 as a work divided into two books, the overall effect of which is exactly like a classic humanist dialogue, leaving the reader rather unclear about where the author stood (though it is most plausible to read it as finally endorsing the legitimacy of the Roman pursuit of imperial greatness; indeed, in *De Iure Belli* (p. 79) Gentili described the second book as having been argued 'with sound reason, and not in a declamatory fashion').[3] The model for this performance was presumably the famous sceptical philosopher Carneades, who had delivered a similar pair of orations for and against Roman imperialism at Rome in 155 BC. Gentili also openly praised Machiavelli in his *De Legationibus* of 1585.[4] Unsurprisingly for someone with his views, he became a close associate of the Earl of Essex and the rest of the war party, including Francis Bacon, in the councils of the last years of Elizabeth's reign.[5]

His major work was his *De Iure Belli*, published in 1588 and (extensively revised) in 1598, and dedicated to Essex. In this we can see all the issues which were in debate between the humanists and the

[2] The best account of Gentili's life and work is Diego Panizza, *Alberico Gentili, Giurista Ideologo nell'Inghilterra Elisabettiana* (Padova, 1981). See p. 157 for the date at which he stopped lecturing.

[3] *De Armis Romanis libri duo* (Hanover, 1599); see also *De Iniustitia Bellica Romanorum Actio* (Oxford, 1590). The quotation from *De Iure Belli* is to be found in the Carnegie Endowment edition, *De Iure Belli*, ed. C. Phillipson, trans. J. C. Rolfe (Oxford, 1933), II, 79.

[4] *De Legationibus libri tres*, ed. E. Nys, trans. G. J. Laing and E. H. Zeydel (Carnegie Endowment, New York, 1924) III. 9; see Panizza, *Alberico Gentili*, 93.

[5] For the significance of this, see my *Philosophy and Government 1572–1651* (Cambridge University Press, 1993), 104–10.

theologians. That debate was not in general over the question of whether war *as such* was legitimate: apart from a few radicals among the early Christians and the sixteenth-century Reformers, there was no one to be found who wholly denied the legitimacy of certain kinds of violence. Instead, the debate was focused on the range of justifications, which I will deal with in turn.

Pre-emptive strikes

The first and in some ways the most important of these was the issue of the *pre-emptive strike*. Much actual warfare, from antiquity to the present day, has been the consequence of one party fearing the power or ill intentions of another, and striking first in order to protect itself. This is clearly a morally fraught matter, as by definition the aggressor has not actually been harmed, and his judgement about the necessity of his action might well be called into question both by the victim and by a neutral observer. Moreover, the fear which the aggressor feels may be of very remote or indirect harm; as we shall see, the imperial annexation of remote corners of the globe was often justified in terms of the hazard which the indigenous inhabitants represented to the imperial power and its citizens.

Gentili certainly had few scruples about action on the basis of fear, rather than any real injury: 'no one ought to expose himself to danger. No one ought to wait to be struck, unless he is a fool. One ought to provide not only against an offence which is being committed, but also against one which may possibly be committed. Force must be repelled and kept aloof by force. Therefore one should not wait for it to come.' (p. 62). The most important case in practice, he believed, was when one state was much more powerful than its rivals:

> it is better to provide that men should not acquire too great power, than to be obliged to seek a remedy later, when they have already become too powerful . . . This it is which was the constant care of Lorenzo de' Medici, that wise man, friend of peace, and father of peace, namely, that the balance of power should be maintained among the princes of Italy . . . But both the peace and the balance of power ended with him, great scion of the Medici and mighty bulwark of his native city and the rest of Italy. Is not this even to-day our problem, that one man may not have supreme power and that all Europe may not submit to the domination of a single man? Unless there is something which can resist Spain, Europe will surely fall. (p. 65)

The contrast between this view and that of the theologians was obvious to contemporaries: Francis Bacon, urging his fellow countrymen in the 1620s to break treaties and make war on Spain because of its overweening power and the threat it represented to England, perceived the difference very clearly.

Howsoever some schoolmen, otherwise reverend men, yet fitter to guide penknives than swords, seem precisely to stand upon it, that every offensive war must be 'ultio', a revenge, that presupposeth a precedent assault or injury; yet neither do they descend to this point, which we now handle, of a just fear; neither are they of authority to judge this question against all the precedents of time. For certainly, as long as men are men, the sons, as the poets allude, of Prometheus, and not of Epimetheus, and as long as reason is reason, a just fear will be a just cause of a preventive war . . .[6]

The roots of this view lay equally clearly in the writings of the ancient orators. Cicero, the most important of them for the Renaissance, repeatedly implied that the violence of enemies did not actually have to be manifested in order to be legitimately opposed by violence. His *Philippics*, intended to enflame the Senate to take action against Marcus Antonius during the months in 44 and 43 in which Antonius was trying to appropriate the political legacy of Caesar, contained many passages appealing for pre-emptive action before the apparent danger to the republic became actual—'every evil is easily crushed at its birth; become inveterate it as a rule gathers strength'.[7] Cassius Dio, in his *Roman History*, represented Cicero at this moment as saying to the Senators (in words that were frequently taken in the sixteenth century to be authentically those of Cicero),

how can you believe that the man who has lived so licentiously up to the present time will not proceed to every extreme of insolence, if he shall also secure the authority given by arms? Do not, then, wait until you have suffered some such treatment and then rue it, but be on your guard before you suffer; for it is rash to allow dangers to come upon you and then to repent of it, when you might have anticipated them . . .[8]

While in the *De Officiis* (in a passage which Hobbes must have pondered) Cicero distinguished between injuries committed as a result of

[6] Francis Bacon, *The Letters and the Life*, VII, ed. James Spedding (London, 1874), 477.

[7] *Works*, XV, ed. and trans. Walter C. A. Ker (London and New York: Loeb Classical Library, 1926), 286–7 (*Philippic*, V. xi. 30–1).

[8] Cassius Dio, *Roman History*, ed. Herbert Baldwin Foster, trans. Earnest Cary (London and Cambridge, Mass.: Loeb Classical Library, 1969), IV, 472–3 (XLV. 35–366).

desire and those which 'often arise from fear, when he who is contemplating harming another, fears that if he does not do so, he may suffer some damage', with the implication that the latter category is morally different from the former.[9]

The idea that potential dangers must be overcome before they could develop, and that the republic was entitled to strike at its possible enemies in this way, applied in Roman eyes not merely to internal threats such as that posed by Marcus Antonius. As Cato is recorded as saying about the destruction of Carthage, 'the Carthaginians are our enemies already; for whoever is directing all his preparations against me, so that he may make war on me at the time of his own choice, is already my enemy, even if he is not yet taking armed action'.[10] Cicero similarly praised Caesar's Gallic conquests as wars in defence of the republic.[11] Paul Veyne has pointed out that it was this willingness to attack any potential danger which made Rome see itself as destined to be mistress of the entire *orbis terrarum*—any independent state was in principle a danger.[12] Safety from these more remote dangers was bound up with the high value which the Romans placed upon *glory*, since glory consisted precisely in the capacity to overawe one's rival and thereby render one's self safe from attack; and in Book I of his *De Officiis*, Cicero justified war for glory, rather than immediate survival, in the following interesting terms: 'the only excuse . . . for going to war is that we may live in peace unharmed' (I. 35), and

> when a war is fought out for supremacy (*de imperio*) and when glory is the object of war, it must still not fail to start from the same motives (*causas*) which I said a moment ago were the only righteous (*iustas*) grounds for going to war. But those wars which have glory for their end must be carried on with less bitterness. For we contend, for example, with a fellow-citizen in one way, if he is a personal enemy, in another, if he is a rival: with the rival it is a struggle for office and position, with the enemy for life and honour. So with the Celtiberians and the Cimbrians we fought as with deadly enemies, not to determine which should be supreme, but which should survive; but with

[9] *De Officiis*, trans. Walter Miller (Cicero's *Works*, XXI, London and New York: Loeb Classical Library, 1913), 24 (I. vii), my translation.

[10] *Oratorium Romanorum Fragmenta*, ed. H. Malcovati (Turin, 1967–79) I, 78 (fr. 195); trans. in P. A. Brunt, 'Laus Imperii', in *Imperialism in the Ancient World*, ed. P. D. A. Garnsey and C. R. Whittaker (Cambridge University Press, 1978), 177.

[11] *Works*, XIII, trans. R. Gardner (London and Cambridge, Mass.: Loeb Classical Library, 1970), 578–81 (*De Prov. Cons.*, xiii. 32–3).

[12] Paul Veyne, 'Y a-t-il eu un imperialisme romain?', *Mélanges de l'école francaise de Rome*, 87 (1975), 793–855.

the Latins, Sabines, Samnites, Carthaginians, and Pyrrhus we fought for supremacy. (I. 38)

The cases where Cicero defended pre-emptive strikes were, of course, all cases where *the republic* was threatened in some way, and in general it is fair to say that the Romans did not believe that *individuals* were entitled to take such desperate measures—though it is true that in his *Pro Milone* Cicero did say, in terms that became proverbial, that

there is a law not of the statute-book, but of nature, . . . that should our lives have fallen into any snare, into the violence and the weapons of robbers or foes, every method of winning a way to safety would be morally justifiable. When arms speak, the laws are silent; they bid none to await their word, since he who chooses to await it must pay an undeserved penalty ere he can exact a deserved one. (10–11)[13]

The occasion was a defence of one of his own supporters who had raised street gangs to fight against the gangs of Cicero's enemy Clodius.

Nevertheless, such a claim was at the very edge of respectability at Rome, and probably well over it. It was clear to the great jurists from Labeo in the time of Cicero, down to Ulpian in the second century, that under the domestic law of Rome, the only 'fear' which could be pleaded in extenuation of an individual's act was an immediate and obvious one. The *Digest* 4.2 contains many discussions of this issue, including a long passage by Ulpian rehearsing the views of Labeo and his successors, and remarking (for example) that it was not a case of justifiable fear if a person 'hearing that some armed man was approaching, abandoned his land'—the armed man had actually to enter the land.[14]

Interestingly, Cicero, who was after all proud of being a jurist himself as well as an orator, seems to have tried to deal with just this issue in the longest and most careful discussion of war which he composed, which would have clarified much about Roman political thought. This was Book III of his *De Republica*, only fragments of which, unfortunately, survive, but which was known to, and extremely carefully studied by, Lactantius and Augustine.

It took the form of a debate organized around the same orations of Carneades which Gentili was to use as his model in his Oxford lectures,

[13] *Works*, XIV (London and Cambridge, Mass.: Loeb Classical Library, 1979), 16–17.

[14] *Digest of Justinian*, Latin text ed. Theodor Mommsen and Paul Krueger, English trans. ed. Alan Watson (University of Pennsylvania Press, 1985), 4. 2. 9.

in which Carneades had *inter alia* ridiculed the idea of justice in international relations—'no people would be so foolish as not to prefer to be unjust masters rather than just slaves'.[15] Carneades himself certainly took his polemic against justice to apply to individuals as well as nations, using among other examples the familiar dilemma posed by two just men in a shipwreck, each trying to get hold of a plank which would support only one. But Cicero's defence of the just empire of the Romans, while using in part arguments about the legitimacy of natural domination (see below), seems to have turned principally on a denial of the parallel between an individual and the *respublica*. He stressed that only a *civitas*, and not a private individual, had an overriding need to survive.

For a *civitas* must be constituted with a view to its eternal continuance. And so death is never natural to a *res publica* as it is to a man. For a man death is not only inevitable but very often even desirable; whereas when a *civitas* is destroyed, wiped out, extinguished, it is (to compare small with great) as if the whole of this world should collapse and perish.[16]

Indeed, the sacrifice of the citizen in the interests of his *respublica* was of course regarded as a particularly glorious thing by all Roman writers; but none of them would have sanctioned the sacrifice of Rome in the interests of human society.

It is against the background of this thought that we should presumably read the other fragments of his argument in the *De Republica* in which he said that 'a war is never undertaken by the ideal State (*a civitate optima*), except in defence of its honour or its safety (*salute*)' and 'those wars are unjust which are undertaken without provocation. For only a war waged for revenge or defence (*ulciscendi aut propulsandorum hostium causam*) can actually be just' (III. 34, 35). Taken out of context by Christian writers, these sentences were made to yield the idea that war only in defence of one's innocent and immediate safety was just, but Cicero is unlikely to have intended anything as clear cut; elsewhere in Book III he observed that 'I agree [presumably with Carneades] that an anxious and hazardous justice is not appropriate to a wise man' (III. 39), and the final message of Book III is likely to have been the same as that

[15] *Works*, XVI trans. C. W. Keyes (London and Cambridge, Mass.: Loeb Classical Library, 1970), 206–7 (III. 28).

[16] III. 34. I have taken the translation from Augustine, *City of God*, ed. David Knowles, trans. Henry Bettenson (Harmondsworth: Penguin, 1972), 1031–2 (XXII. 6), as it is considerably more accurate than the Loeb translation of the *De Republica*.

of the *De Officiis*, that the apparent injustice of an imperial hegemony could be defended as being in the necessary interests of Rome.

Although the Romans were the most powerful voices in antiquity in defence of what we may reasonably term this *raison d'état* view, they had predecessors in the Greek world among the very men against whom the philosophers had defined their own position, the sophists (whom the Roman rhetoricians later termed *oratores* and praised as their own precursors).[17] Views very like those of the Romans are to be found (for example) in the writings of Thucydides, whom Cicero praised as the finest of the Greek 'oratorical' historians (a group which he distinguished from the 'philosophical' historians such as Xenophon):[18] the *History of the Peloponnesian War* abounds in such 'Roman' sentiments as the observation that the war was caused by 'the growth of Athenian power and the fear which this caused in Sparta' (I. 23), or the famous argument of the Mytelenians that they were entitled to attack the Athenians even though

> Athens had not yet taken action against us . . . For if we had the same ability as they have for planning action and then putting it off, we should be their equals, and there would be no need for us to be their subjects. As it is, they are always in the position where they can take the initiative in aggression; we should be allowed the initiative in self-defence. (III. 12)[19]

The idea that war could legitimately be made for imperial power and glory never vanished from European minds, though throughout the Middle Ages it was a contested notion, found largely among historians and other 'literary' figures rather than among philosophers. It survived in large part because one of the chief critics of Roman culture, Augustine, was at the same time gripped by the imaginative and emotional force of Roman history. I will deal with his criticisms in my next chapter, but here it is more relevant to point to the (albeit qualified) endorsement he gave to these Ciceronian values. One of the central thoughts of the *Civitas Dei* was the idea that much Roman writing about civic virtue was indeed applicable to a Christian, if the *respublica* which the citizens served was seen as the *Civitas Dei*. On this account,

[17] See e.g. Cicero's remarks in his *Brutus*—*Works*, V (*Brutus* and *Orator*), trans. G. L. Hendrickson and H. M. Hubbell (London and Cambridge, Mass.: Leob Classical Library, 1962), 36–9 (VII. 26–9).

[18] *Works*, III, trans. E. W. Sutton and H. Rackham (London and Cambridge, Mass.: Loeb Classical Library, 1967), 238–41 (*De Oratore* II. xiii–xiv. 55–8).

[19] Quotations from the Penguin edn., ed. Moses Finley, trans. Rex Warner (Harmondsworth, 1972).

Roman values were a kind of model for civic values in general: thus, writing about the Roman empire in the *City of God*, he praised the relative freedom from vice of the rulers of Rome in its heroic period, and remarked that

> it was that Empire, so far-spread and so long-lasting, and given lustre and glory by the heroic quality of its great men, that gave to them the return they looked for as a recompense for their resolution, while it sets before us Christians examples whose message we cannot but heed. If we do not display, in the service of the most glorious City of God, the qualities of which the Romans, after their fashion, gave us something of a model, in their pursuit of the glory of their earthly city, then we ought to feel the prick of shame. (V. 18)[20]

> The Roman Empire was not extended and did not attain to glory in men's eyes simply for this, that men of this stamp should be accorded this kind of reward. It had this further purpose, that the citizens of that Eternal City [the City of God], in the days of their pilgrimage, should fix their eyes steadily and soberly on those examples [the examples of devotion to the *respublica* among the early Romans] and observe what love they should have towards the City on high, in view of life eternal, if the earthly city had received such devotion from her citizens, in their hope of glory in the sight of men. (V. 16)

The self-sacrifice even to death of the ancient Romans for their city was a model for Christian self-sacrifice.

By using republican Roman values as a model for Christian values in this fashion, Augustine in a sense resolved the tension between them; but in another sense, he merely perpetuated it, for the old Roman values were on his account still to be inculcated as part of the education of a modern Christian. The old problem about the relationship between liberty for one's own *respublica* and subordination for other people's remained, for Augustine could not but respond sympathetically to the struggle for liberty celebrated in the pages of Sallust; republican Romans had been diverted from much worse vices by their twin pursuits of glory and liberty. 'This unbounded passion for glory, above all else, checked their other appetites. They felt it would be shameful for their country to be enslaved, but glorious for her to have dominion and empire; and so they set their hearts first on making her free, then on making her sovereign' (V. 12). And he distinguished between the ambition for glory leading to dominion, and the ambition for

[20] Quotations are from the Penguin edn., ed. David Knowles, trans. Henry Bettenson (Harmondsworth, 1972).

dominion alone (V. 19)—the former was morally more acceptable than the latter.

This ambiguous attitude to the values of Rome was inevitable, given the meliorative character of Augustine's overall enterprise; but it bequeathed an equally ambiguous legacy to his successors. For example, the Roman stress on republican liberty, the force of which Augustine had acknowledged without exactly recommending it as a central modern value, was eloquently defended in what was, in effect, a supplement to the *City of God* put out by Augustine's pupil and friend Paulus Orosius, the *Histories Against the Pagans* (*Historiarum adversus paganos libri septem*). Orosius's work was tremendously influential in early medieval Europe, and in it his readers could find (for example) praise for the recovery of Athenian liberty by Thrasybalus from the Thirty Tyrants,[21] and sympathy for the plight of Gaul at Caesar's hands:

> Wretched Gaul panted when, at the point of a sword, she was forced to profess a promise of eternal slavery, with her hostages in addition torn from her; she panted, as I have said, for that sweetness of liberty well known to all and so delightful, as for a draught of cold water, and the more she realized that it was being taken from her, the more eagerly did she desire it.[22]

The Roman Empire, according to Orosius, was only really acceptable at the point at which its constituent nations voluntarily accepted unity in the interests of a common religion, and at which any individual was free to settle anywhere in the empire.[23] It is not surprising that King Alfred had Orosius translated into English in the midst of his kingdom's struggle for independence against the Vikings.

The survival of Roman values in the Latin texts, and the ambiguous attitude of Augustine and Orosius towards them, meant that throughout the early Middle Ages, and despite the influence of the theologians, it was possible to praise vigorous military action in the interests of one's *respublica*, including the establishment of secure imperial domination over other peoples. The medieval so-called 'renaissances', those of the Carolingian period and the twelfth century, were in reality simply periods in which this continued 'Romanism' or 'humanism' was particularly obvious. *Glory* remained a clear and relatively uncontentious goal for rulers—Hincmar of Rheims, for example, writing in the ninth

[21] Paulus Orosius, *The Seven Books of History Against the Pagans*, trans. Roy J. Deferrari (Catholic University of America Press, 1964), 71–2.

[22] Ibid. 255. [23] Ibid. 173–7.

century, quoted extensively from Book V of the *City of God* and from Orosius, and in one striking passage reproduced Orosius's account of the Spartans at Thermopylae who had had God on their side in their struggle for liberty and glory.[24] His contemporary the Irishman Sedulius also praised war as making citizens more vigorous and united,[25] and talked a lot about the glory of a successful ruler (though he was equally at pains to stress that a truly glorious ruler would be especially devoted to the Church). This language was particularly easily applicable to the Carolingian empire, but some of the best examples come from another extremely self-confident and effective regime, Angevin England, where this kind of language was used about enterprises such as the conquest of Ireland by the Anglo-Norman lords of the twelfth century.

Ireland was, after all, a Christian country that had never been ruled either by the Romans or by the English, and yet it was successfully invaded on rather tenuous juridical grounds (the Anglo-Normans went in on behalf of a dispossessed Irish prince Dermot mac Murchard). Giraldus Cambrensis wrote the history of the conquest in about 1187, employing a wide range of humanist themes (for example, 'it is better for a prince to be loved than to be feared; but it is expedient that he should be feared also, so that the fear proceeds rather from good-will than from coercion . . .)[26], and dedicated to the future King Richard I 'in order that the record of the glorious achievements performed by your father may augment your own glory'.[27] He depicted the conquest in entirely Roman terms: on the one hand, the native Irish are represented as fighting for their 'country and liberty' in an honourable way, and as believing that the Normans should be crushed quickly—'it is always best to meet difficulties half-way, and check the first approaches of disease'.[28] The Normans, on the other hand, are represented as saying that they come to reinstate the rightful prince, but also that

> it may be the consequence of this enterprise that . . . the dominion of the whole kingdom devolve on our posterity. If the victory be won by our prowess, and Mac Murchard be restored, and the realm of Ireland be secured by our enterprise for us and our heirs for ever, how great will be our glory, how worthy of being achieved even by the loss of life and the contempt of

[24] *De Regis Persona et Regio Minesterio*, in Migne *Patrologia Latina*, 125 coll. 843–4.
[25] *On Christian Rulers*, ed. Edward G. Doyle (Binghamton, NY, 1983), 84.
[26] Giraldus Cambrensis, *Historical Works*, ed. Thomas Wright (London, 1982), 185.
[27] Ibid. 171. [28] Ibid. 198.

death . . . We must all die, because that is the inevitable and common fate of mankind; and though no splendid or glorious actions may have made us illustrious during life, by our deaths, at least, we may make our names memorable in future ages.[29]

Something of the same spirit may be glimpsed in the remarks of John of Salisbury on warfare in his *Policraticus*, also against the background of an expanding and confident Angevin England.[30]

Of course, when the Roman texts were accorded overwhelming respect, as began to happen in fifteenth century Italy, Roman ideas about the need for a city to use relatively unscrupulous violence in the pursuit of liberty and glory naturally resurfaced in a strong form—most famously and distinctively in the case of Machiavelli. As we can now see, however, in this area he simply put very clearly indeed something which had always been present in the Roman texts, the character of which does not need further repeating. But the same was true to a surprising extent in all recognizably humanist writing, including that of the jurists—see, for example, the treatise *De Re Militari et de Bello* of the Piedmontese Pietrino Belli, an adviser to the court of Emmanuel Philibert of Savoy, where the principles of modern statecraft were closely studied and acted upon. Writing in the year of Cateau-Cambresis (1559), Belli was happy to acknowledge that wars waged 'for empire and for glory' were justifiable.[31]

The twist which some humanists in the Renaissance gave to this theme, however, was to deny that it was applicable to a modern city state; instead, they argued that only the *respublica Christiana* was an appropriate object of such loyalties. The most creative of the humanist jurists, Andrea Alciato, made the point quite clear:

some nations were subject to Rome . . . others were left completely free and under their own laws, but were understood to respect the majesty of the Roman people with due courtesy . . . others were enemies (*hostes*), like the Parthians and the Germans, the former always contending with the Romans out of rivalry (*aemulatio*), the latter for liberty . . . Others were neither enemies nor in any way associated with the Romans, like the Scythians . . . But since under the Antonine law all who were in the Roman world were made Roman

[29] Ibid. 201.

[30] See *Policraticus*, ed. and trans. Cary J. Nederman (Cambridge University Press, 1990), VI, Chs. 1–19.

[31] *De Re Militari et Bello Tractatus*, ed. A. Cavaglieri, trans. H. C. Nutting (Carnegie Endowment, Oxford, 1936), II. 61.

citizens, it follows that all Christians are today the Roman people; this principle (*ius*) excludes from citizenship those who in Asia, Africa and other provinces do not profess the faith of CHRIST. They are enemies of the Roman people and lose the rights of the Roman *civitas*. This is why when war is declared against Turks and Saracens, there are the rights of *postliminium*, and those taken in war become the property of the captors. But it is otherwise among Christians, for under the law of CHRIST all men are brothers, so that war between them is even worse than civil war; so there is no right of *postliminium* in this case.[32]

These jurists on the whole rejected the idea that the emperor was lord of the world,[33] and correspondingly focused on the separate identity of Christian Europe as the equivalent of a single *respublica*. The notion of a *respublica Christiana* was in fact much more recent, and more tied to a clearly humanist view of the world, than has usually been recognized. Medieval historians (including even the late Walter Ullmann)[34] have used it freely as a description of medieval Christendom, but it is actually rather uncommon as a term in medieval documents; *Christianitas* or the *populus Christianus* are the standard terms, neither of which, of course, have the specifically political overtones of the *respublica Christiana*. It was used by Pope Clement III in the course of his appeal for the Third Crusade, but was not used by the popes of the thirteenth century.[35] Not until the pontificate of the first fully humanist pope, Pius II (Aenio Silvio Piccolomini) in the mid-fifteenth century, do we find it used extensively, as part of his campaign to foment a crusade against the Turks after the fall of Constantinople. Pius II talked in his orations and letters about the 'glory' which a war on behalf of the *Christiana respublica* would bring, and (interestingly) called one of the first pan-European peace conferences, at Ratisbon, in order to plan the crusade—the *respublica* had to have an institutional character separate from that of the old imperial Europe.[36]

[32] *Opera*, I (Basle, 1571) col. 274; *in tit. de verb. signif. comment, lex* 117. See also the early fifteenth-century jurist Raphael Fulgosius, *In Primam Pandectarum Partem Commentarii* (Lyons, 1554), 8ᵛ (*De iustitia et iure*, '*Ex hoc iure*' §5).

[33] See e.g. Alciato *Opera*, III, col. 180.

[34] *Principles of Government and Politics in the Middle Ages* (London: Methuen, 1961), 224.

[35] Piero Zerbi, *Papato, Imperio e 'Respublica Christiana dal 1187 al 1198*, *Pubblicazionidell'Universita Cattolica del S. Cuore*, NS 15 (Milan, 1955), 48–9 and n. 177; G. Vismara, *Impium foedus—la illiceita delle alleanze con gli infideli nella respublica christiana medioevale* (Milan, 1950).

[36] Pius II, *Orationes Politicae, et Ecclesiasticae*, I (Lucca, 1755), 167, 264, 266. Denys Hay, in *Europe: The Emergence of an Idea* (rev. edn. Edinburgh, 1968), observed that the term *respublica Christiana* came into vogue at this time, though he rather oddly attributed its popularity to the requirements of Latin prosody (p. 87).

The Medici pope, Leo X (1513–21), also used the term on a widespread scale, as part of the immense propaganda campaign which he too organized on behalf of an anti-Turkish crusade. The court of Leo X represented the first occupation by humanists of one of the high grounds of international politics, so much so that when the expression 'Renaissance' first became common, in the mid-eighteenth century, it was applied specifically to Leo's pontificate,[37] and the term *respublica Christiana* was used repeatedly by the humanists such as Sadoleto who drafted the pope's letters and manifestos.[38] The common theme was that Christian Europe was a political entity threatened by an external enemy, the Turks, upon whom it was both entitled and, indeed, obliged to make war; but correspondingly, warfare between Christian princes was condemned as *civil* war, the worst fate that could befall a republic in Roman eyes. Leo struggled to make peace between the Christian rulers in order that the *respublica Christiana* could fight the Turks, not because he believed that war *as such* was undesirable or illegitimate.

The works of even the most apparently pacifist of the sixteenth-century humanists, the Christian Northerners such as Erasmus and More, fit into this context. Certainly their works (particularly those of Erasmus) contain many deeply felt attacks on warfare within Christian Europe. But these humanists combined their profound Ciceronianism and equally profound Christianity precisely by seeing themselves as members of a *respublica Christiana*, a *civitas* defined by the Christian texts, as the *civitas* of Rome had been defined by the Roman law—an analogy Erasmus drew explicitly in his influential *Ciceronianus*. It was during Leo's campaign for Christian unity against the Turks that Erasmus published his early essays about the evils of war.[39] The most famous, *Dulce Bellum Inexpertis*, which appeared in the 1515 edition of his *Adagia*, was an enlarged version of a letter he had written in March 1514 to a diplomat involved on the Habsburg side in the great struggle between the Habsburgs and the kings of France (a struggle which had

[37] See J. E. Sandys, *A History of Classical Scholarship*, II (Cambridge University Press, 1908), 3.

[38] Kenneth M. Setton, 'Pope Leo X and the Turkish Peril', *Proceedings of the American Philosophical Society*, 113 (1969), 367–424. See especially pp. 377, 387, 391, 396, 397, 398, 408, 417.

[39] The standard work on this is still Robert P. Adams, *The Better Part of Valor* (Seattle: University of Washington Press, 1962), though he greatly underestimates the hostility to the Turks which runs throughout the writings of all the 'Erasmians'.

recently culminated in the ejection of the French from Italy). Erasmus's politics were broadly speaking pro-French in these struggles, and his hostility to war at this time was partly connected to his sense that the French should not be attacked by a grand coalition. 'Now Italy has been liberated from the French. What has been achieved by all this bloodshed, except to set a new governor in place of the king of France? And the country is no longer as prosperous as it was before.'[40] *Dulce Bellum Inexpertis* contains a famous denunciation of war between Christians, but it stops short of denouncing in equally strong terms a combined war by Christians against Turks, and praises Leo X's policies.

Two years later, Erasmus was appointed a counsellor to Prince Charles of Burgundy by the faction within the state who wanted appeasement with France, and he again wrote both letters and an essay (the *Querela Pacis*) urging peace with France. 'Is the Christian world to be leagued together against the most spotless and flourishing part of Christendom (*Christiana ditio*)? France alone remains not infected with heretics, with Bohemian schismatics, with Jews, with half-Jewish marranos, and untouched by the contagion of Turkish neighbours, as are some other countries which everyone can recognise for himself without naming any names.'[41] This time, he was clearer in his support for a war with the Turks: 'if war . . . is not wholly avoidable, that kind would be a lesser evil than the present unholy conflicts and clashes between Christians. If mutual love does not bind them together, a common enemy will surely unite them after a fashion, and there will be a sort of a common purpose, even if true harmony is lacking.'[42] And when he returned to this question in 1530, pressed on just this issue by a German anxious about Lutheran pacifism, Erasmus insisted that he should not be understood as opposing war by united Christians against Turks, as long as the war was 'for the tranquillity of the Christian republic' rather than 'desire of wider rule or greed for possessions'.[43]

[40] Erasmus, *Collected Works*, II (University of Toronto Press, 1975), 282 (letter 288, 14 March 1514, to Antoon van Bergen).

[41] *Collected Works*, IV (University of Toronto Press, 1977), 279 (letter 549, 10 March 1517 to Riccardo Bartolini, published in Erasmus's *Epistolae elegantes* of 1517). An almost identical passage, making the same point, is to be found in the *Querela Pacis* itself—*Collected Works*, XXVII (University of Toronto Press, 1986), 306, though there the countries are named as Italy, Hungary, and Spain. For Erasmus's politics and the context of the work, see ibid. 290.

[42] *Collected Works*, XXVII, p. 314 (*Querela Pacis*).

[43] *Opera Omnia*, V. 3 (Amsterdam: North-Holland, 1986), 58 (*Utilissima Consultatio de Bello Turcis Inferendo, et Obiter Enarratus Psalmus XXVIII*, ed. A. G. Weiler, ll. 483–4).

When even Erasmus thought this, it was easy for other humanists to take war for glory and dominion, including pre-emptive strikes, to be justifiable for a modern European state.[44] In this respect, as in most others, Gentili was simply putting forward a humanist commonplace.

The Relativism of Patriotism

The idea that our state is entitled to seek glory and imperial power in order to protect itself from its rivals obviously raises immediately the question of whether *another* state is similarly entitled. If it is right to be a strenuous patriot for Rome, should it not also be right to be a strenuous patriot for Carthage? It was the relativist implications of the value of patriotism which led to much of the criticism directed at the 'oratorical' view by Greek philosophers and Christian theologians, but again Gentili was unafraid to draw the obvious conclusion. As he said, 'it is the nature of wars for both sides to maintain that they are supporting a just cause'. It is true that the

> purest and truest form of justice . . . cannot conceive of both parties to a dispute being in the right . . . But we for the most part are unacquainted with that truth. Therefore we aim at justice as it appears from man's standpoint. In this way we avoid the objection of Baldus [the last of the great scholastic jurists], that when war arises among contending parties, it is absolutely inevitable that one side or the other is in the wrong. (p. 31)

And he observed drily that 'it will not occur very often, as you will learn forthwith, that injustice is clearly evident on one of the two sides' (p. 32). Gentili was even prepared to say that it could be just to defend oneself even if one had provoked the war: 'to defend our own property is a necessary defence . . . And even though we have provoked the war which is made upon us, this is a just cause' (p. 59).

Again, this idea about the possibility of justice lying on both sides in a war was an authentic restatement of the Roman view. Many of the Roman writers expressed sympathy for the patriotic struggles of their own enemies—thus Caesar could allow that his Gallic opponents were fighting for liberty, 'for which all men naturally strive' (*De Bello Gallico*, 3. 10. 3), and Sallust could voice persuasively the anti-Roman sentiments

[44] See, e.g., the extraordinary defence of the St Bartholomew's Day Massacre by Guy de Pibrac, to which I drew attention in my *Philosophy and Government* (Cambridge University Press, 1993), 41.

of Mithridates, King of Pontus.[45] Even the Roman jurists' discussion of war, and in particular of enslavement as a result of war, openly treated the Romans' enemies as in some sense on a moral par with the Romans, and as being equally justified in enslaving their prisoners. Commenting on the law of *postliminium*, the principle that Roman citizens taken as prisoners by an enemy were slaves in the eyes of Roman law also, until they returned to Roman jurisdiction, the Roman jurist Pomponius remarked, in a passage which was much cited in the Renaissance, that *postliminium* could operate in peace as well as in war,

> for if we have neither friendship nor *hospitium* with a particular people, nor a treaty made for the purpose of friendship, they are not precisely [*quidem*] enemies, but that which passes from us into their hands becomes their property, and a freeman of ours who is captured by them becomes their slave, and similarly if anything of theirs passes into our hands.[46]

This was a startling vision of an international order, in which any nations who had not made explicit treaties with one another were entitled to enslave one another's citizens, and in which the Romans were involved in a struggle for power with morally equal rivals.

Of all the Roman views, this was the one that medieval writers found hardest to take, for obvious reasons, and it seems that it was not until the first generation of genuinely humanist jurists that anyone was prepared to restate it. Gentili believed that the first to do so was Raphael Fulgosius of Piacenza, writing in the second or third decade of the fifteenth century: Fulgosius picked up the remarks of Pomponius in the *Digest* about *posliminium*, and argued expressly against all previous jurists that a war could be said to be just on both sides. Prior to the conflict, no one could assess the legitimacy of their cause, and only victory would decide—'Victrix causa deis placuit', he observed, citing Lucan.[47] However, the most influential defender of this idea was, once again, Andrea Alciato. He argued that war could be just on both sides

[45] On this, and much more of the Roman view of imperialism, see P. A. Brunt, 'Laus Imperii', in *Imperialism in the Ancient World*, ed. P. D. A. Garnsey and C. R. Whittaker (Cambridge University Press, 1978), 183 and n. 84.

[46] *Digest of Justinian*, Latin text ed. Theodor Mommsen and Paul Krueger, English trans. ed. Alan Watson (University of Pennsylvania Press, 1985), 48.15.5.

[47] *In Primam Pandectarum Partem Commentarii* (Lyons, 1554), 8^r (*De iustitia et iure*, '*Ex hoc iure*' §1). The quotation from Lucan is from *Pharsalia*, I. 128. Fulgosius (1367–1427) taught at Padua 1407–27, and was a legal adviser to the Venetian Republic—see Luigi Mensi, *Dizionario Biografico Piacentino* (Piacenza, 1899), s.n.

under the *pristina* law of nature, and reminded his readers of Plutarch's anecdote about Brennus, the King of the Senones.

When a Roman mission asked him why he was besieging Clusium in Etruria, he replied 'I do it by natural *ius*, by which he who is the weaker is obliged to submit to the stronger . . . You Romans too followed this, when you subjugated the Fidenates, the Ardeatas, the Veians, and the Volscians, with no other reason than that you have men who surpass those people in the virtue of arms (*illis praestantiores virium virtute habebamini*).' Remember also what Aristides said, in his oration to the Rhodians: 'the law of nature comes from the more powerful. It is very clear that the lesser obey the greater: and anyone who thinks that liberty is accordingly extinguished, is very far from being right: it no more follows than it would if us puny humans (*homunciones*) were to conspire together and assemble aginst the gods like the giants did, or enviously believe them to be as nothing.'[48]

Alciato's star pupil, and one of the clearest-headed of all the humanist jurists, François Connan, picked up this last thought in his *Commentarii*, written probably during the 1540s and published posthumously in 1553 (he had died in 1551). In them, he observed brutally about the law of war that 'you can investigate and speculate all you like, but you will find no other reason why ownership of things is acquired by *accessio* under the law of nature, than that . . . by a tacit law of nature the weaker give way to the more powerful; from which single principle all the laws of war derive'.[49] Pietrino Belli, writing (as we have seen) slightly later, was even prepared to use Pomponius's remarks on *postliminium* to justify the Spanish conquest of the New World:

not only in war does enslavement take place, but also apart from it. For if a person should go among a people with whom his countrymen had no ties of hospitality or friendship, or if any one from such a place should come amongst us, he would be the slave of the person seizing him. With good right, therefore, the Spaniards enslaved those Indians of the West, who live far away from our

[48] *Paradoxorum iuris civilis libros VI*, II. 21, *Opera* (Basle, 1571), III, col. 63. The references are to Plutarch, *Camillus*, XVII. 2–4 and Aristides, *Oration XXIV to the Rhodians: Concerning Concord*. Alciato's Latin version (which I have translated) is tendentious: e.g. Aristides actually described the natural law as 'promulgated by the gods, our superiors'. For a correct translation, see Aristides *The Complete Works*, II, trans. Charles A. Behr (Leiden: E. J. Brill, 1981), 52. See also Alciato's *Commentaria in Digestorum, seu Pandectarum Iuris Civilis Titulos Aliquot*, I. 26–31, *Opera*, V coll. 5–7.

[49] *Commentariorum Iuris Civilis Libri X* (Paris, 1558), 147^{v}. For Connan, see C. Bergfeld, *Franciscus Connanus 1508–1551* (Cologne, 1968).

world, and were unknown to the Greeks and Romans, but who were discovered in our times through perilous and bold navigation.[50]

The Natural Society of the Human Race

I

Alongside this far-reaching argument for the legitimacy of war on behalf of one's own preservation, Gentili also urged that war could be legitimate in the interests of a wider 'human society'. 'Nature has established among men kinship, love, kindliness, and a bond of fellowship . . . the law of nations is based upon this association of the human race' (p. 67). Each state should behave in this world society like an individual in an actual state:

> the rule which governs a private citizen in his own state ought to govern a public citizen, that is to say a sovereign or a sovereign people, in this public and universal state formed by the world . . . And since we are one body, just as the other members would aid the one that was injured, if one member should desire to harm another, since it is for the interest of the whole body, even of the offending member, that each of the members be preserved: exactly so men will aid one another, since society cannot be maintained except by the love and protection of those who compose it . . . The Lazi said to the King of Persians that he was not just merely because he committed no unjust act, if he did not also defend those who were unjustly oppressed; and indeed it was in that way that they secured help and forces to use against the Romans. It is the duty of a man to protect men's interests and safety. (pp. 68–9)

The implications of this were far-reaching, for Gentili used the idea of a world community, among other things, to justify the Spanish conquest of the New World:

> Therefore, I approve the more decidedly of the opinion of those who say that the cause of the Spaniards is just when they make war upon the Indians, who practised abominable lewdness even with beasts, and who ate human flesh, slaying men for that purpose. For such sins are contrary to human nature, and the same is true of other sins recognized as such by all except haply by brutes

[50] It should be said that Belli continued, rather oddly, 'with good right, I say, the Spaniards enslaved those Indians, as allowed by the law just cited; unless one were to assume that this law refers to a foreigner captured as he goes among strangers, and not to foreigners captured in a strange land. (On this principle, perhaps, the [rulers of Spain], actuated by the Christian spirit, which they cultivate to a high degree, gave orders that if those people accepted the religion of Christ, they should live in freedom under their own laws).' *De Re Militari et Bello Tractatus*, ed. A. Cavaglieri, trans. H. C. Nutting (Carnegie Endowment, Oxford, 1936), II, 85.

and brutish men. And against such men, as Isocrates says, war is made as against brutes . . .

It is right to make war upon pirates, and the Romans justly took up arms against the Illyrians, Balearians, and Cilicians, even though those peoples had touched nothing belonging to the Romans, to their allies, or to any one connected with them; for they had violated the common law of nations. And if a war against pirates justly calls all men to arms because of love for our neighbour and the desire to live in peace, so also do the general violation of the common law of humanity and a wrong done to mankind. Piracy is contrary to the law of nations and the league of human society. Therefore war should be made against pirates by all men, because in the violation of that law we are all injured, and individuals in turn can find their personal rights violated; is it not so?

Therefore, since we may also be injured as individuals by those violators of nature, war will be made against them by individuals . . . Marriage, the begetting of children, and education belong to this law which they have violated, and they deprive all men, whose kindred and associates they are, of their natural rights. (pp. 123–4)

And Gentili linked this idea to the notion of 'natural' slavery, though he was appropriately cautious about endorsing the wholly Aristotelian theory: 'with this view also a disquisition of Aristotle on the natural origin of slavery is in harmony. For although the philosopher is speaking of those who have servile dispositions, yet his arguments apply to those who become slaves because of their wickedness and sins' (p. 330). He was reluctant, however, to conclude that *all* barbarians were, as he thought the Greeks had believed, natural slaves—in I. XII he set out the arguments for and against such an idea, and concluded that although such antagonism was not strictly natural, it was the result of education, 'which is a second nature', and of Christian experience of the treachery of peoples such as the Turks.

Gentili also allowed his disgust at the behaviour of barbarians to lead him to reject the legitimacy of ever making treaties with them (a matter in great debate in the course of the sixteenth century). He endorsed the view of some radical Protestants that Christians should never ally themselves with non-Christians, partly on Scriptural grounds, but partly on the grounds that barbarians lay outside normal morality.

It is characteristic of infidel barbarians to burn, pillage, and destroy. It is their way to use unfair wiles, to fight with poison, to wage a merciless war, at any rate to inflict slavery, which has been abolished in all Christian warfare. Hence

I do not approve the treaty of the King of France with the Turks, because of which once so many thousands of men, boys, and women were captured and led off into everlasting and intolerable servitude. Moreover you cannot trust the infidels. For although the impious oath of an infidel may be accepted, yet what trust can be put in an unbeliever? (p. 402)

The balance found in Gentili between the priority of self-preservation and the needs of a wider human society is going to be in many ways the key theme of this study, repeated again and again with appropriate modifications by writers in the seventeenth and eighteenth centuries as they dissociated themselves from the Aristotelian traditions. What we have to understand from the beginning is that human society, for these humanist and post-humanist writers, was a much thinner idea than it was for the Aristotelians: it completely lacked the dimensions of friendship and self-sacrifice which a true political community possessed. Consequently, in their works we can see them struggling to find an appropriate vocabulary to express this idea, and to capture the particular degree of sympathy and fellow-feeling which they believed human beings would naturally manifest towards one another.

This struggle was already under way in the Roman texts. The notion of a human society is found abundantly in Cicero: for example, 'those who say that we should think about the interests of our fellow-citizens, but not those of foreigners, destroy the common society of the human race [*communem humani generis societatem*]'.[51] But when he tried to explain what he meant by this society, he often emphasized its weakness and etiolated character. Writing in his *De Amicitia*, for example, he drew a distinction between *amicitia* ('friendship') or *benevolentia* ('goodwill'), and *propinquitas* (a term which is hard to translate in this context—the Loeb text uses simply 'relationship').

It seems clear to me that we were so created that between us all there exists a certain tie [*societas*] which strengthens with our proximity to each other. Therefore, fellow countrymen are preferred to foreigners and relatives [*propinqui*] to strangers, for with them Nature herself engenders friendship, but it is one that is lacking in constancy. For friendship exceeds *propinquitas* in this, that goodwill [*benevolentia*] may be eliminated from *propinquitas* while from friendship it cannot; since, if you remove goodwill from friendship the very name of friendship is gone; if you remove it from *propinquitas* the name of *propinquitas* still remains. Moreover, how great the power of friendship is may

[51] *De Officiis*, III. vi. 28, my trans.

be most clearly be recognized from the fact that, in comparison with the infinite ties uniting the human race and fashioned by Nature herself, this thing called friendship has been so narrowed that the bonds of affection always unite two persons only, or, at most, a few.[52]

This thin notion of natural *propinquitas*, expressly contrasted in this passage with the richness of friendship, clearly underlies the famous remarks in the *De Inventione* (which was without a doubt a model for Rousseau) in which Cicero described the natural life of men as one led 'scattered in the fields and hidden in sylvan retreats', where 'no one had seen legitimate marriage nor had anyone looked upon children whom he knew to be his own; nor had they learned the advantages of an equitable code of law.'[53] Such a picture of the natural life of man is very common in Roman sources, and it has always been recognized as essentially Epicurean in origin (it is found eloquently set out, for example, in Lucretius).

Both in antiquity and in the Renaissance, Epicurus's doctrine was regarded as the philosophy most opposed to the idea of a rich natural sociability; Hobbes was, for example, consistently accused of being an Epicurean. It is true that Epicureanism saw itself as in opposition to the prevailing accounts of natural affection among men, both Aristotelian and Stoic;[54] but it is not immediately clear what its own doctrines on the matter were. It is sometimes supposed by modern scholars that Epicurus's claim that 'natural justice is a symbol or expression of expediency'[55] was radically incompatible with *any* theory of natural sociability, however thin;[56] but it is not obvious that this was so in antiquity. There is a long and convincing summary of a work by Hermachus, Epicurus's successor, in Porphyry's *On Abstinence from Animal Food*, in

[52] Loeb Classical Library edn. of Cicero's works, XX, ed. and trans. William Armstead Falconer (London and Cambridge, Mass.: 1946), 128–9 (v. 19–20).

[53] Loeb Classical Library edn. of Cicero's works, II, ed. and trans. H. M. Hubbell (London and Cambridge, Mass., 1976), 4–7 (I. ii. 2).

[54] For an account of the Stoic concept, see S. G. Pembroke, 'Oikeiosis', in *Problems in Stoicism* ed. A. A. Long (University of London Press, 1971), 114–49. As Pembroke makes clear, the Stoic account is highly complex: at one point it touches on Epicureanism (as Carneades the sceptic in fact alleged—p. 129, while at another it touches on Aristotelianism (pp. 132–6)). Renaissance accounts of the matter are equally confused, and little is to be gained by attributing to any writer a 'Stoic' notion of natural sociability, without a great deal of further exposition about what they might actually have believed.

[55] Diogenes Laertius, *Lives of Eminent Philosophers*, II (trans. R. D. Hicks, London and Cambridge, Mass.: Loeb Classical Library, 1965), 672–5 (X. 150).

[56] See e.g. Diogenes of Oinoanda, *The Epicurean Inscriptions*, ed. Martin Ferguson Smith (Naples: Bibliopolis, 1993), 479.

which Hermachus argued that the universal ban on murder arose from 'a certain natural alliance which exists in men towards each other, through the similitude of form and soul', as well as the obviousness of the fact that murder 'did not contribute to the whole nature and condition of human life'. In the original state of mankind, before cities were created, wise men refrained from murder 'and punished it with no casual disgrace' in order to 'preserve that communion which greatly contributes to the peculiar safety of each individual'.[57] And later Epicureans were quite prepared to say even that all men are citizens of a single country.[58]

When Cicero talked about 'the common society of the human race', he may have meant little more than this: that there is a kind of mutual recognition between men which differs from the relationship between men and the rest of the natural world,[59] and which involves an appreciation of the mutual benefits which men can provide for one another, without requiring of us the sacrifice which a fully developed system of mutual aid will entail. In the *De Officiis*, indeed, he made clear the limits of natural sociability, when he observed that the principles of 'the society of everyone with everyone else' (*omnibus inter omnes societas*) require that we should

> bestow even upon a stranger what it costs us nothing to give. On this principle we have the following maxims: 'Deny no one the water that flows by'; 'Let anyone who will take fire from our fire'; 'Honest counsel give to one who is in doubt'; for such acts are useful to the recipient and cause the giver no loss. We should, therefore, adopt these principles and always be contributing something to the common weal. But since the resources of individuals are limited and the number of the needy is infinite, this spirit of universal liberality must be regulated . . . in order that we may continue to have the means for being generous to our friends. (I. xvi. 51–2)

[57] Porphyry, *On Abstinence from Animal Food*, trans. Thomas Taylor, ed. Esme Wynne-Taylor (London, 1965), 25, 27 (I. 7, 10). Grotius had certainly read this work before he published *De Iure Belli ac Pacis*, where he described as 'a famous passage' (*insignis locus*) an interesting remark by Porphyry on the claims of necessity. See *De Iure Belli ac Pacis*, II. 20. 21, referring to *On Abstinence from Animal Food* III. 18 (p. 127). He does not, however, mention Porphyry in *De Indis*.

[58] Diogenes of Oinoanda, *The Epicurean Inscriptions*, ed. Martin Ferguson Smith (Naples: Bibliopolis, 1993), 195–6 (text), 381 (trans.), 479 (note).

[59] Or would differ given the assumptions of antiquity about animals. Our own time's notion that we have some kind of moral relationship with at least the higher animals would probably correspond quite well to the ancient concept of the relationship we have with strangers.

The contrast here between the impoverished relationship with the stranger and the rich relationship with the 'friend' is exactly the contrast which we are trying to understand.

Even Seneca, though much more of a conventional Stoic than Cicero, stressed the connection between the global society and our own self-interest, remarking (in words which were clearly the model for Gentili) that

> to injure any man is a crime, for he is your fellow-citizen in the greater commonwealth. What if the hands should desire to harm the feet, or the eyes the hands? As all the members of the body are in harmony one with another because it is to the advantage of the whole that individual members be unharmed, so mankind should spare the individual man, because all are born for a life of fellowship [*coetum*], and society [*societas*] can be kept unharmed only by the mutual protection and love of its parts. We would not crush even a viper or a water-snake or any other creature that harms by bite or sting if we could make them kindly in the future, or keep them from being a source of danger to ourselves and others. Neither, therefore, shall we injure a man because he has done wrong, but in order to keep him from doing wrong.[60]

However fundamentally weak natural human sociability might be, the notion of a global society, for the Romans just as much as for Gentili, legitimated some quite extensive intervention in the affairs of other nations—as long, of course, as one's own preservation, or the preservation of one's republic, had been secured. Seneca, again, put the point most clearly, when in his *De Beneficiis* he discussed the question of whether one should repay a debt owed to a blood-thirsty tyrant.

> If he had bestowed something upon me, and yet bore arms against my country [*patria*], he would have lost all claim upon me, and it would be considered a crime to repay him with gratitude.[61] If he does not assail my country, but is the bane of his own, and, while he keeps aloof from my own people, harrows and rends his own, nevertheless, even if such depravity does not make him my personal enemy [*invicum*], it makes him hateful [*invisum*] to me, and regard for the duty that I owe to the whole human race is, in my eyes more primary and pressing than the duty I owe to a single man . . . I am free to act as I please

[60] *Works*, I (*Moral Essays*, I) (London and Cambridge, Mass.: Loeb Classical Library 1985), 234–7 (*De Ira*, II. xxxi. 7–8).

[61] The same point is made in Cicero's *De Officiis*—one should not repay a loan to the enemy of one's country, because the *respublica debet esse carissima*, (III. xxv. 95).

toward him, from the moment when by violating all law he put himself beyond the pale of the law . . . [Though it is worth noting that Seneca proceeded to urge moderation in such action, limiting it principally to a refusal to supply arms.][62]

The idea that piracy is an example of conduct which can be attacked by anyone, and which leads to the pirate being treated as an outcast from human society, is also extremely common in the Roman texts: thus in the *De Officiis* Cicero observed that it would not be wrong to fail to pay a ransom agreed with a pirate,

> not even if one should fail to deliver the ransom after having sworn to do so; for a pirate is not included in the number of lawful enemies [*perduellium*], but is the common foe of all the world; and with him there ought not to be any pledged word nor any oath mutually binding. (III. xxix. 107–8)

Like Gentili, the Romans also seem to have tentatively associated the notion of human society with that of natural slavery. It is well known that in general writers of the Hellenistic and Roman period were unhappy with the fully fledged Aristotelian account of the natural slave, but they were quite prepared to argue for the forcible enslavement of thse who 'violated the common code of mankind' (as Polybius said in justifying the enslavement of the Mantineans in 227 BC).[63] In the lost Book III of the *De Republica*, Cicero too seems to have endorsed such an idea: part of his response to Carneades was to say that 'Do we not observe that dominion has been granted by Nature to everything that is best, to the great advantage of what is weak? For why else does God rule over man, the mind over the body, and reason over lust and anger and the other evil elements of the mind?' And he appears to have distinguished between 'a kind of unjust slavery, when those who are capable of governing themselves are under the domination of another' and some kind of just slavery—presumably of those who were not capable of governing themselves (III. xxv. 37).

II

Although one might have expected the idea of a general human society to be reasonably popular among the Christians of the Middle Ages, in

[62] *Works*, III (*Moral Essays*, III) (London and Cambridge, Mass.: Loeb Classical Library, 1975), 502–5 (*De Beneficiis*, VII. xix. 9–xx. 1).

[63] *Histories*, trans. W. R. Paton (London and Cambridge, Mass.: Loeb Classical Library 1967), I, 382–5 (II. 58).

fact (as we shall see in the next chapter) they were surprisingly hesitant about it, and about the conclusions which the Romans had drawn from it. Their hesitancy was, of course, reinforced by the discovery of Aristotle, since a global society is impossible on an Aristotelian view of the 'perfect' community, which must be a relatively small *polis*—even Babylon was too large, in Aristotle's eyes, to count as a single *polis* (*Politics*, 1276a25). But once again the Renaissance saw the full recovery of the idea, together with its implications for such things as the enslavement of barbarians. As we shall also see in the next chapter, the Thomist tradition had been very uneasy about natural slavery, but Renaissance authors threw aside all restraints, and ran Aristotle and the Romans together to justify their position.

Thus in the late fifteenth century the Florentine Donato Acciaiuoli, in one of the first and most impressive of humanist commentaries on Aristotle's *Politics*, completely endorsed the Greek account of natural slavery, and pointed to the contemporary application of it: Aristotle 'said that a war was just in which men hunt wild animals and those, for example barbarians and infidels (*infideles*) who deserve servitude, but refuse it'.[64] Erasmus's friend Jacques Lefevre d'Etaples also straightforwardly repeated Aristotle's views in his commentary on the *Politics*,[65] and it was probably this Parisian humanist Aristotelianism which influenced John Mair in his well-known remarks defending the conquest of the islanders of the Caribbean in these terms.[66] Other friends and followers of Erasmus agreed with Lefevre: for example, Josse Clichtove in his *De Bello et Pace* of 1523 distinguished between warfare among Christians, which he utterly condemned, and warfare against other religions, which he unhesitatingly approved of—calling in particular for offensive war to destroy 'abominable' religions.[67] Juan Luis Vives, close to Erasmus on so many issues, implied the same in his dialogue *De Europae Dissidiis, et Bello Turcico* of 1526, in which a spokesman for Habsburg imperialism is allowed to outline at length his scheme for a glorious pan-European onslaught on the Ottomans and the annexation of their empire, aided by the 'feminine' character of Asiatics (though

[64] Donato Acciaiuoli, *In Aristoteles libros octo Politicorum Commentarii* (Venice, 1566), 30^r; see also 218^r.

[65] Aristotle, *Politicorum libri octo* . . . (Paris, 1511), 9^r. See 6^r for his views about slavery in general.

[66] For Mair, see Anthony Pagden, *The Fall of Natural Man* (Cambridge University Press, 1982), 38–41.

[67] *De Bello et Pace Opusculum* (Paris, 1523), 28^v–29^r.

the point is also repeatedly made that only through true faith in Christ can the internecine struggles of Europe be overcome).[68]

Perhaps the best example of the early humanist recovery of the Roman ideas about aggressive war and enslavement on behalf of the human society, however, is from another friend of Erasmus—More's *Utopia*. In many ways, the point of *Utopia* is to explore the implications of the ideas found in Seneca's *Dialogi*,[69] and the account of the Utopians' warfare in Book II picks up the themes we have seen in Seneca: the Utopians 'go to war only for good reasons: to protect their own land, to drive invading armies from the territories of their friends, or to liberate an oppressed people, in the name of humanity, from tyranny and servitude' (pp. 89–90); they believe that 'they would deserve well of all mankind if they could exterminate from the face of the earth that entire vicious and disgusting race' the Zapoletes (despite their utility as mercenaries for the Utopians). Prisoners taken in these wars were enslaved (pp. 80, 95). It should be acknowledged, though, that More was anxious to acquit the Utopians of any charge of 'glorying' in war.[70]

By the 1530s the notion of natural slavery had become a commonplace among humanists; thus the most famous humanist Aristotelian of all, Agostino Nifo (notorious to modern readers as the plagiarist of Machiavelli's *Prince*), could remark in his essay 'On Wealth' of 1531 that 'The wealth which can be acquired by war consists of barbarians and their goods, for (as Aristotle says) war is only just for Greeks and Latins if it is against barbarians. Barbarians are natural slaves, and Greeks and Latins natural masters. So barbarians and their goods are for the common use of all Greeks and Latins.'[71] 'Barbarians', for Nifo, included the 'Ethiopians and their neighbours' and the Arabs. Influenced by this Aristotelianism, humanist jurists began to take up the theme; thus Connan (who as well as being a pupil of Alciato was a friend of the great French Aristotelian Louis Le Roy) remarked in a sentence that summed up the deep assumption of all humanists, that 'liberty was born with servitude . . . there was no one free, when no one was a slave: as among Christians no one is called free, since none of them is a slave'.

[68] Juan Luis Vives, *Opera Omnia*, VI (Valencia, 1785), 473–81.

[69] See the note on the subject by J. M. Parrish, 'A new source for More's *Utopia*', *Historical Journal*, 40 (1998), 493–9.

[70] *Utopia*, ed. George M. Logan and Robert M. Adams (Cambridge University Press, 1989), 87–95. See also More's refutation of the Lutheran view about war against the Turks in his *A Dialogue Concerning Heresies* (*Complete Works*, VI. 1 (Yale University Press, 1981), 415), discussed by Adams, *The Better Part of Valor*, pp. 274–5.

[71] Agostino Nifo, *Opuscula* (Paris, 1645), I, 62. See also p. 56 for a brief endorsement of Aristotle's view of slave hunting.

He went on to endorse the naturalness of slavery for those lacking 'virtue, prudence or industry', of whom 'we see many; indeed very many, even those born and brought up in the grandest families; such were all Asiatics in the opinion of Agesilaus King of Sparta, who said they were good slaves, but bad freemen'.[72]

The willingness of sixteenth-century humanists, even including those in Erasmus's circle, to countenance war on behalf of the *respublica* against its enemies, explains what has otherwise puzzled many commentators, that one of the most startling accounts of the legitimacy of war by Christians on non-Christians came from the pen of an absolutely stereotypical humanist, Juan Ginés de Sepulveda.[73] Sepulveda was an almost embarrassingly good example of an early-sixteenth century ultra-Ciceronian humanist, who was employed at the papal court in the mid-1520s as a translator of Aristotle into Ciceronian Latin—the pre-eminently humanist approach to Aristotle, rendering the Greek philosopher (as I have observed elsewhere)[74] a participant in a Roman philosophical discourse. Sepulveda's allegiance is neatly illustrated (*inter alia*) by the fact that his translation and edition of Aristotle's *Politics* is entitled *De Republica*—a feature of all truly Ciceronian translations of the *Politics* in the sixteenth century (for *politica* was of course a barbarous term, a mongrel piece of Greco-Latinity).[75] His own political writings from the 1520s onwards extol the need for men to pursue glory (as in his dialogue *Gonsalus, sive de Appetenda Gloria*), and in 1529 he added his voice to the chorus demanding an immediate war against the Turks. In this oration to Charles V, he urged peace in Europe (which he repeatedly described as the *respublica Christiana*), and called on his audience to fight 'for our country, for our children, for our hearths and homes, and above all for security and freedom, and for our religion itself' (*pro patria, pro liberis, pro aris et focis, ad summa pro salute et libertate, proque ipsa religione*).[76] In words clearly directed at the

[72] François Connan, *Commentariorum Iuris Civilis Libri X* (Paris, 1558), 72^{r}–73^{r}.

[73] The best account of Sepulveda's life is in *Contemporaries of Erasmus*, III, ed. Peter G. Bietenholz and Thomas B. Deutscher (University of Toronto Press, 1987), 240–2. Henri Mechoulan in *L'Antihumanisme de J. G. de Sepulveda* (Paris, 1974) provides a thoroughly misleading account of Sepulveda as a critic of Erasmus on war, ignoring (for example) Erasmus's *Consultatio* about war against the Turks; the article in *Contemporaries of Erasmus* is much more sensitive about the relationship between Sepulveda and Erasmus.

[74] *Philosophy and Government 1572–1651* (Cambridge University Press, 1993), 13–19.

[75] Aristotle, *De Republica Lib. VIII*, ed. and trans. J. Gines de Sepulveda (Cologne, 1601); see preface (sig. A3) for Sepulveda proclaiming himself a loyal Ciceronian.

[76] *Cohortatio ad Carolum V ut facta cum Christianis pace, bellum suscipiat in Turcas* (Bologna, 1529), in Sepulveda, *Opera*, IV (Madrid, 1780), 359.

Lutherans, he attacked those who said that Turks should not be resisted by Christians.[77]

He followed this up while still in Italy with a full-scale dialogue discussing the same issue, entitled *Democrates* (Rome, 1535); but after his return to Spain he wrote a sequel, *Democrates alter* (*c*.1544), which occasioned a great and famous controversy in Spain. The work could not be printed until 1892, though Sepulveda's *Apologia* for it was known. The disturbing feature of this book was of course that he explicitly extended the arguments widely used among humanists about defending the *respublica* with the claim that according to Aristotle war in order to rule natural slaves was justified; as Democrates' interlocutor exclaimed at this point, 'You are saying extraordinary things, beyond anything accepted by learned men'.[78] But Sepulveda's Ciceronian translation of the *Politics* already contained the clearest and most accurate translation of the Aristotelian passages about the acquisition of natural slaves, breaking the medieval tradition of construing the passages in a more humane light (see Chapter 2), and, as we have seen, his views would not have been extraordinary in Italian or French humanist circles.

Moreover, despite the comprehensive defeat which Sepulveda's views suffered in Spain, broadly similar ideas continued to be put forward by humanist jurists outside Spain. As I said in the Introduction, the change from a humanism based on Cicero to one based on Tacitus which I have traced in a recent book,[79] made little difference in this area: for the dissension with Cicero was over the need for the citizen to put liberty at the heart of his moral and political life. That the state should treat its own independence and power as pre-eminently important, was not in doubt. Thus the greatest of these late-sixteenth-century Tacitists, Justus Lipsius, talked about war in terms very similar to those of the earlier humanists, and made their point very clearly when he remarked that 'invasion can be legitimate, even without a precedent injury, as in the case of Barbarians and other people who are wholly abhorrent to us in customs or religion: especially if they are powerful, and themselves invade or have invaded other countries.'[80]

[77] *Cohortatio ad Carolum V ut facta cum Christianis pace, bellum suscipiat in Turcas* 362–3.

[78] *Miranda narras Democrates, et praeter receptam doctorum hominum opinionem. Democrates Segundo*, ed. Angel Losada (Madrid, 1951), 19.

[79] *Philosophy and Government 1572–1651* (Cambridge University Press, 1993).

[80] From Lipsius's *Politicorum*, ch. V (1589), (Antwerp, 1623), 150. *Iam & invasio quaedam legitime videtur, etiam sine iniuria. ut in Barbaros, & moribus aut religione prorsum a nobis abhorrentes: maxime si potentes ij, & aliena ipsi invaserunt aut invadunt.*

The most striking practical instance of this approach is in the justification produced by French writers for their colonizing projects. As we shall see in Chapter 2, after the mid-century and the defeat of Sepulveda, the Spanish were very unwilling at any high intellectual level to justify their conquests in terms of a civilizing mission; instead, they insisted on a strict reading of the laws of war between developed countries. As we shall see in Chapters 3 and 4, the Dutch and the English were equally unwilling, preferring (unsurprisingly) a kind of economic argument (see also the next section of this chapter). But the French remained remarkably loyal to the early humanist idea that one is entitled to conquer and rule the less civilized with the intention of civilizing them.

Like their rivals the Dutch and the English, the French were led initially into colonial projects by fear of the threat posed to them by the Spanish world empire—it is no coincidence that all three nations were involved in bitter fighting against Spain's European domination in the late sixteenth century. All through the sixteenth century there were small-scale attempts by the French and English to establish permanent settlements on the land of native peoples, particularly in North and South America, which could be used as bases from which to harass the Spanish Empire, and from the early seventeenth century the French succeeded in constructing permanent bases in the outer Caribbean islands and in the northern part of North America. In practice these settlements were devoted to trade rather than agriculture and colonial occupation, and the numbers of people involved were very small—in 1627 there were only 107 Frenchmen in Canada;[81] but the French government and ecclesiastical establishment had theoretically intended these early settlements to be full colonies, despite the fact that the actual explorers usually recognized that the only effective economic basis for their activities would be trade with the native peoples, along the lines of the Portuguese Eastern trade.

Thus the commissions issued in the mid-sixteenth century to Cartier and Roberval for their abortive schemes on the St Lawrence envisaged the planting of colonists and the cultivation of the land. These schemes did not find much practical expression, however, until the 1620s (at the same time as the Dutch also began larger scale annexation of land). The arrival of missionaries among the fur traders led to extensive debates

[81] See James Axtell, *The Invasion Within: The Contest of Cultures in Colonial North America* (New York: Oxford University Press, 1985), 36.

within 'New France' about the scope of the colonies, and whether they should be turned into agricultural communities using both French and Indian labour.[82]

In these debates, the French advocates of expansion drew on the kinds of ideas about war put forward by the humanist writers (many of whom were French—for example, Jacques Lefevre, Josse Clichtove, and François Connan). In particular, they stressed that the justification for colonization would be its civilizing effect, including its success in bringing the native peoples to Christianity. The patent which Henri IV gave to Pierre de Gua for a colony on the Atlantic coast in 1603 said that the principal point of the settlement was 'to cause the people which do inhabit the country, men (at this present time) barbarous, atheists, without faith or religion', to be converted to Christianity, and from the beginning the kings of France made it at least a theoretical condition of grants of trading rights to new colonies that the grantees should arrange for missionaries. As a corollary, Louis XIII declared that all Indian converts would become full French citizens, entitled to settle in France and acquire property—the long history of participation by colonial peoples in metropolitan French life had formally been inaugurated.[83]

Lescarbot, the first historian of New France, and a man very sympathetic to the missionary programme, explained the connection between the programme and the introduction of agriculture by settled European colonists:

> tillage of ground . . . is the chiefest thing that may draw men to believe as one would, by reason that out from the earth cometh all that which is necessary for the life . . . Whosoever then shall give bread and clothing to this people, the same shall be, as it were, their God: they will believe all that he shall say to them, even as the Patriarch Jacob did promise to serve God if he would give him bread to eat and garments to cover him.[84]

This stress on Christianity corresponded to French practice in their wars within Europe itself, where the French were very ready to employ the language of the Christian mission; thus replying to Jansen's *Mars Gallicus*, which had called into question the legitimacy of war against another Christian prince, the King of Spain, with arguments which

[82] See James Axtell, 36–40.

[83] Ibid. 38; the decree about citizenship is in *Recueil géneral des ancienes lois* (Paris, 1822–7), XVI, 222.

[84] Marc Lescarbot, *The History of New France*, ed. H. P. Biggar and W. L. Grant, trans. W. L. Grant (Toronto, 1907–14), I, 163.

were, unsurprisingly, very similar to those of Erasmus, Daniel de Priézac asserted in 1638 that

the glory and conservation of the Christian Empire seems to be so clearly tied to, and absolutely dependent upon, [France's] endless survival, that if the predictions of the oracles are to be believed, Roman greatness will not perish as long as there are Kings of France, for it will always be supported by them and preserved by their help.[85]

The same basically humanist argument seems to have been used about slavery; at least, it was widely believed in the French Antilles in the eighteenth century that there had been a traditional ban in French law on subjects of the King of France being slaves, and that this had so worried the first settlers in the Antilles that they had asked Louis XIII for a ruling on the matter. He is said to have decreed that enslavement for the purpose of conversion to Christianity was legitimate.[86] It is hard to know what the origin of this story was, but it sounds as if it was based on a half-remembered argument about the natural slavery of the non-Christian savage, of the kind often used in sixteenth-century France.

The Occupation of Vacant Land

Gentili drew one further conclusion from the notion of a human society, which was to be of great importance in the seventeenth century, and which most of his humanist precursors did not draw. In I. XVII, discussing the grounds for making offensive war 'out of necessity', he claimed both that exiles are always entitled to fight for somewhere to live, and that vacant spaces may always be colonized by those who need them and can use them.

The Ansibarii [a people whose forced exile is narrated in Tacitus's *Annals*] well said . . . 'As the Gods have Heaven, so the Earth was given to Mankind, and what is possessed by none, belongs to every one. And then looking up to the Sun and Stars as if present, and within hearing, they asked them, whether they could bear to look on those uninhabited lands, and whether they would not rather pour in the Sea upon those who hindered other to settle on them'.[87]

[85] W. F. Church, *Richelieu and Reason of State* (Princeton University Press, 1972), 400.

[86] Montesquieu, *The Spirit of the Laws*, trans. and ed. Anne M. Cohler, Basia Carolyn Miller, and Harold Samuel Stone (Cambridge University Press, 1989), III. 15. 4, p. 249; J-B Labat, *Nouveau voyage aux isles de l'Amerique*, IV (1748), 422.

[87] Instead of the Carnegie Endowment translation for this quotaation from Tacitus, I have used the translation of the same passage found in the edition of Grotius's *De Iure Belli ac Pacis*, which I cite later—*The Rights of War and Peace, in Three Books . . . To which are added, all the large notes of Mr. J. Barbeyrac . . .* (London, 1738), 156 (II. 2. 17).

True indeed, 'God did not create the world to be empty'. And therefore the seizure of vacant places is regarded as a law of nature . . . And even though such lands belong to the sovereign of that territory . . . yet because of that law of nature which abhors a vacuum, they will fall to the lot of those who take them, though the sovereign will retain jurisdiction over them . . . Are there today no unoccupied lands on the earth? Is it not, pray, being reduced more and more to the wilderness of primeval times? What is Greece today, and the whole of Turkey? What is Africa? What of Spain? It is the most populous country of all; yet under the rule of Spain is not almost all of the New World unoccupied? (pp. 80–1)

Although Gentili quoted Tacitus in this passage, the Roman historian's own view of the Ansibarian argument was rather different: he recorded that the Roman legate to whom the argument was addressed 'was impressed. But he replied that men must obey their betters, that the gods they invoked had empowered the Romans to decide what to give and take away and to tolerate no judges but themselves'.[88] And indeed, in general the Roman view was that any land had a ruler, and that the ruler could determine what happened to it. It is true that the general requirement imposed on us by human society to share our goods was recognized by many of the 'orators': we have already seen Cicero saying that the principles of *omnibus inter omnes societas* require that we should 'bestow even upon a stranger what it costs us nothing to give', while in the same work he observed that 'they do wrong who would debar foreigners from enjoying the advantages of their city and would exclude them from its borders . . . to debar foreigners from enjoying the advantages of the city is altogether inhuman' (*De Officiis*, III. xi. 47). Similarly, Plutarch records a discussion at a Roman dinner table (appropriately enough) about the obligation to allow others to share our unwanted food.[89] Many ancient cities allowed settlers to have squatters' rights on public land, a practice eloquently defended by Dio Chrysostom, the Greek orator who was a contemporary of Tacitus, in his Seventh or 'Euboean' Discourse;[90] but even Dio did not say clearly that waste land could simply be taken by those who need it.

[88] *The Annals of Imperial Rome*, trans. Michael Grant (Harmondsworth: Penguin, 1959), 300–1 (XIII. 55).

[89] *Moralia*, IX, trans. Edwin L. Minaar, F. H. Sandbach, and W. C. Helmhold (London and Cambridge, Mass.: Loeb Classical Library, 1961), 36–7 (VII. 4, 703).

[90] *Works*, I (*Discourses I–IX*), trans. J. W. Cohoon (London and Cambridge, Mass.: Loeb Classical Library, 1971), 304–7.

Later writers were, on the whole, equally hesitant about drawing this conclusion, despite their frequent endorsement of the need to avoid waste.[91] Since Roman law did not sanction the *occupatio* of vacant land, on the principle that all land must be owned by someone, the general view among civilians (expressed for example by Alciato)[92] was that the sovereign owned all unoccupied land and could distribute it.[93] In the late Middle Ages some canonists (notably Francesco Accolti, who was active in the first half of the fifteenth century, and who seems to have been particularly interested in this issue, prompted by a law case at Mantua) argued that private individuals could acquire proprietorial rights in unoccupied land by cultivating it;[94] but no one in the Middle Ages seems to have thought that such rights could be acquired against the express wishes of the local sovereign. The person who apparently put into a clear and developed form the idea which Gentili was later to pick up was, interestingly enough, More in his *Utopia*, a work which Gentili often cited with enthusiasm (for example, p. 342).

If the population throughout the entire island exceeds the quota, they enrol citizens out of every city and plant a colony under their own laws on the mainland near them, wherever the natives have plenty of unoccupied and uncultivated land. Those natives who want to live with the Utopians are taken in. When such a merger occurs the two peoples gradually and easily blend together, sharing the same way of life and customs, much to the advantage of both. For by their policies the Utopians make the land yield an abundance for all, though previously it had seemed too barren and paltry even to support the

[91] See e.g. Ambrose, *De Officiis*, III. vii. 45, *Select Works and Letters* (Oxford and New York: Select Library of Nicene and post-Nicene Fathers Series II, 1896), 75.

[92] *Opera*, VI, col. 143–4.

[93] For the Roman view, see W. W. Buckland, *A Text-Book of Roman Law* (Cambridge University Press, 1975), 207. Ownership of land could be acquired by *usucapio*, that is, long-term possession of a thing in good faith that one was entitled to it; but in the clearest passage in the *Digest* where this is discussed (a passage of Gaius, known now to us through the complete text of his *Institutes*, but not so known to the Middle Ages and Renaissance) the example is a piece of land left vacant through the 'negligence' of the owner, occupied by someone and then transferred to a third party: 'if the taker transfers this possession to one who receives it in good faith, the transferee will be able to acquire the land by usucapion; and even though he who took the vacant possession knows that the land is nother's, this is no obstacle to the *bona fide* possessor' (*The Institutes of Gaius*, ed. Francis de Zulueta (Oxford University Press, 1946), 78–79 (II. 51); *Digest*, 41. 3. 37). This is the equivalent of the English rule about the bona fide possession of stolen goods, and of course presupposes that the initial occupation of vacant land was unjustifiable.

[94] Franciscus [Accolti] de Aretio, *Consilia* (Lyons, 1536), 14^r (*consilium*, XV. 3). This was presumably also the reasoning behind European laws such as that referred to by Locke (*Two Treatises of Government*, ed. Peter Laslett (Cambridge University Press, 1988), 293 (II. 36)). Contrary to the popular idea, there was no common-law right of squatting in England—see William Holdsworth, *A History of English Law*, VII (London, 1926), 479–80.

natives. But those who refuse to live under their laws the Utopians drive out of the land they claim for themselves; and on those who resist them, they declare war. The Utopians say it's perfectly justifiable to make war on people who leave their land idle and waste yet forbid the use and possession of it to others who, by the law of nature, ought to be supported from it.[95]

But few even among More's successors agreed with him, until Gentili put the idea firmly into the minds of people engaged in constructing colonies in the New World; the subsequent fortune of this idea, particularly in the hands of the Dutch and the English (for, as I said in the previous section, it was rarely used by French or Spanish writers), will be a central theme of the following chapters.

[95] *Utopia* ed. George M. Logan and Robert M. Adams (Cambridge University Press 1989), 56.

2

SCHOLASTICISM

Ancient Philosophy

To turn from the pages of Gentili's *De Iure Belli* to the disputations *de bello* in Luis de Molina's *De Iustitia et Iure* is to move to a completely different view of war, put forward in a wholly different literary genre. Gone is the dense array of references to ancient authors; instead, we have the characteristic scholastic repertory of Christian fathers and modern (that is, medieval) philosophers. The first edition of Molina's book appeared in 1593, but it was based on lectures delivered at Evora in 1582, in the form of a commentary on Thomas Aquinas's *Secunda Secundae* Qu. 40.[1] It came towards the end of a long and distinguished series of works on the subject by Spanish Thomists, many of them (though not Molina himself) Dominicans associated with the University of Salamanca. Molina's most famous immediate predecessor was Francisco de Vitoria, the only one of this group whose works are at all well known today.

Molina's views are easily summarized; indeed, he himself provided a summary at the head of each disputation. First, he distinguished between *defensive* and *offensive* war. The former was open to anybody, private or public, as long as the victim was genuinely suffering an immediate and actual attack, and could retaliate in some moderate and proportionate fashion (p. 269). The latter involved either the punishment of some state for an injury committed by its ruler or its subjects, or the recovery of some property which had wrongly been withheld; it was restricted to legitimate sovereigns (pp. 267, 291), unless men were living in a 'barbaric' situation, without developed government, such as those in *Brasilica regione*, when the leaders of *familia* or *pagi* were effectively the sovereigns and could act as the *ministri Dei* in securing

[1] For the text, see Manuel Fraga Iribarne, *Luis de Molina y el Derecho de la Guerra* (Madrid, 1947). Details of the work's origins are on pp. 33–8.

vengeance (p. 273). Wars in pursuit of glory, or pre-emptive strikes, were utterly forbidden (p. 343); war could not be just on both sides (pp. 343, 190); warfare against barbarians was unjustifiable, unless it was to protect innocent victims of their aggression, and even then it should not usually lead to the occupation of their lands by a foreign power, but to the liberation of their victims (p. 351). All of these views, it will be clear, are expressly opposite to those of Gentili and the other humanists.

The theological tradition of which *De Iustitia et Iure* was a part began, we can say, before Christianity itself, for it drew initially on the kinds of criticism of the pagan orators which had been made in antiquity itself, by the Greek philosophers of the Socratic school. It should not be forgotten that these philosophers had come to their ethical beliefs as a result of a struggle against a group of men who represented in the Greek cities very much the same values as the Romans later espoused—the sophists (whom the Roman rhetoricians later termed *oratores* and praised as their predecessors). The parallel was particularly marked in the case of the *Gorgias*, where Socrates's opponent is depicted both as elevating oratory above philosophy, and as being untroubled about the struggle for personal and political domination. Against the orators, the philosophers (particularly Plato and Aristotle) had insisted that the highest good for man, or the best way of life, was not the practical life of the citizen, but the virtuous contemplation of the philosopher. This was true even of Aristotle, despite the undoubted weight he gave to life within the *polis*, for the good life in the *polis* was ultimately inferior to the life of contemplation depicted in Book X of the *Ethics*.

A natural implication of this was that military activity by the citizen was also regarded somewhat warily; as Aristotle said in the *Politics* (1333a41): 'men must be able to engage in business and to go to war, but leisure and peace are better; they must do what is necessary and indeed what is useful, but what is honourable is better'. And he observed of the Spartans that 'many modern writers'

> commend the Lacedaemonian constitution, and praise the legislator for making conquest and war his sole aim, a doctrine which may be refuted by argument and has long ago been refuted by facts. For most men desire empire in the hope of accumulating the goods of fortune; and on this ground Thibron and all those who have written about the Lacedaemonian constitution have

praised their legislator, because the Lacedaemonians, by being trained to meet dangers, gained great power. But surely they are not a happy people now that their empire has passed away, nor was their legislator right.[2]

Plato, it should be said, had a more complex approach to the issue. In his *Laws* he set up a debate between Clinias the Cretan, who remarked (in words which presumably influenced Hobbes, and certainly influenced Bacon[3]) that 'humanity is in a condition of public war of every man against every man' (626), and the Athenian Stranger who reproved him for this view and urged that a state should not primarily be designed for war (628, 638). On the other hand, Plato's *Republic* (as the discussion of the origin of the state at 372–4 illustrates) takes it for granted that the primary purpose of the Guardians will be to make war, and to conquer other cities in the interests of preserving and protecting their own. From the point of view of later readers, however, it seems to have been the views in this area of the *Laws* rather than the *Republic* which carried most weight.

There was one important and revealing qualification in these accounts of war and empire, made most brutally by Aristotle. Men should not

> study war with a view to the enslavement of those who do not deserve to be enslaved; but first of all they should provide against their own enslavement, and in the second place obtain empire for the good of the governed, and not for the sake of exercising a general despotism, and in the third place they should seek to be masters only over those who deserve to be the slaves. (1333b39–1334a2)[4]

This passage ties in with the chilling remark at 1256b22 that 'the art of war is a natural art of acquisition, for the art of acquisition includes hunting, an art which we ought to practise against wild beasts, and against men who, though intended by nature to be governed, will not submit; for war of such a kind is naturally just'.[5] Warfare for the glory and advancement of one's *polis* was frowned on in the Aristotelian (and, arguably, the wider Greek) tradition; but warfare for the principle of governing inferiors—Hellenes over barbarians, as Isocrates (for example) constantly called for—had a moral justification. The Greek

[2] *The Politics*, ed. Stephen Everson (Cambridge University Press, 1988), 177–8.
[3] *The Letters and the Life*, VII, ed. James Spedding (London, 1874), 476.
[4] *The Politics*, ed. Stephen Everson, p. 178. [5] Ibid. 11.

philosophers' view (speaking broadly) was thus that the construction of an ethical order was the principal justification for making war, and that patriotism of the Roman kind was not enough.

The early Christians' attack on the culture of pagan Rome, and particularly on the culture of the pagan orators, went (of course) much further than the philosophers' attack had gone. The ferocity of this onslaught should not be understimated, nor its cogency in exposing apparent inconsistencies in the orators' views. For example, in the early fourth century the North African Christian Lactantius, in his *Divine Institutes*, launched a bitter attack on the whole of the Ciceronian culture—a culture in which he himself had been trained and about which he was an expert. As he rightly pointed out, Cicero was ambiguous: on the one hand, he talked about 'the common society of the human race', but on the other he praised those who put 'the interests of our country in the first place'. 'What are the interests of our country', wrote Lactantius, 'but the inconveniences of another state or nation?—that is, to extend the boundaries which are violently taken from others, to increase the power of the state, to improve the revenues,—all which things are not virtues, but the overthrowing of virtues.'[6] And he quoted from Carneades, as Cicero had done, but with complete approval: 'all nations which flourished with dominion, even the Romans themselves, who were masters of the whole world, if they wish to be just, that is, to restore the possessions of others, must return to cottages, and lie down in want and miseries.'[7] Lactantius concluded

> Whoever, then, has gained for his country these goods (as they themselves call them)—that is, who by the overthrow of cities and the destruction of nations has filled the treasury with money, has taken lands and enriched his countrymen—he is extolled with praises to the heaven: in him there is said to be the greatest and perfect virtue. And this is the error not only of the people and the ignorant, but also of philosophers, who even give precepts for injustice, lest folly and wickedness should be wanting in discipline and authority. Therefore, when they are speaking of the duties relating to warfare, all that discourse is accommodated neither to justice nor to true virtue.[8]

And he remarked, 'it will be neither lawful for a just man to engage in warfare, since his warfare is justice itself, nor to accuse any one of a capital charge, because it makes no difference whether you put a man

[6] *Works*, I trans. William Fletcher (Edinburgh: Ante-Nicene Christian Library XXI, 1871), 366.

[7] Ibid. 328. [8] Ibid. 367.

to death by word, or by the sword, since it is the act of putting to death itself which is prohibited'.[9]

Augustine

If Lactantius's wishes had prevailed, the culture of pagan Rome, including Cicero's works, would have been destroyed; but, as we saw in Chapter 1, the culture was saved in part by the ingenuity of Augustine, and by the force of his argument that the Roman values could be seen in a way as models for Christian values. But Augustine's approach to these issues was notoriously complex, and its complexity lingered in much of the subsequent theological writing about war. While it is true that he believed that the Roman struggle for glory was in a sense a model for the Christian, he was very clear that this was only at the level of the *Civitas Dei*—patriotic striving for the glory of one's *civitas terrena* was not justifiable for the Christian, who had to recognize the essentially illusory character of terrene values (in his *Contra Academicos* he drew the analogy between this idea and Platonism, observing that 'civic virtues' (*virtutes civiles*) were part of the sensible world which was only a flawed imitation of the intelligible one).[10] On the other hand, a Christian could use violence on behalf of his city, as long as it was used without *libido*—that is to say, as long as it was clearly recognized that it was a deeply unfortunate duty brought about by a clear case of injustice in the world, and that the violence was intended to protect 'those things in accordance with the law by which peace and human society are preserved—insofar as they *can* be preserved on the basis of such things'.[11] It followed that a wise magistrate, taking due cognizance of the situation, could order his soldiers both to repulse an enemy 'by an equal force for the protection of the citizens',[12] and to make offensive war when doing so could 'revenge the injuries caused when the nation or *civitas* with which war is envisaged has either neglected to make recompence for some illegitimate act committed by its members, or to return what has been injuriously taken'.[13] As he said in the *Civitas Dei*, 'it is the injustice of the opposing side that lays on the wise man the

[9] Ibid. 407.

[10] *Answer to Skeptics*, ed. Rudolph Arbesmann, trans. Denis J. Kavanagh (New York, 1943), 214–15 (III. xvii. 37).

[11] *On Free Choice of the Will*, ed. and trans. Thomas Williams (Indianoapolis: Hackett, 1993), 25 (I. 15).

[12] Ibid. 9 (I. 15).

[13] *Quaestiones in Pentateuchum*, Migne, *Patrologia Latina*, xxxiv, col. 781.

duty of waging wars'[14]—competitive rivalry of states, for example, could never count as a justification. The scope left to an individual citizen to use violence was also much less, given that even the preservation of one's self was not something which was likely to be embarked upon without *libido*: the magistrate in a sense was sacrificing himself for his city, and therefore for other men, but a citizen who clung to his own life was guilty of unchristian conduct. He put into the mouth of one of the characters in *On Free Choice of the Will* (the early work in which he explored all these issues in the most compelling way) the following sentiment, which seems to be treated sympathetically within the dialogue.

A soldier who kills the enemy is acting as an agent of the law, so he can easily perform his duty without inordinate desire (*libido*). Furthermore, the law itself, which was established with a view to protecting the people, cannot be accused of any inordinate desire . . . [But as for someone who defends his own life, for example against a highway robber], I do not see how they can be excused, even if the law itself is just. For the law does not force them to kill; it merely leaves that in their power. They are free not to kill anyone for those things which can be lost against their will, and which they should therefore not love [i.e. their earthly life].[15]

This austere view of violence, in which it had to be thoroughly dissociated from self-interest of any kind, was clearly in practice the antithesis to the orators' vision of the competitive struggle for domination among men and cities. Even such features of their view as the idea of a general human society were questionable, at least in so far as they had been presented as fulfilling an individual's wants: Book XIX of the *Civitas Dei* contained a critical discussion of this notion, which no doubt helped to make it less central in the theological tradition than one might have expected.

What consolation have we in this human society, so replete with mistaken notions and distressing anxieties, except the unfeigned faith and mutual affections of genuine, loyal friends? Yet the more friends we have and the more dispersed they are in different places, the further and more widely extend our fears that some evil may befall them from among all the mass of evils of this present world. (p. 862)[16]

[14] *City of God*, ed. David Knowles, trans. Henry Bettenson (Harmondsworth, 1972), 862 (XIX. 7).

[15] *On Free Choice of the Will*, p. 9 (I. 5).

[16] *City of God*, p. 862 (XIX. 8),

What Augustine left to his successors was, therefore, an ambiguous legacy. On the one hand (as we saw in the previous chapter), he helped to preserve something of the spirit of the Roman rhetorical writers, but on the other hand he helped to make a very tight linkage between the principles of human *law* and the conduct of warfare. War had to be strictly parallel to the jurisdictional act of a magistrate, and could not be justified by the much looser conditions which the Romans had allowed—Cicero's distinction, for example, between the immortal *civitas* and the mortal citizen would have been deeply offensive to Christian sensibilities (which may, of course, be why the relevant portion of the *De Respublica* is lost). The linkage between the theologians and the lawyers, in this area, persisted throughout the Middle Ages, and is the most distinctive feature of the theology of war throughout the period. It is found particularly strongly expressed in the principal theological discussions of war for the later Middle Ages which were centred on the *Decretum* and the *Decretals*—the very existence of 'canon law' being testimony to the salience and the pervasiveness of the link by that date. Thus, by a careful selection of Ciceronian and Augustinian texts (in particular avoiding Book I of the *De Officiis* and Book V of the *City of God*), Gratian (the twelfth-century compiler of the *Decretum*) and his successors represented both the Ciceronian and the Christian tradition as exclusively endorsing the narrowly penal or juridical view of war (a representation which has continued to mislead even modern writes such as F. H. Russell).[17] All Gratian's citations, in Russell's words, 'emphasised the similarity between a judicial process and the just war',[18] including the claim that nations and their rulers could be treated as equivalent to private individuals in Roman law, and that the Roman principles of private law applicable to self-defensive violence could straightforwardly by applied to them.[19]

But it is important to recognize that in this area there was a two-way traffic: the lay students of civil law in the Middle Ages were not anything like as interested in the 'laws of war' as their clerical colleagues, for the simple reason that (as we have already seen) the Roman law did not contain any particularly helpful discussion of international affairs—the most obvious passages, such as Pomponius on *postliminium*, must have seemed very alien to medieval writers. It was clerics trying to

[17] See Frederick H. Russell, *The Just War in the Middle Ages* (Cambridge University Press, 1975), ch. 1 *passim*.

[18] Ibid. 63. [19] Ibid. 96–8, 131–3.

extend some of the principles of Roman law into the new territory of international affairs who produced the most distinctive theories.

Dominium Mundi

A good example of this is one of the most famous and curious medieval claims, that the emperor is lord of the world. It is often supposed that this was a straightforward survival of Roman attitudes, but as we saw in Chapter 1, Latin writers and Roman lawyers were hesitant in claiming that their state was *de jure* the ruler of the world, and where it was claimed, it is usually clear that it was merely hyperbole. There is only one passage in the *Digest* in which such a claim is formally made (14. 2. 9): this is a passage taken from the writings of Volusius Maecianus on the Rhodian sea law (the set of conventions which Mediterranean sailors used to sort out disputes over wrecks, etc.), which records the answer of the Emperor Antoninus to the petition of a shipwrecked sailor: '"I am master of the world (*kosmos*), but the law of the sea must be judged by the sea law of the Rhodians when our own law does not conflict with it." Augustus, now deified, decided likewise.'[20] This is the modern translation, based on the Greek text which became available in the Renaissance. Throughout the Middle Ages, this passage was accessible only in a Latin version, which went as follows (my translation): 'I am master of the world: and the law of the sea. Marine affairs are to be judged by the law of the Rhodians: the law makes no conflict between our rights and that law. Augustus, now deified, decided likewise.'[21] The original text makes a rather broken-backed case for world sovereignty and for imperial rights over the sea—presumably, the seaman had described Antoninus in the usual fulsome terms as 'master of the world', and the emperor was busy disavowing any practical legal consequences to the title. The medieval text is a little more sweeping, but so obscure as to be almost useless without substantial support.

[20] *Digest of Justinian*, Latin text ed. Theodor Mommsen and Paul Krueger, English trans. ed. Alan Watson (University of Pennsylvania Press, 1985), 14. 2. 9.

[21] *Ego quidem mundi dominus: lex autem maris. Lege rhodiorum iudicet nautica: in quibus nulla nostrarum ei lex adversetur: hoc autem ipsum et divus augustus iudicavit*. (*Digestum Vetus* (Paris, 1510), 382^r). The translation of '*in quibus . . . adversetur*' is hazardous; I have taken it to mean literally '[that] law opposes nothing of ours in those matters to it [i.e. the *lex Rhodia*]'. The sentence attracted much discussion among the commentators until the proper text clarified it—a classic instance of what Renaissance scholars resented about their predecessors.

Between the disappearance of the Roman law texts in the West and their rediscovery in the twelfth century, this kind of claim is scarcely ever made by emperors—A. J. Carlyle wisely observed in his history of political thought that the Carolingians claimed to be lords of 'Europe' or of the *populus Christiana*, but not of any wider entity. Augustine, moreover, did not think of the Roman Empire as *global*, though he did of course believe in its world-historical significance. And even after the *Digest* was read again the early glossators such as Accursius tended to treat this passage as possessing little significance. What seems to have marked a major change was the activity of the 'Decretists'—the commentators on Gratian's *Decretum*, the principal early codification of canon law.[22] By the end of the twelfth century canonists could freely say (in the words of Alanus Anglicus) that 'the ancient law of nations held that there should be only one emperor in the world' and that 'infidel rulers' have no right to the sword.[23] This idea gathered pace among the canonists and became enshrined in the mid-thirteenth-century *Decretals*, the supplement to the *Decretum*. There, the gloss to a papal bull dealing with the 'translation' of the empire to the Germans said expressly that *regnum mundi* was translated, and that the emperor was *princeps mundi et dominus* (I. VI. 34, *Venerabilem*).

The reason why it was the canonists rather than the civilians who led the way was, of course, that unlike the Roman writers and lawyers they already possessed a coherent account of world rule, in the form of the idea that the Pope was 'Vicar of Christ' with rights of some kind over all the peoples of the earth. The origins of this idea lay in the ninth century, when Popes such as Nicholas I could say that they were set up as princes over the whole earth,[24] and it was clearly a more plausible view than the belief that the Roman emperor had been lord of all the world: the emperor's claims were straighforwardly refuted by the facts of geopolitics, but the Pope's claims belonged to a different scheme of things and could not be refuted (in principle) by the existence of any number of independent principalities. Since the canonists also believed that imperial power had been conferred on the Christian emperors by

[22] For both the *Decretum* and the *Decretals*, see *Corpus Iuris Canonici*, ed. E. L. Richter and E. Friedberg (Graz, 1959). The relevant *quaestiones* in the *Decretum* are II. c. 23 qu. 1, 2 (I, 889–95).

[23] See A. M. Stickler, 'Alanus Anglicus als Verteidiger des Monarchischen Papsttums', *Salesianum*, 21 (1959), 362, 363.

[24] See e.g. Walter Ullmann, *A History of Political Thought: The Middle Ages* (Penguin, 1965), 78.

the Pope, it simply followed for them that the emperors must possess *dominium mundi* by virtue of certain fundamental features of Christianity.

Throughout the late Middle Ages, canonists pursued these two ideas: that the Pope was in some sense lord of the world; and that he had transferred some of his powers to an emperor who also had a global responsibility. In practice, what one might term the reserved rights of the papacy came to be of greater significance, as emperors proved (for example) to be broken reeds over such matters as crusades; it came to be commonly held that the Pope could exercise his global jurisdiction by calling on any secular rulers to implement his decisions. As for the character of papal jurisdiction over infidels (for, of course, his jurisdiction over Christians was much less problematic), the standard view was that put forward by Sinibaldo Fieschi, later Pope Innocent IV, in the mid-thirteenth century. Infidels were not *as such* enemies of the Christian world, nor deserving of punishment; indeed, physical punishment for unbelief violated one of the prime dogmas of Christianity, that unbelievers should not be converted by force. But the Pope as Christ's vicar had a general responsibility for ensuring that all men obeyed God's laws, and he could therefore punish infidels, as well as Christians, for breaking them. It was not part of God's law in this sense that one should be a Christian—there was no natural obligation on men to follow the gospel. But it was part of God's law (according to Innocent) not to commit sodomy or idolatry, since both these sins could be recognized as such even by natural men, and infidels could be punished by Christian arms, as the behest of the Pope, for sins of this kind.

They could also be punished for denying access by Christian missionaries to their territory: this was another aspect of their obligation to obey God's law, since it was a general requirement on men at least to listen to the truth. Unlike many later writers, Innocent actually faced up to the question of whether infidels could similarly send missionaries into Christian lands, and replied stiffly that they could not, 'because they are in error and we are on the righteous path'. Papal intervention to protect Christians tyrannized by infidels was also legitimate, on the same grounds as intervention by the papacy in the affairs of any kingdom to protect its subjects was justified.[25] Though Innocent's view was undoubtedly the most authoritative within the church, there was a

[25] See James Muldoon, *Popes, Lawyers, and Infidels: The Church and the Non-Christian World 1250–1550*, (University of Pennsylvania Press, 1979), 5–15.

more radical tradition, represented particularly by his pupil Henry of Segusio ('Hostiensis'), which held that infidels were by definition sinners who had forfeited any right to hold property or political office, and who could therefore in principle legitimately be governed directly by Christian rulers under the general direction of the Pope.[26] In the fourteenth century, this view came to be smeared with heresy, through its similarity to the heretical doctrine that *dominium* rested on grace, and the Innocentian view survived as the orthodox papalist theory. It is accordingly found in writers such as Augustinus Triumphus, who argued that all pagans can be punished by the Pope for breach of any law which they themselves accept 'and which they profess to observe', such as (he alleged) the law of nature. To meet the objection that the Pope does not in fact possess jurisdiction over pagans, Augustinus replied that 'Pagans are not subject to the Pope *de facto*, but they are *de iure*, since *de iure* no rational creature can remove itself from his dominion, any more than from the dominion of God'.[27] The same argument is still found in a standard late-medieval textbook, which was to be very influential throughout the sixteenth century, Sylvestro Mazzolini's *Summa Summarum*.[28]

Some civil lawyers were ready to incorporate the canonists' views into their own work; thus Frederick II proclaimed that he was *dominus mundi* in an imperial constitution which became incorporated into the *Corpus Juris Civilis*. Commenting on this, and on *Digest* 14. 2. 9, Bartolus of Sassoferrato in the fourteenth century produced an influential formulation. Citing the same array of biblical texts which the canonists had used, Bartolus accepted that 'after Christ all *imperium* was in Christ and his Vicar; and was transferred by the Pope onto the secular prince' with the result that the Emperor became *dominus mundi*;[29] indeed, 'he who says the Emperor is not lord and monarch of the whole world is a heretic'.[30] But he recognized the force of the argument that there are many peoples who have never accepted the rights of the emperor, and who might even believe (as in the case of the 'Grant Cham' of the

[26] Ibid. 16–17. This seems to be similar to the remarks of Alanus Anglicus, n. 23.

[27] *De Potestate Ecclesiastica*, qu. 23 (1584), 137. The same view is found later in Antonius of Florence's *Summa*, III. 22. 5. 8.

[28] 'De Papa', qu. 7 (Nuremberg, 1518), 358r.

[29] *Post Christum vere omne imperium est apud Christum; & eius Vicariam: & transfertur per Papam in principem saecularem*. On *Extravagantes*, *Quomodo in laesae maiestatis*, tit. 1, *Ad respicium* (*Corpus Juris Civilis*, V (Geneva, 1625), sig. PP1r).

[30] Bartolus, *In Digestum Novum Commentarii* (Basle, 1562), 983–4 (on 49. 15. 24).

Tartars) that it is their ruler who is in fact *dominus mundi*.[31] His solution was to employ the same distinction as Augustinus: infidels are subject to the Emperor *de jure* but not *de facto*.

Bartolus's view remained common among civilans who worked with and were sympathetic to canonists and theologians, but it came under fire from Renaissance jurists, fuelled by the vision of Rome which I dealt with in Chapter 1. Alciato (as always, the representative humanist jurist) expressed scorn for the idea of the *Doctores* that the whole world is subject to the Emperor *de jure*.

> I do not agree with this, partly because there are many areas which do not obey the Romans, such as Scythia and Sarmatia, and all the East beyond the Euphrates . . . And although some Emperors called themselves lords of the world, either that should be taken as hyperbole, or their remarks should be discounted, as being in their own interests.[32]

He also dissented from the claim that the Pope could exercise jurisdiction over infidels, at least where their conduct had no effect on Christians; in doing so, he said (interestingly), he was lining up with most of the other *moderni*.[33]

Despite this, the first voyagers to the New World, who were Alciato's contemporaries, began by using medieval accounts of world *dominium* to justify their activities. Portuguese expansion in Africa and the Atlantic islands was usually accompanied by papal bulls legitimating the conquest of infidels in those territories along Innocentian lines, and Pope Alexander VI in 1493 issued a famous set of bulls making the same point about Portuguese and Castilian conquests in the New World, and calling on the governments to settle a demarcation line between them (duly accomplished in the Treaty of Tordesillas the following year).[34] Though it is sometimes said that the Pope was merely wishing to act as an arbitrator, the text of the bulls strongly suggests that Alexander's lawyers believed that he had the right to allocate unknown lands. When the Spanish government in the first years of the

[31] Ibid.

[32] *Sed haec ipse non probo: tum quia multa sunt provinciae quae non paruerunt Romanis, ut Scythia & Sarmatia, et ultra Euphratem fluvium universus Oriens . . . Et quamivis quandoque Imperatores orbis dominos se appellent, id vel per hyperbolem accipiendum est, vel eorum dictis minime credendum, quia in causa propria*. *Opera*, III, col. 180.

[33] *Opera*, IV, 449.

[34] See e.g. Muldoon, *Popes, Lawyers, and Infidels*, pp. 137–9. For the bulls, see Frances Gardiner Davenport ed., *European Treaties Bearing on the History of the United States and its Dependencies to 1648* I (Washington, DC, 1917), 56–83.

new century consulted experts about the legitimacy of its conquest, it too received strong advice that papal authority entitled Christian rulers to occupy the lands of infidels. Its advisers stressed in particular both the need to protect missionaries, and the sins of the Indians against natural law in matters of sexual morality, as justifications for papal intervention.[35] By the 1520s, however, this was far less commonly claimed—partly (as we shall see) because it no longer fitted Spanish policy, but partly because the views of the *moderni* had won out among the jurists who provided professional advice to the government.

THE LAW OF THE SEA

The practical issue which was often at the forefront of the civilians' minds as they discussed the notion of the emperor as *dominus mundi* was not, however, the question of infidel rights. Instead, it was the issue raised in the very fragment of Volusianus Maecianus which was their text—the question of rights over the sea. Though many historians have been strangely reluctant to admit it, it is fairly clear that the Romans simply assumed that in principle (though not necessarily, as we have seen, in practice) the powers of the emperor extended to the high seas, and that this was the actual point of the remark made by Antoninus in *Digest* 14. 2. 9. The *Digest* also contains many passages in which it is said that the sea is 'common' to all mankind, in the sense that no estates can be carved out of it; but imperial legal rights over the sea are obviously compatible with the claim that the sea cannot be owned in the same sense as the land.

After the general use of Roman law lapsed in the West, the new kingdoms tended to claim rights against one another in their seas; but the recovery of the *Corpus Juris Civilis* led the civil lawyers to reconsider the possibility that the emperor had some general jurisdiction over the oceans. Some early readers of the *Digest* took this passage from Maecianus to mean (according to Accursius) that 'no law can go against

[35] The Burgos *junta* of 1512 at which these issues were first extensively discussed in Spain is dealt with in Pagden, *The Fall of Natural Man* (Cambridge University Press, 1982), 47–50. The extensive treatises which were submitted to the king in the same year by two members of the *junta*, Juan López de Palacios Rubios and Matías de Paz, are translated in *De las Islas del mar Océano [and] Del dominio de los Reyes de España sobre los indios*, trans. Agustín Millares Carlo, ed. Silvio Zavala (Mexico City: Fondo de Cultura Económica, 1954), and are discussed in Pagden *The Fall of Natural Man*, pp. 50–6 and Muldoon *Poets, Lawyers, and Infidels*, p. 142. De Paz was particularly critical of the Dominican tradition as represented by Durandus—see *De las Islas del mar Océano*, pp. 234–9.

the custom of the sailors' (*nulla lex possit adversari consuetudine nautarum*), but Accursius himself said this was a bad interpretation (*male*), and that in fact it means that the Rhodian law must be followed in those matters which 'our laws' do not contradict.[36] So from the time of Accursius, it was clear to Roman lawyers that the emperor could in principle legislate for the sea. As another gloss said, things such as the sea and the coastline 'are common with respect to use and ownership [*dominium*], but with respect to protection [*protectionem*] they are the Roman people's'. A later note to this gloss explained that 'protection' meant 'jurisdiction', which is 'Caesar's'.[37]

What did 'protection' or 'jurisdiction' mean in the context of the sea? It is fairly clear from imperial *acta* in the thirteenth century, and from the writings of late-medieval legists, that jurisdiction covered such things as the right to levy tolls on navigation and to tax and even to organize sea-fisheries, as well as less controversial matters such as preventing piracy and policing shipboard crime etc.[38] These were rights over the *person*—as the gloss said, the 'sea' in 14. 2. 9 means 'those who travel over the sea, and their possessions',[39] and estates could not be created consisting of areas of the sea; but most of the rights which later states have claimed over their territorial waters were claimed for the emperor by thirteenth-century lawyers. It seems to have been generally assumed that a ruler could not actually *forbid* such things as peaceful passage and fishing, but since it was also assumed that these activities could be taxed and organized, the right to ban them was not needed much in practice by a government.

Characteristically, nations like the English were unconvinced by these new imperial claims: an anonymous early fourteenth-century English jurist remarked that the law of nature (on which Roman law was, of course, supposed by these writers to be based) was followed 'less in England than anywhere else in the world' because the King of England claimed jurisdictional rights in the seas around his country.[40]

36 *Digestum Vetus* (Lyons, 1569), coll. 1465–6.

37 *Digest*, 1. 8. 2, *Digestum Vetus* (Lyons, 1569), col. Fenn's discussion of this passage is very unreliable: he attributes it to 43. 8. 3, and confuses the later *additio* (which dates from the late Middle Ages) with the original gloss. Percy Thomas Fenn, *The Origin of the Right of Fishery in Territorial Waters* (Cambridge, Mass., 1926), 38.

38 Ibid. 53, 65.

39 *Digestum Vetus* (Lyons, 1569), col. 1465. See also Bartolus's observation that one can prohibit *people* from fishing, without that implying anything about the ownership of the sea—*In Tertium Tomum Pandectarum, Digestum Novum Commentarii* (Basle, 1562), 347.

40 *Select Passages from the Works of Bracton and Azo*, ed. F. W. Maitland (Selden Society, VIII, London, 1895), 125.

Similar rights were claimed in the Northern seas, even over to Greenland and beyond, by the kings of Denmark. Bartolus and his followers were able to cope with these claims in precisely the same way as they coped with the existence of infidel rulers, by arguing that although the emperor was ruler of the world *de jure*, *de facto* he had to concede the rights of local rulers to manage their own affairs. Consequently, they accepted that individual cities such as Venice and Genoa (the cases they were particularly concerned with, rather than the less familiar cases of the Northern seas) might possess the imperial authority over their seas as much as over their lands. Bartolus proposed a one hundred mile limit.[41] Beyond this limit (we can assume) he believed that the emperor had *de jure* authority and no one else had *de facto* jurisdiction—nor, of course, was the emperor usually likely to possess it.

Digest 14. 2. 9 was useful here, as it implied that it was reasonable for the emperor to recognize local customs and prescriptions in maritime matters, and it became a standard claim that the rights of Venice in the Adriatic rested on such a prescription. Some Bartolists (particularly those connected with the French court, according to Alciato)[42] went so far as to claim that the passage implied that the emperor had always had to respect the rights of other authorities over the sea, but as Alciato waspishly observed this was *perridiculum*, and was certainly not a common view; after the Renaissance rediscovery of the Greek text it was seldom asserted. It should be said that despite his implication that Antoninus's claim was an example of the *hyperbole* he attributed to some emperors, Alciato did believe that the sea 'as far as sovereignty [*superioritatem*] is concerned' is under the emperor's jurisdiction.[43] But (like many of the humanists) nowhere did he give a clear account of modern rights over the sea.

Natural Slavery

A further claim which some medieval theological writers were led to make about international affairs was influenced by their reading of Aristotle in the years after the recovery of the Aristotelian corpus. As I have said, there was intrinsically a great deal of respect for Greek

[41] See Percy Thomas Fenn, *The Origin of the Right of Fishery in Territorial Waters*, pp. 103–4.

[42] *Dispunctionum*, II. 5, *Opera*, II (Basle, 1571), col. 22.

[43] See his remarks on the subject, *Opera*, V, col. 11.

philosophy within Christianity, and even Aristotle's most startling idea, that there are natural slaves, was taken seriously. There were two passages in the *Politics* upon which the commentators expended their energy. The first was at 1255b35: 'The art of acquiring slaves, I mean of justly acquiring them, differs from both the art of the master and the art of slave, being a species of hunting or war.'[44] Clearly, this passage could be construed by later commentators as assuming that there is a distinction between acquiring slaves and *justly* acquiring them, and that in principle all the apparatus of a conventional just war could lie behind the just acquisition of slaves (captives in a just war were always seen by later writers as legitimately enslaved). Much more important was the second passage, at 1256b20–25: 'The art of war is a natural art of acquisition, for the art of acquisition includes hunting, an art which we ought to practise against wild beasts, and *against men who, though intended by nature to be governed, will not submit; for war of such a kind is naturally just* [my italics].[45] It is clear in the modern translation that this passage unequivocally states that hunting natural slaves is *ipso facto* just—it is the fact that the victims of the raid are natural slaves which makes the activity just. This was the passage which was to prove most contentious in the late Middle Ages and the Renaissance, with (it should be said) some of the contention arising from the obscurity of the Latin translation of the passage, which rendered the last part of it as reading '. . . against any men who are born to subjection but do not wish it, as if by nature this fundamental and primary war is just'.[46] However, the first readers of this text clearly construed it as meaning that slave-raiding is *ipso facto* just. For example, Albert the Great in his commen-

[44] *The Politics*, ed. Stephen Everson (Cambridge University Press, 1988), 9.

[45] Ibid. 11.

[46] This is a complicated matter, but important for our understanding of the way the Dominicans handled the matter (see below). The first Latin translation of the *Politics*, possibly an early draft by William of Moerbeke of his later standard translation (*c.*1260), rendered the clause in italics above as follows: '. . . *ad hominum quicumque nati sunt subici et non volunt, velut natura iustum hoc existens bellum primum*'. ('Translatio imperfecta', *Aristoteles Latinus*, XXIX. 1, ed. Petrus Michaud-Quantin) (Bruges, 1961). This is most reasonably translated: '. . . against those men who are born to subjection and do not wish it, as if by nature this primary war comes to be just'. It is not particularly clear precisely what this means, but the revised version suggests that the translator was seeking to tone it down still further, by omitting *existens*. This version, which became the standard text for the next two centuries, reads '. . . *ad homines quicumque nati subiici non volunt, tamquam natura iustum sit hoc praedativum bellum et primum*'. (See e.g. the text in *Libri Politicorum . . . cum commento multum utile et compendioso Joh. Versor* (Cologne, 1497)). This is another characteristically opaque rendering, but it can be translated (as I have done in my text) '. . . against any men who are born to subjection but do not wish it, as if by nature this fundamental and primary war is just'.

tary on the new work (which was precisely designed to clarify its obscurities) remarked:

Whoever are born to subjection and are naturally slaves (as was shown earlier), if they refuse to be subjected, ought according to nature to be subjected (for it is just according to nature that they be subjected). Consequently just war can be made on them, and this was the cause of the first war.[47]

Throughout the late Middle Ages this remained a possible view. The Frenchman John Buridan, in the middle of the fourteenth century, argued in his *Quaestiones* on the *Politics* that, while it is true that natural servitude must be *libera* and not the result of violence (f. ix), it is also true that war is legitimate against those *iustos natos subici* (f. x). His pupil Nicole Oresme said something similar in his translation of and commentary on the *Politics* (*c.*1370): he translated the relevant clause of 1256b20–5 from the Latin as follows: '. . . *contre quiconque hommes qui sunt naiz ou ordenés de nature pour estre subjects et ne le veulent estre. Aussi comme se ceste bataille ou guerre predative estoit juste par nature et premiere.*' In the commentary, he explained what this meant:

It is a just war because it is a just thing to suppress and bring back under nature's decree by force any thing which is naturally in subjection, if it opposes this and rebels against it. Such a war is called *primary* because it does not have a new servitude as its cause, but (as far as slaves are concerned) is for the rebellion which they make out of their malice against the decree of nature, which made them slaves at birth.[48]

It may in part have been this French tradition which lay behind what is now the well-known move by Jean Mair, to use of the idea of natural slavery to vindicate the occupation of the West Indies; but the other tradition which will have influenced him was the nascent humanist one, in which (as I showed in Chapter 1) the notion of natural slavery was being considered with favour from the early fifteenth century onwards.[49]

[47] *Quia quicumque nati sunt subiici & naturaliter, supple, sunt servi, sicut ante determinatum est, si illi nolunt subiici, cum secundum naturam subiici debeant (hoc enim secundum naturam iustum est, ut subiiciantur) illis potest iuste moveri bellum: & haec fuit causa primi belli. Opera* IV. 2 (Lyons, 1651), 29 (I. 1. 6).

[48] *Elle est juste pourtant, car toute chose qui est naturelement subjecte, si elle contrarie et fait rebellion, ce est juste chose de la reduire et ramener a son ordenance naturel par force. Et tele guerre est dicte* premiere *pource qu'elle ne est pas pour cause de nouvel seurvenue, mes quant as sers elle est pour la rebedllion qu'il ont de leur mauvestey contre l'ordenance de nature, qui les fist ders dez leur nativité. Le Livre de politique d'Aristote*, ed. A. D. Menut, *Transactions of the American Philosophical Society*, NS 60. 6 (1970), 62.

[49] One aspect of this is that the new humanist translations and commentaries increasingly made Aristotle's views unambiguous: thus the first, Leonardo Bruni's, translated

Thomism

Although canonists, and the civil lawyers influenced by them, might make these strong claims for world domination, either by emperor or pope, there was another powerful tradition in the later Middle Ages which was extremely unhappy about such claims. This was the tradition to which Molina himself belonged (despite being a Jesuit), that of the Dominicans, beginning with Thomas Aquinas. The marked feature of this tradition was that, while they agreed wholeheartedly with the Augustinian and the canonist theory of war as governed by the general principles of a civil law code, they disagreed equally profoundly with any theory of world authority, preferring instead a vision of a world of independent and equal political communities. A powerful basis for this view was of course Aristotle's account of the proper *polis* as a relatively small unit: no Aristotelian could easily accept the idea of a world state, whether it was couched in the language of papalism or in that of humanism (the *societas* or *respublica humana*). Aquinas himself was somewhat equivocal on the subject of infidel societies: in the *Secunda Secundae* of the *Summa*, he wrote

> Dominion or authority [*dominium vel praelatio* . . . is an institution of human law, whereas the distinction between the faithful and infidels is by divine law. Now divine law, which is from grace, does not do away with human law, which is from natural reason. Consequently the distinction between the faithful and infidels, considered in itself, does not cancel the dominion or authority of infidels over the faithful. However this right can be justly taken away by the sentence or ordinance of the Church which has the authority of God, for infidels by their infidelity deserve to forfeit power over the faithful.[50]

This referred only to the special case of infidels ruling over Christians; he later seemed to extend the discussion, though again in an equivocal fashion, when he remarked

the disputed clause (in terms surprisingly similar to Moerbeke's rejected version) as '. . . *contra eos homines qui ad parendum nati sunt, nec volunt parere: quia natura id bellum iustum existat*', of which the last phrase can be translated as 'since by nature this becomes a just war' (Aristotle, *Opera*, II (Basle, 1538), 132). Périon in his translation said something similar—'quod iustum sit hoc bellum natura' (Basle, 1549), p. 16. (For the significance of Périon as a humanist translator of Aristotle, see my *Philosophy and Government 1572–1651* (Cambridge, 1993), 16–17.) Sepúlveda (as one might expect) made the meaning of the passage brutally obvious: '. . . *in eos homines, qui cum sint ad parendum nati, imperium recusant: est enim huiusmodi bellum natura iustum*'. That is, 'against those men who, while they are born to obey, refuse authority: for war of this kind is just by nature'. (*Opera* (Cologne, 1601), *De Republica libri VIII*, p. 22).

[50] *Summa Theologiae*, XXXII ed. and trans. Thomas Gilby (London, 1975), 68–71 (II. IIae 10,10).

one who sins by infidelity can be sentenced to deprivation of his dominion, as also on occasion for other faults. The Church, however, is not competent to penalize unbelief in those who have never received the faith, according to St Paul's disclaimer [1 Corinthians 5: 12]. Yet she can sentence to punishment the unbelief of those who received the faith . . .[51]

But many of his Dominican followers were more outspoken. John of Paris, for example, in his famous defence of French kingship against Boniface VIII, *De Potestate Regia et Papali* of 1302–3, argued that

there can be different ways of living and different kinds of state conforming to differences in climate, language, and the conditions of men, with what is suitable for one nation not so for another . . . Accordingly, the Philosopher shows in the *Politics* that development of individual states and kingdoms is natural, although that of an empire or [universal] monarchy is not.[52]

The fact that this was in many ways a *Dominican* rather than purely a *Thomist* tradition is illustrated by the fact that Durandus of San Porciano, who was the most anti-Thomist of the early Dominicans, agreed with this view, and applied it to infidel societies. He wrote that infidel rulers not harassing Christian subjects could not be deprived of their *dominium*, and that 'pagans and infidels are outside the church and we have no right to judge them'.[53]

By the time of the discovery of the New World, this view was commonplace among Dominicans: thus Cajetan, the most authoritative Dominican writer of the late fifteenth century, who was also a loyal Thomist, declared firmly

Some infidels do not fall under the temporal jurisdiction of Christian princes either in law or in fact (*nec de iure nec de facto*). Take as an example the case of pagans who were never subjects of the Roman Empire, and who dwell in lands where the term 'Christian' was never heard. For surely the rulers of such persons are legitimate rulers, despite the fact that they are infidels and regardless of whether the government in question is a monarchical régime or a commonwealth (*politico regimine*); nor are they to be deprived of dominion

[51] Ibid. 100–1 (II. IIae 12,2).

[52] John of Paris, *On Royal and Papal Power*, trans. Arthur P. Monahan (Columbia University Press, 1974), 15.

[53] *De Iurisdictione Ecclesiastica* (Paris, 1506), 4^r; see also his *In Petri Lombard Sententias Theologicas Commentariorum Libri IIII* (Venice, 1571), 206^v. For a short account of Durandus, see *Dictionnaire de biographie française*, s.n. For a similar view from a Thomist layman, see Aquinas's pupil Pierre Dubois's opposition to a universal temporal monarchy in his *The Recovery of the Holy Land*, trans. and ed. Walther I. Brandt (New York: Columbia University Press, 1956), 121–2 (p. 3 for the fact that he attended Aquinas's lectures).

over their own peoples on the ground of lack of faith . . . No king, no emperor, not even the Church of Rome, is empowered to undertake war against them for the purpose of seizing their lands or reducing them to temporal subjection. Such an attempt would be based upon no just cause of war . . . Thus I do not read in the Old Testament, in connection with the occasions on which it was necessary to seize possession by armed force, that war was ever declared against any nation of infidels on the ground that the latter did not profess the true faith. I find, instead, that the reason for such declarations of war was the unwillingness of the infidels to concede the right of passage, or the fact that they had attacked the faithful (as the Midianites did, for example), or a desire on the part of the believers to recover their own property . . . Men of integrity ought to be sent as preachers to these infidels, in order that unbelievers may be induced by teaching and by example to seek God; but men ought not to be sent with the purpose of crushing, despoiling and tempting unbelievers, bringing them into subjection, and making them twofold more the children of hell [see Matthew 23: 15].[54]

At the same time, the Dominicans firmly denied the suggestion that war could legitimately be made against natural slaves. His own denial involved Aquinas in an extremely generous reading of the text of the *Politics*, but his authority was sufficient to render war for the purposes of enslavement unacceptable to most of his medieval readers. This fact has been obscured by the odd circumstance that the crucial texts were systematically rewritten in the Renaissance, but it is one of considerable importance for understanding the Hispanic Dominicans' hostile reaction to Sepulveda. The Dominican position on natural slavery turned on the translation of the relevant passage of the *Politics*, which (as we have just seen) was far from clear. In his commentary on the *Politics* Aquinas wrote about this passage, in sharp contrast to his master Albert, that such war should be made 'against barbarous men who are naturally slaves, as was said above, and if this is first a just war according to nature'.[55] This completely changed the sense of the passage, by insisting that the conventional criteria for a just war had already to be met before natural slaves could be brought under subjection. Aquinas seems in general to have been hesitant about a full-bloodedly

[54] On Aquinas, *Secunda Secundae*, qu. 66 art. 8 (Aquinas, *Secunda Secundae* (Lyons, 1552), 109[r]). The translation is taken from Grotius, *De Iure Praedae*, I trans. Gwladys L. Williams (Oxford University Press, 1950), 225, where Grotius quotes this passage *in extenso* against the claims of the Portuguese and the Spaniards to rights over the Indians.

[55] *Ad homines barbaros qui sunt naturaliter servi, ut supra dictum est, ac si hoc sit primum iustum bellum secundum naturam. Opera iussu Leonis XIII P.M. edita*, XLVIII (Rome, 1971), A99.

Aristotelian account of natural slavery: in his eyes it was closer to the natural subordination of women to men, and other natural hierarchies which do not admit of violence and which presuppose a high degree of mutual recognition of the asymmetrical relationship. His followers directly questioned the category of natural slave as such—for example Guy of Rimini, writing in the early fourteenth century.[56]

Aquinas's authority was such that throughout the late Middle Ages it was often difficult to return to the first, straightforward reading of the Aristotelian text (in this as in many other instances). Jean Dunbabin has observed of his commentary that 'many, if not most, other medieval commentators simply plagiarised it wholesale',[57] though she has also noted that there were some exceptions to this, and her exceptions include writers like Buridan and Oresme. But it would probably be fair to say that it was not until a humanist understanding of Aristotle became more widespread that Aquinas's interpretation was generally called into question. One extraordinary consequence of the spread of humanism was that humanist readers of Aquinas rewrote his commentary on the *Politics* in such a way that it was made to say (in this area) the opposite of what Aquinas had intended. The general story of this rewriting has been told by Conor Martin and the editors of the Leonine edition of Aquinas:[58] they have shown that at the turn of the fifteenth and sixteenth centuries, Aquinas's commentary was reissued in print attached to the Bruni translation of Aristotle's text. In order to make the commentary fit the new translation, it was extensively emended, and one of the most extreme pieces of surgery was performed on this passage (though I believe this has hithero been overlooked). In place of Aquinas's original remark that war could be made on natural slaves '*ac si hoc sit primum iustum bellum secundam naturam*', the new text used by the sixteenth-century printed versions read: '*ac si hoc sit, bellum fit iustum secundam naturam*'[59]—that is, 'and in this case, war becomes just according to nature'. However, the oral tradition within the Dominican order

[56] *Sed ut hoc videtur crudele dictum et contra naturalem amorem qui debet esse inter homines et contra doctrinam et pietatem Christianae religionis* . . . See Jean Dunbabin, 'The Reception and Interpretation of Aristotle's *Politics*', in *The Cambridge History of Later Medieval Philosophy*, ed. N. Kretzmann, A. Kenny, and J. Pinborg (Cambridge University Press, 1982), 728.

[57] Ibid.

[58] Conor Martin, 'The Vulgate Text of Aquinas's Commentary on Aristotle's *Politics*', *Dominican Studies*, V (1952), 35–64; and Aquinas, *Opera iussu Leonis XIII P.M. edita*, XLVIII (Rome, 1971), 17–21.

[59] See e.g. Venice ed. 1568, p. 9.

was presumably based on the old text, and Francisco de Vitoria, the most important transmitter of Thomist ideas to the new Spain, would have been taught from it.

A scepticism about the legitimacy of European dealings with the rest of the world was thus integral to the Dominican tradition by the early sixteenth century, and it is not at all surprising that the Dominicans of Spain came to be the most notable critics of their country's American adventure. What is surprising is that their criticisms were given such great weight by the Spanish government itself. There are two principal reasons for the seriousness with which the government took the criticism. The first and most important one is that the Spanish rulers were not at all keen on either imperial or papalist defences of American colonization: the Kings of Spain were insistent that they did not owe their American possessions to the grant of any other power. Their anti-papalism was particularly encouraged by the bull of *Praecelsae devotionis* of Pope Leo X in 1514, which apparently handed the Pacific over to the Portuguese—a papal decree which the Castilians were clearly not going to accept. The next fifteen years were marked by a long diplomatic struggle over the Pacific between Spain and Portugal in which the papal decision was eventually disregarded and a bilateral treaty between the two powers settled the issue.[60] The second reason for the government's increasing unwillingness as the century wore on to use the kind of arguments put forward at the Burgos *junta* of 1512 may simply have been the tremendous cultural influence in the Spanish church which Vitoria and his pupils came to enjoy; it is noteworthy in this context that by *c.*1556 the Portuguese government, despite its originally strong papalism, had also come round to the Dominican way of thinking.[61]

The initial Dominican view was that there may be *no* legitimacy to

[60] See Muldoon, *Poets, Lawyers, and Infidels*, p. 139; Davenport, *European Treaties*, pp. 112–17.

[61] There is surprisingly little research on Portuguese ideas about empire. Some ideas can be obtained from Luís Filipe F. R. Thomaz, 'Estrutura Política e Administrativa do Estato da India n. séc. xvi', in L. de Albuquerque and I. Guerreiro eds., *Actas do II Seminario Internacional de Historia Indo-Portuguesa* (Lisbon, 1985), 525–6. The interest in governmental circles by the mid-century in Thomist ideas is shown by the important document in the royal archives entitled *Por que causas se pode mover guerra justa contra infieis*, printed in A. da Silva Rego ed., *As Gavetas da Torre do Tombo*, II (Lisbon, 1962), 676–85. (Though it should be said that the proposed date of this document is rather unconvincing: its citations look like a standard apparatus from earlier in the century, with in particular nothing from Vitoria.)

the conquest of America. For example, one of the leading Dominican theologians of early sixteenth-century Spain, Domingo de Soto, devoted a section of his *Relectio De Dominio* of 1534–5 to the question of 'the temporal dominion of Christ and the Pope, and the right by which the Spaniards maintain an overseas empire'. He concluded that the pope had no kind of temporal authority, direct or indirect, over the world.

So by what right do we maintain the overseas empire which has recently been discovered? To speak truly, I do not know. In the Gospel we find: 'Go ye into all the world, and preach the Gospel to every creature' (Mark 16[: 15]); this gives us a right to preach everywhere in the world, and, as a consequence, we have been given a right to defend ourselves against anyone who prevents us from preaching. Therefore if we were in danger, we could defend ourselves from them at their expense; but I do not see that we have any right beyond this to take their goods or subject them to our rule . . . [The Lord said in Luke 9: 5] 'whosoever will not receive you, when ye go out of that city, shake off the very dust from your feet for a testimony against them'. He did not say that we were to preach to an unwilling audience, but that we should go and leave vengeance to God. I do not say this to condemn everything that has taken place with those islanders; for God's judgements have many depths, and God perhaps wishes those people to be converted in ways unknown to us. Let this be enough for the present on these topics.[62]

De Soto's doubts about the Spanish conquest of the Americas were tackled from within the Dominican order three years later by his colleague Francisco de Vitoria, in his *relectio* on dietary law (1538). Vitoria carefully and fully dealt with the Innocentian case in this work, using the issue of cannibalism as the peg on which to hang his discussion, and putting forward the basic idea which he was to develop fully in his famous *relectio De Indis* the following year. Vitoria argued, first, that there were indeed no grounds upon which the Pope could claim special rights over infidels. Second, the fact that an action was against the law of nature could not be pleaded as justification for intervention. Third, if infidels (or anyone else) injured the innocent by such practices as human sacrifice, then any ruler could intervene to stop them, even if the victims 'neither seek nor wish this help; it is lawful to defend an

[62] *Relección 'De Dominio'*, ed. Jaime Brufau Prats (Granada, 1964), 158 and 162–4. See also Prats, *La Escuela de Salamanca ante el Descrubimento del Nuevo Mundo* (Salamanca, 1989), 152.

innocent man even if he does not ask us to, or even if he refuses our help . . .'. But

> the belligerent does not thereby have the power to eject the enemy from their dominions and despoil them of their property at whim; he can act only as far as is necessary to ward off injustices and secure safety for the future. It follows that, if there is no other method of ensuring safety except by setting up Christian princes over them, this too will be lawful, as far as necessary to secure that end.[63]

The distinction between the second and third of these points is, of course, far from clear, particularly as Vitoria argued that crimes against the law of nature such as murder or theft, as well as more obviously victimless crimes like sodomy, could not justify intervention. The main force of his argument that the law of nature was not a good basis for intervention was, however, directed against the Innocentian claim that the *Pope* could be the judge of whether the law had been breached; Vitoria was in general very unhappy about complicated systems of what a later generation would call 'natural jurisprudence', observing in the *De Indis* that 'not all sins against natural law can be demonstrated to be so by evidence, at least to the satisfaction of all men'.[64] The point about the blatant injury of innocent people was both that it was clearly wrong, and, most importantly, that according to conventional jurisprudence any suitably constituted political authority could act to stop it; in *De Indis* Vitoria conceded that 'in this case, there is truth in the opinion held by Innocent IV . . . that sinners against nature may be punished' (one manuscript adds revealingly 'when their sins are to the detriment of the innocent').[65] In one of his earlier works, a lecture on 'civil power' delivered in 1528, Vitoria had even been prepared to use the humanist idea of the global republic—an idea which, as I have suggested already, was in general a difficult one for Aristotelians to accept.

> The whole world, which is in a sense a commonwealth, has the power to enact laws which are just and convenient to all men; and these make up the law of nations [*ius gentium*]. From this it follows that those who break the law of nations, whether in peace or in war, are committing mortal crimes, at any rate in the case of graver transgressions such as violating the immunity of ambassadors. No kingdom may choose to ignore this law of nations, because it has the sanction of the whole world.[66]

[63] *Political Writings*, ed. Anthony Pagden and Jeremy Lawrance (Cambridge University Press, 1991), 225–6; see the same points in *De Indis*, ibid. 288.

[64] *Political Writings*, p. 274. [65] Ibid. 288. [66] Ibid. 40.

In his later and more considered works on this subject, however, Vitoria avoided referring to a global commonwealth.

Despite these difficulties Vitoria's argument swiftly became the most popular official defence of the conquest, no doubt precisely because it had come from an order whose doubts about the enterprise were well known. De Soto, it should be said, remained rather sceptical even of this justification of the conquest, remarking about it later that since the Indians committed such acts out of ignorance

> I do not see why it gives us the right to take arms against them before we have persuaded them of the truth of our faith . . . And this is worth thinking hard about, that according to Christ we should be careful when punishing criminals, 'lest while ye gather up the tares, ye root up also the wheat with them' [Matthew 13: 29]. So if in protecting a thousand people, or actually a few hundred, we leave as corpses hundreds of thousands of the innocent, we have not only not fulfilled our charitable obligation, but have made ouselves hateful and tainted to the Indians, and incapable of converting them to our faith.[67]

De Soto was not alone in thinking this: at about the same time we can find this argument, in almost identical words, being put forward by the most famous critic of the Spanish conquest, Bartolomé de Las Casas, in his *Argumentum Apologiae* in defence of the Indians.[68] De Soto's comparative isolation from the general Vitorian compromise is illustrated by the fact that the work in which he seems to have discussed these issues most extensively, *De Ratione Promulgandi Evangelium*, was not generally available and is now lost, no doubt because of the criticisms of Spanish imperialism it is likely to have contained.[69]

[67] Juan de la Peña, *De Bello contra Insulanos: Intervencion de España en America*, ed. L. Pereña, V. Abril, C. Baciero, A. Garcia, J. Barrientos, and F. Maseda, *Corpus Hispanorum de Pace*, IX (Madrid, 1982), 592. The *relectio* was given at Salamanca in 1552; see Luciano Pereña Vicente, *Mision de España en America 1540–1569* (Madrid, 1956), 245. There is a problem about the text as printed in the de la Peña volume: the last sentence begins 'Unde si in protectionem mille, immo centium centies millenas nos nocentissimas mortes perpetramus . . .'. In view of the similarity between this passage and that in Las Casas's *In Defense of the Indians* referred to below, together with the general tenor of de Soto's argument, it seems plausible that this should read 'nos innocentissimas mortes . . .'. De Soto, it should be said, was also sceptical about the notion that some kind of global commonwealth could underlie the *ius gentium*—see his remarks on the difference between *ius civile* and *ius gentium* in his manuscript *Utrum Idem Sit Ius Gentium cum Iure Naturali*, printed in Francisco Suarez, *De Legibus*, IV, ed. L. Pereña, V. Abril, and P. Suñer, *Corpus Hispanorum de Pace*, XIV (Madrid, 1973), 244.

[68] *In Defense of the Indians*, trans. and ed. Stafford Poole (DeKalb, Ill.: Northern Illinois University Press, 1974), 205–6.

[69] Mentioned by De Soto in his *De Iustitia et Iure* (1553–4), V. 3. 5. See *De Iustitia et Iure*, ed. P. Venancio Diego Carro (Madrid, 1967), I. lvi, III. 431.

Depsite this, unhappiness about European empires continued at Salamanca. In the late 1550s a friend of De Soto in the law faculty, Fernando Vazquez y Menchaca, started lecturing to the *adolescentia* of the university on a series of *paradoxa* in jurisprudence.[70] When they were published in 1563 they were organized as an idiosyncratic defence of the dignity and power of the Kings of Spain; but part of Vazquez's case consisted of a thoroughgoing and unusual attack on the idea of monopolistic maritime empire. Chapter 20 expressed hostility to the whole idea of navigation, urging that peoples separated by God should remain separate, while Chapter 89 contained a famous attack on any claim by a state to *dominium* over the sea—famous because Grotius later quoted freely from it. Vazquez's discussion was certainly remarkable, particularly because in some of his remarks he anticipated Grotius's keen sense of the practical economic basis of property rights: thus he explained the difference between land and streams, which could be appropriated, and the sea, which could not, in the following terms:

> In the case of lands or streams, it was expedient that the law should operate thus, whereas it was not expedient in regard to the sea. For it is generally agreed that, if a great many persons hunt or fish upon some wooded tract of land or in some stream, that wood or stream will probably be emptied of wild animals or fish, an objection which is not applicable to the sea.[71]

Moreover, Vazquez was not prepared to concede that in principle a state might have *jurisdiction*, rather than ownership, over any part of the high seas: in his view, it seems, the oceans were a realm of complete moral freedom. To this extent, as we shall see, he went rather further than Grotius was prepared to go.

But his remarks on the sea were, for all their force and originality, only hints at a complete theory. Vazquez lacked Grotius's single-mindedness, and was prepared to employ a wide range of arguments to establish his point. It is probable that his remarks were aimed principally at the Portuguese rather than the Spanish: these were the years in which the Spanish Crown had decided to try to break the Portuguese monopoly in the Far East trade, a policy which culminated in the

[70] See Kurt Seelmann, *Die Lehre des Fernando Vazquez de Menchaca vom Dominium* (Köln, 1979), 30–6; quotation pp. 35–6. Vazquez had read De Soto's *De Ratione Promulgandi Evangelium*: see the *Controversiae*, 10. 10, where he says that De Soto attacked the war made 'Indorum gentibus et regionibus' by the king of Portugal on the grounds of natural slavery.

[71] See Grotius, *De Iure Praedae*, trans. G. L. Williams, p. 253.

settlement of the Philippines in 1563. The thrust by the Spanish into the Far East even led to a brief military confrontation with the Portuguese: for three months in 1568 a Spanish garrison in the Philippines was besieged by a Portuguese fleet.[72] The Spanish project turned out to be entirely successful, and the direct exchange of American silver for Far Eastern manufactures, cutting out the Portuguese middle men, proved to be the economic centrepiece of Spain's extra-European empire. What Vazquez seems to have been suggesting to his king was that the principle of bilateral maritime monopolies worked against the interests of Spain, and that its abandonment by both Portugal and Spain would benefit Spain most. However, the success of the Philippines project and, even more, the amalgamation of Spain and Portugal under the Spanish Crown in 1580, removed this as an issue from Spanish politics.

Nevertheless, though they represented the more extreme end of the Salamanca scholastic tradition, the views of De Soto and Vazquez on war and imperialism illustrate the strength of Thomist ideas in the heartland of world empire. When Molina came to teach this material at Evora, specifically as a lecture series on Aquinas, he was naturally led to incorporate all these views, and to create a *Summa* of his own which could act as a convenient reference work for writers of the new century. The constraints imposed by a combination of Augustine, Aristotle, and Aquinas persisted among the Iberian theologians: even Francisco Suarez, the most influential of the Jesuits, who has sometimes been regarded as breaking through these bounds, was notably hesitant about doing so. His substantive view of war and international relations was broadly that of Molina; and though at one point in his *De Legibus* of 1612 he argued that the *ius gentium* was based on the 'quasi-political and moral unity' of the human race, he was at pains elsewhere to stress that this did not mean that there was or ever had been a real global commonwealth: the *ius gentium* was (in part) the result of agreement between autonomous commonwealths.[73] But outside Iberia, these constraints were far less powerful; we shall see in the next chapter just how feeble they could prove when someone brought up in the humanist tradition began to think about the morality of war.

[72] For the struggle between Spain and Portugal for the Far Eastern trade, see Nicholas P. Cushner, *Spain in the Philippines: From Conquest to Revolution* (Manila, 1971), especially pp. 63–4.

[73] *De Legibus*, II. xix. 9 contrasted with III. ii. 6. See Francisco Suarez, *De Legibus*, IV, ed. L. Pereña *et al.*, *Corpus Hispanorum de Pace*, XIV (Madrid, 1973), 135 and 155.

3

HUGO GROTIUS

Introduction

It was Hugo Grotius who was generally reckoned by writers at the end of the seventeenth century to have created a new science of morality by inventing a new way of talking about international relations; and what I outlined in the first two chapters was the intellectual context in which Grotius had to work. As we saw, there were (broadly speaking) two traditions of thinking about war and peace by the beginning of the seventeenth century. One, the more familiar to modern historians, was the scholastic tradition, represented principally by the Dominicans and Jesuits of Spain and Portugal, which persisted in judging warfare by the Thomist criteria, and which was therefore inevitably critical of much actual modern military activity (and in particular the conquest of Central America). The other was what I have termed the humanist tradition, which applauded warfare in the interests of one's *respublica*, and saw a dramatic moral difference between Christian, European civilization and barbarism. In this chapter, I want to turn to what Grotius did, and the significance of his new ideas.

By birth and upbringing, Grotius belonged wholly to the humanist world;[1] he was a spectacularly precocious classical scholar, who devoted the first twenty-five years of his life to the traditional pursuits of the young humanist, the writing of poetry and history. Indeed, though he is often spoken of as a jurist, he had no formal juristic training, and he was employed first in the typically humanist roles of political adviser (to Jan van Oldenbarnevelt) and historiographer—from 1601 to 1607 his only paid employment was indeed as official historiographer to the States of Holland, the assembly which governed the Province of Holland, the richest and most powerful province in the United Prov-

[1] For fuller details about this, see my *Philosophy and Government 1572–1651* (Cambridge University Press, 1993), 155–69.

inces. Subsequently he became the equivalent of attorney-general to the States, and then Pensionary of Rotterdam with a seat in the States. His early political writings were very much in the modern humanist tradition, tracing out an argument for the aristocratic republic, though stressing above all the need for it to engage in commerce and manufacture in order to secure its liberty against its enemies, particularly of course Spain. From the beginning of his intellectual career in the late 1590s he praised the activities of those Dutch sailors who were carrying the war against Spain into the Spanish overseas empire of the East Indies (something they had been doing from 1595 onwards); indeed, one of his first publications (in 1599) was a Latin translation of a Dutch work on navigation by means of the magnetic compass, which Grotius dedicated to the Republic of Venice with a preface drawing attention to the parallels between the two great commercial republics. His family was (like many aristocratic mercantile families in the United Provinces) quite heavily involved in the Indies trade: cousins included directors of the United East India Company and admirals in its service, while his father as burgomaster of Delft was responsible for nominating to one of the seats on the company's board.

De Indis: The Foundations

In these circumstances, it was not surprising that he was led to write a major apology for the whole Dutch commercial expansion into the Indies. The primary issue which he addressed was the capture by Jacob van Heemskerk (one of Grotius's cousins, as it happens)[2] in 1602 of a Portuguese ship carrying copper from Japan, silk and porcelain from China, and bullion from Mexico and Peru. Its value was over three million guilders[3]—which represented the equivalent of about half the total capitalization of the East India Company—and it may well be that it was this prize which led to the formation of the United East India Company, which was long to dominate the Indies trade, out of the smaller provincial companies which had been operating since 1595. (The United Company was formed in between the taking of the prize and the auction of its contents at

[2] Grotius's grandmother on his father's side was a van Heemskerk; Jacob's grandson Johan was later to be helped by Grotius in his career as a lawyer because of the relationship between them. See A. I. van Aa, *Biographisch Woordenboek der Nederlanden* (Amsterdam, 1867) *s.n.* Cornelis De Groot and Johan van Heemskerk.

[3] See George Masselman, *The Cradle of Colonialism* (New Haven, 1963), 131.

Amsterdam in 1603.)[4] To understand the scale of the sums involved, the value of this prize was not far off the total annual expenditure of the English government at the time; the company paid out annually a dividend equivalent to about a third of that expenditure.[5]

The seizure of a prize on this scale was something quite unprecedented, and it seems to have occasioned general consternation in Europe, for it brought home to contemporaries that the United Provinces, having formerly been engaged wholly in a war of rebellion and self-defence against Spanish power in the Netherlands, was now engaged in a spectacular war of aggression. By 1603 the security of the United Provinces (it was generally recognized) was established, and indeed James VI of Scotland, coming to the English throne in that year, decided formally to end the war with Spain which the English had been waging as long as the new republic seemed unsafe. In 1605 Dutch aggression reached even greater heights, when they took a fort at Amboyna from the Portuguese. Very quickly, and by what is to us a familiar combination of finance and military threat, the Dutch either won over native rulers or arranged their overthrow by rival factions, and secured a firm grip on the spice trade from the Indies to Europe and (probably more importantly) on the intra-Asian trade in all kinds of commodities. The advanced industrial and commercial skills of the Dutch, once they were allowed to operate in Asia, turned out to be as competitive as they had already proved to be in Europe, and princes in Japan, China, and the Indies became as reliant on Dutch capital as those in Germany, England, and France.

The novelty of all this must be recognized. The Dutch were not waging a defensive war in the Indies to protect either their homeland or existing trade patterns: they were waging an offensive war, in order to open up trade routes and make a lot of money. Moreover, they were not even doing so through conventional political structures: until the United East Indies Company was formed in 1603, the Dutch companies (for one of whom Heemskerk was working) were governed by charters issued by the States of Holland which said nothing about military force,

[4] See E. H. Kossmann's article, 'The Low Countries', in *The New Cambridge Modern History*, II (Cambridge University Press, 1970), 367–8.

[5] For the dividend, see Kossmann 'The Low Countries'. For the comparable figures for England, see the totals of government expenditure 1598–1608 in F. C. Dietz, *English Public Finance 1558–1641* (London, 1964), 113: they average £470,000 p.a. The pound at this period was worth ten guilders—see the table in *The Cambridge Economic History of Europe*, IV (Cambridge University Press, 1967), 458.

and even after that date the States-General of the Union (which authorized the United Company) gave only a very general and rather vague permission to the company to use force to preserve law and order.[6] It was not even clear to neutral observers that the States-General, let alone the States of Holland, were legitimate sovereign bodies: Holland was a 'province' of the Netherlands whose status was disputed, while the States-General represented a union of provinces in revolt against their king (the King of Spain). The Dutch thus seemed to be violating some of the most fundamental principles of international relations. Grotius's commitment to defend them accordingly forced him to a fundamental revision of those principles, and in the process (it is, I think, no exaggeration to say) he fundamentally revised Western political thought itself.

His ideas were embodied in a treatise which he always referred to as the *De Indis*, but which its nineteenth-century editor entitled *De iure praedae*. It was to remain in manuscript for some three centuries, only being discovered in a sale of the De Groot family papers in 1864. It was then realized that Chapter XII of the work had been prepared separately for publication as the famous *Mare Liberum*, at the express request of the East Indies Company in November 1608, who wished to influence the peace negotiations then in progress. (The book actually appeared in 1609.) It was also realized that much of Grotius's major work, the *De Iure Belli ac Pacis* of 1625, had been developed from this early essay, though in one of the areas with which I am concerned it did differ in a particularly interesting way, as we shall see. Some fragments of Grotius's working papers for the *De Indis* survive, which show that he was interested in contrasting his own views with those of Vitoria;[7] but in general (it is fair to say) he was not well versed in the modern scholastic literature.

Grotius made his vital move in a passage discussing the right of punishment, or the *ius gladii*—the fundamental right to use force, possessed (according to every traditional theorist) by the civil magistrate and only the civil magistrate (or his equivalent, such as the head of a family—as we saw Molina was arguing at almost the same time as Grotius was writing the *De Indis*).

[6] For the formation of the united company and the status of its predecessors, see Jan den Tex, *Oldenbarnevelt* (Cambridge University Press, 1973), 300–12.

[7] See Peter Borschberg, *Hugo Grotius: 'Commentarius in Theses XI'* (Berne, 1994), and '"De Pace": Ein unveröffentlichtes Fragment von Hugo Grotius über Krieg und Frieden', *Zeitschrift der Savigny-Stiftung für Rechtsgeschicte*, Rom. Abt. 113 (1996), 268–92.

Is not the power to punish essentially a power that pertains to the state [*respublica*]? Not at all! On the contrary, just as every right of the magistrate comes to him from the state, so has the same right come to the state from private individuals; and similarly, the power of the state is the result of collective agreement . . . Therefore, since no one is able to transfer a thing that he never possessed, it is evident that the right of chastisement was held by private persons before it was held by the state. The following argument, too, has great force in this connexion: the state inflicts punishment for wrongs against itself, not only upon its own subjects but also upon foreigners; yet it derives no power over the latter from civil law, which is binding upon citizens only because they have given their consent; and therefore, the law of nature, or law of nations, is the source from which the state receives the power in question.[8]

This last argument is of course identical to the one used later by Locke and described by him as 'a very strange doctrine';[9] but he would not have found it in *De Iure Belli ac Pacis*, and it appears in that part of *De Indis* which was not known until 1864. This must count as one of the most striking examples of intellectual convergence.

Grotius had thus made the claim that an individual in nature (that is, before transferring any rights to a civil society) was morally identical to a state, and that there were no powers possessed by a state which an individual could not possess in nature. The kind of state he had in mind, moreover, was one which was sovereign in a strong sense: he remarked that '*supra rempublicam nihil est*', and (interestingly) used the Roman legate's answer to the Ansibarii (see above p. 48) to vindicate this view—'the gods had empowered the Romans to tolerate no judges but themselves'.[10]

Grotius's idea of state sovereignty at this stage in his life was important, and has been little studied; but the consequences of his assimilation of individuals to states would have been quite different had he possessed a weaker notion of sovereignty. As the passage above illustrates, he believed that any *respublica* was formed by the voluntary union of

[8] *De Iure Praedae Commentarius*, I trans. Gladys L. Williams and Walter H. Zeydel (Carnegie Endowment for International Peace, Oxford University Press, 1950), 91–2. For the Latin text, the easiest source (since the Carnegie Endowment text is a photocopy of the manuscript) is still the original edn. by H. G. Hanaker (The Hague, 1868), 91. See also Peter Borschberg, *Hugo Grotius: 'Commentarius in Theses XI'*, pp. 244–5 for an early statement of this idea, in the manuscript which seems to be part of the working papers for the *De Indis*.

[9] *Two Treatises of Government*, ed. Peter Laslett (Cambridge University, Press 1988), 272 (II. 9).

[10] *De Iure Praedae Commentarius*, I 24–5.

individuals to make a civil society; but he also seems to have believed that any society with a suitable set of representative institutions would count as a *respublica*. It was upon this basis that he defended in the *De Indis* the Dutch revolt against the King of Spain, arguing that the States of Holland represented the people of Holland and that the magistrate (the king) was always under their authority.

It was also upon this basis that he defended his own vision of the constitution of the United Provinces. The Union had been born in the revolt, and had been formally created by the Treaty of Utrecht in 1579, in which a number of the countries[11] of the Northern Netherlands (dominated in practice by Grotius's own country, Holland) bound themselves together to resist the king. The Union's affairs were governed by an assembly, the States-General, meeting at The Hague, but each country also had its own States, meeting as its supreme government. As with many later unions, the constitution of the United Provinces was far from clear, and in particular it was unclear to what extent the individual countries remained sovereign states—this became a major personal issue for Grotius in 1618, when he and his master Oldenbarnevelt had their careers destroyed by the institutions of the Union (see below).

Grotius's answer to this question, long before the crisis of 1618, was unequivocal: the countries were sovereign states, as they had always been, since each continued to possess its own States. The Union was an alliance in which no participating country had shared any part of its sovereignty. He enlarged on this theme after 1618, in a defence of his political conduct (his *Apologeticus*),[12] in which he argued that the Union handled the conduct of war on behalf of the constituent countries, but left the *summa potestas* in the hands of the aristocratic assemblies (the

[11] Grotius uses two terms in his Latin writings to describe the 'provinces' such Holland. One is *natio*—see e.g. *De Antiquitate Reipublicae Batavicae*, ed. Collegium Classicum c.n. EDEPOL (Arnham, 1995), 78 (VII. 5) (*Federatae nationes*), while the other is *respublica*—see *De Iure Praedae Commentarius*, ed. H. G. Hanaker (The Hague, 1868), 270, and the *De Antiquitate Reipublicae Batavicae* throughout ('Batavia' is used strictly by Grotius to mean Holland—see Chs IV and V). The Treaty of the Union of Utrecht speaks in Dutch of 'Landen' and 'Provintien', though generally of 'Provintien', the usage followed by all modern historians. I have chosen to call them 'countries', in deference to Grotius's views. For an English text of the treaty, see *Texts Concerning the Revolt of the Netherlands*, ed. E. H. Kossmann and A. F. Mellink (Cambridge University Press, 1974), 165–73.

[12] *Apologeticus eorum qui Hollandiae Westfrisiaeque & vicinis quibusdam nationibus ex legibus praefuerunt ante mutationem quae evenit anno CI) I) CXVIII (The Defence of the Constitutional Rulers of the Countries of Holland and West Frisia and their Neighbours Before the Revolution of 1618).* I have used the Paris edn. of 1630.

primores) governing each country. The Union was acknowledged to be a union of 'free nations and rulers. The word "free" undoubtedly means "sovereign" ';[13] in this respect, it resembled Switzerland, in which (Bodin had shown) each canton was sovereign.[14] In the *De Indis* he was not even willing to go this far: in that work, he scrupulously treated the States of *Holland* as the sovereign body which could make peace or war and whose pronouncements were relevant to Dutch activity in the Far East.[15]

This was the kind of sovereign *respublica*, then, which Grotius had in mind when he argued that the natural individual was, morally speaking, like a miniature sovereign state, to which the vocabulary of liberty and sovereignty could be applied:

> God created man αὐτεξουσιον, 'free and *sui iuris*', so that the actions of each individual and the use of his possessions were made subject not to another's will but to his own. Moreover, this view is sanctioned by the common consent of all nations. For what is that well-known concept, 'natural liberty', other than the power of the individual to act in accordance with his own will? And liberty in regard to actions is equivalent to ownership in regard to property. Hence the saying: 'every man is the governor and arbiter of affairs relative to his own property'.[16]

And the relationship between men in a civil society was broadly like the relationship of the sovereign republics of the United Provinces in their Union: guarded co-operation, with a great deal held back by the parties and with a great deal requiring unanimity.

As I said in the Introduction, we take for granted that the language in which we still describe this autonomous, right-bearing individual is in fact a language used originally to describe states or rulers. When Hart in his famous 1955 essay 'Are there any Natural Rights' said about promising that 'the promisee has a temporary authority or sovereignty

[13] This refers to the Truce of 1609 concluded with the Archdukes of the Spanish Netherlands: *In pactis quooque induciarum continetur, haberi ab Archiducibus Federatas nationes pro liberis nationibus atque proceribus. Libertatis autem nomine certum est designari ius imperandi summum* (p. 15).

[14] Page 3. Bodin's discussion of Switzerland, in Book I of his *République*, may be found in *The Six Bookes of a Commonweale*, ed. K. D. McRae (Cambridge, MA, 1962), 76–7.

[15] This fact is obscured in the Carnegie Endowment translation, which is very confused about the separate identity of the States General and the States of Holland. But it is clear in the Latin text, where he talks about the *Ordines reipublicae Hollandiae*: see e.g. the Hanaker edition pp. 270–5 compared with the Carnegie translation, pp. 284–91.

[16] *De Iure Praedae Commentarius*, I, p. 18.

in relation to some specific matter over the other's will',[17] he was drawing on precisely this tradition which we find articulated clearly for the first time in the *De Indis*: that we can best understand the rights which individuals possess *vis-à-vis* one another (outside the arbitrary and contingent circumstances of their civil agreements) by looking at the rights which sovereign states seem to possess against one another.

Having made this remarkable claim, that there is no significant moral difference between individuals and states, and that both may use violence in the same way and for the same ends, Grotius had of course accomplished one of his primary tasks—to show that private trading companies were as entitled to make war as were the traditional sovereigns of Europe. But he still had to accomplish one of his other tasks, a justification of the kind of war which Heemskerk had made. As we have seen, that was an equally difficult task, for on the face of it the violent incursions into the Indies had not been made straightforwardly for defensive purposes. In order to answer this question, Grotius once again went back to theoretical fundamentals. He set out his ideas in the *Prolegomena* to the *De Indis*. It began with two fundamental laws of nature:

> first, that It shall be permissible to defend [one's own] life and to shun that which threatens to prove injurious; secondly, that It shall be permissible to acquire for oneself, and to retain, those things which are useful for life. The latter precept, indeed, we shall interpret with Cicero as an admission that each individual may, without violating the precepts of nature, prefer to see acquired for himself rather than for another, that which is important for the conduct of life. Moreover, no member of any sect of philosophers, when embarking upon a discussion of the ends [of good and evil], has ever failed to lay down these two laws first of all as indisputable axioms. For on this point the Stoics, the Epicureans, and the Peripatetics are in complete agreement, and apparently even the Academics have entertained no doubt.[18]

Grotius then stipulated two further laws, 'Let no one inflict injury upon his fellows' and 'Let no one seize possession of that which has been taken into the possession of another. The former is the law of inoffensiveness; the latter is the law of abstinence.' He devoted much of the *Prolegomena* to explaining the meaning of these two laws and their

[17] H. L. A. Hart, 'Are there any Natural Rights?', *Philosophical Review*, 64 (1955), 184.
[18] *De Iure Praedae Commentarius*, I, pp. 10–11.

relationship to the first two. He was at pains to stress that self-preservation was the prior obligation:

the order of presentation of the first set of laws and of those following immediately thereafter has indicated that one's own good takes precedence over the good of another person—or, let us say, it indicates that by nature's ordinance each individual should be desirous of his own good fortune in preference to that of another, which is the puport of the proverbs, 'I myself am my own closest neighbour', γόνυ κνήμης ἔγγιον [My knee is closer than my shin], 'My tunic is closer than my cloak'.[19]

As I emphasized in *Philosophy and Government*, this meant that it was only if one's own preservation was secured that one would be obliged to care about the preservation of another person—the first consideration must always override the second.[20] The only respect in which, in nature, men were obliged to think about actually helping their neighbours was, Grotius argued, that they ought always to return like for like—punishing men who transgressed the principles of inoffensiveness and abstinence and not harming those who did not. 'The function of such justice is twofold, namely: in regard to good, the preservation thereof; in regard to evil, its correction. Hence these two laws arise: first, *Evil deeds must be corrected*; secondly, *Good deeds must be recompensed*'.[21] The laws of inoffensiveness and abstinence, together with this obligation to punish, thus gave in general an extremely minimal picture of the natural moral life. Although Grotius glossed them as expressions of 'love', they required men merely to abstain from injury, and not to give any positive help to their fellows. He summed up his view by saying that 'Horace should not be censured for saying, in imitation of the Academics, that expediency might perhaps be called the mother of justice and equity' (a passage to which we shall return in discussing the *De Iure Belli ac Pacis*).[22] It is worth observing at this point that this was of

[19] *De Iure Praedae Commentarius*, I, p. 21.

[20] *Philosophy and Government*, p. 174.

[21] *De Iure Praedae Commentarius*, I, p. 15.

[22] *Utilitas justi propre mater et aequi* (*Satires*, I. iii. 98). *De Iure Praedae Commentarius*, I, p. 9. Two things should be observed about this passage: first, Grotius describes it as 'Academic', i.e. sceptic, whereas it was well known that it was Epicurean—an interesting example of the two philosophies being treated as very similar, as they often were in the response to Hobbes and Gassendi. Second, the same passage had been used in the same context to make the opposite point by the great jurist Jacques Cujas, whom Grotius had certainly read (see pp. 109, 121, 161, 164, 236, 247). 'Epicurus did not derive universal law [*ius commune*] from nature . . . but from general Utility—from convenience, benefit, profit or necessity—which impels us to follow the *ius gentium* or universal law; not out of principle, but because it is inscribed in us by our utility [*sic*]. Utility by itself does not

course precisely Rousseau's account of the natural life of man, though (as we shall see) it was not presented in anything like so clear a fashion in Grotius's printed works.

However, Grotius also argued at some length that it was these principles which gave rise to 'that brotherhood of man, that world state, commended to us so frequently and so enthusiastically by the ancient philosophers and particularly by the Stoics' (p. 13), and especially by Cicero and Seneca, whom he quoted extensively on the subject (pp. 12–14, 93). Although one might suppose that the two visions of natural human life were diametrically opposed, we have already seen that this was not necessarily so in the minds of the Romans whom Grotius cited; and Grotius made clear what he had in mind, not in the passages where he directly described the world state, but in the passages where he depicted the transition from the state of nature (as we can fairly call it, though he did not) to civil society (pp. 19–23). Civil societies developed

> not with the intention of abolishing the society which links all men as a whole, but rather in order to fortify that universal society by a more dependable means of protection, and at the same time, with the purpose of bringing together under a more convenient arrangement the numerous different prooducts of many persons' labour which are required for the uses of human life. For it is a fact (as Pliny so graphically points out) that when universal goods are separately distributed, each man's ills pertain to him individually, whereas, when those goods are brought together and intermingled, individual ills cease to be the concern of any one person and the goods of all pertain to all. (p. 19)

As a consequence, in civil society two more rules apply.

> First, *Individual citizens should not only refrain from injuring other citizens, but should furthermore protect them, both as a whole and as individuals*; secondly, *Citizens should not only refrain from seizing one another's possessions, whether these be held privately or in common, but should furthermore contribute individually both that which is necessary to other individuals and that which is necessary to the whole* . . . These two laws, then, are directed in a certain sense to the common good, though not to that phase of the concept with which the laws of the third order [those concerned with punishment] are concerned, namely, the good of

give rise to *Ius*; for what Horace said, "Utility, Mother of Justice and Right", is Epicurean; Horace belonged to that tradition [*familia*]. We follow the Stoics, who derive from nature the law common to all men, and the law which is special to each city from its common utility, that is, from whatever benefits the city . . .' (*Opera Postuma quae de iure reliquit*, III (2nd edn., Paris, 1637), col. 50, on *Digest*, 1. 1. 9. The first edn. was *Recitationes ad titulum Digestorum de justitia et jure nunc primum in lucem editae* (Speyer, 1595).

the different individuals composing the community. [These laws] relate rather to the common good interpreted as the good of the unit and therefore as one's own. (p. 21)

And in civil society, he went on, the natural ordering of the fundamental principles does not apply, since the individuals concerned had agreed to subordinate their own interests to that of the community.

It is clear from this that natural society, for Grotius, was very unlike civil society in an essential respect, in that it wholly lacked a genuine community of interests or resources. Its sociability extended only as far as was necessary to justify the private right of punishment, and indeed he made this point absolutely clear in his discussion of that right.

One point . . . remains to be clarified. If the state is not involved, what just end can be sought by the private avenger? The answer to this question is readily found in the teachings of Seneca, the philosopher who maintains that there are two kinds of commonwealth, the world state and the municipal state. In other words, the private avenger has in view the good of the whole human race, just as he has when he slays a serpent; and this goal corresponds exactly to that common good towards which, as we have said, all punishments are directed in nature's plan. (p. 93)

Another ways of appreciating Grotius's idea is through a consideration of his account of *justice*—something about which Pufendorf was later to express puzzlement.[23] As is well known, in the Aristotelian tradition, justice was divided into 'general' and 'particular' or 'special'. Understood in its general sense, justice was the sum of moral virtue, and was therefore universal in a very strong sense: no civil societies were needed for general justice to be displayed by moral agents. Understood in its particular sense, justice was the virtue involved in administering a civil society, and was itself divided into 'commutative' justice, the right administration of punishment, and 'distributive' justice, the right distribution of the goods of the society. Although particular justice was restricted in its scope in this way, the Aristotelian writers assumed that the underlying principles upon which acts of particular justice were based were to be found among the principles of universal justice. Grotius, very extraordinarily in the eyes of contemporary Aristotelians, insisted that these distinctions were misleading: universal justice should be regarded as the commutative justice of the Aristotelian tradition, and particular justice was solely distributive justice.

[23] *De Iure Naturae et Gentium*, I. 7. 9, 11.

In other words, Grotius claimed that in some sense the universal relations of men were like a civil society, in that commutative justice could straightforwardly apply to their dealings in the state of nature; but these relations were like a very thin version of human society, since they excluded considerations of distributive justice. This fracturing of the Aristotelian notion of social life was at the heart of Grotius's enterprise, and was to remain characteristic of many of his followers. So when Grotius talked about human sociability in the *De Indis*, he did not mean—and acknowledged through the ancient texts he cited, such as Horace, that he did not mean—that natural men were sociable in anything like the *Aristotelian* sense. Instead, we might say that they were sociable in the *Epicurean* sense, for, as we saw in Chapter 1, Epicureanism did permit a thin notion of human sociability.

De Indis: Practical Implications

There were two significant implications of this claim that natural individuals are like states, and are governed by a minimal morality comparable to that governing international relations. The first was that Grotius, like the good humanist he was, had of course endorsed the claim that we may punish men over whom we do not posses political rights—for on his account of the *ius gladii*, punishment in nature must be exercised by men who do not possess political authority over the objects of their vengeance. So Grotius was even led (in the context of discussing punishment) to assert that Aristotle was not mistaken 'when he says that certain persons are by nature slaves, not because God did not create man as a free being, but because there are some individuals whose character is such that it is expedient for them to be governed by another's sovereign will rather than by their own' (p. 62). In the critical struggle between humanist and scholastic over the right to inflict violence on barbaric peoples, Grotius (contrary to his popular reputation) supported its infliction—and as we shall see, went on in *De Iure Belli ac Pacis* to make his support for it even more explicit.

The second implication of the argument related specifically to the commercial conflict in the Indies. Grotius's theory implied that it was a fundamental right possessed by all private individuals to acquire as many goods as possible, and to protect them, as long as they did not thereby take away the legitimate goods of another person. The Dutch therefore had a fundamental right to seek trade in the East Indies, and attempts by the Portuguese to debar them could only be legitimate if the Portuguese could lay a reasonable claim to own the seas across which the Dutch were sailing. Grotius's argument to show that they could not, was of course the chapter separately published as *Mare Liberum*; and it took the form, once again, of a fundamental re-examination of the idea of property.

The essence of Grotius's new theory can be described as the claim that we have rights to those things—and only those things—in which we have a personal interest: once again, his origins as a humanist are vital to an understanding of his views, for he took the old humanist account of the pursuit of self-interest by individuals or cities, and made it the foundation of an account of rights.[24] When it came to property, this technique elegantly differentiated between the sea and the land: for, as Grotius argued in *Mare Liberum*, one can have true, private property only in things which one can either personally consume or personally transform in some way, for it is only in such things that one can be said to have a personal interest. The fisherman needs to protect his catch from rivals, but he does not need to protect the sea itself, for there is (Grotius argued) always enough for other fisherman in it:

> all that which has been so constituted by nature that though serving some one person it still suffices for the common use of all other persons, is today and ought to remain in the same condition as when it was first created by nature . . . The air belongs to this class of things for two reasons. First, it is not susceptible of occupation; and second its common use is destined for all men. For the same reasons the sea is common to all, because it is so limitless that it cannot become a possession of any one, and because it is adapted for all, whether we consider it from the point of view of navigation or of fisheries.[25]

So far, Grotius had said nothing that would contradict the conventional view, which I outlined in the previous chapter, that the sea could not be owned in the same way as the land could be, but it could come under a state's jurisdiction. But when he turned to this issue, which was the critical one for his case, Grotius argued the following. First, if something cannot become private property, it cannot come under the control of a state either:

[24] See my *Philosophy and Government*, pp. 346–8.
[25] *The Freedom of the Seas*, ed. J. B. Scott, trans. R. van D. Magoffin (Carnegie Endowment for International Peace, Oxford University Press New York, 1916), pp. 27–8.

Ownership [*Occupatio*] . . . both public and private, arises in the same way. On this point Seneca [*De Beneficiis*, VII. 4. 3] says: 'We speak in general of the land of the Athenians or the Campanians. It is the same land which again by means of private boundaries is divided among individual owners'.[26]

And to make clear his ideas, Grotius argued in the key passage:

Those who say that a certain sea belonged to the Roman people explain their statement to mean that the right of the Romans did not extend beyond protection and jurisdiction; this right they distinguish from ownership [*proprietas*]. Perchance they do not pay sufficient attention to the fact that although the Roman People were able to maintain fleets for the protection of navigation and to punish pirates captured on the sea, it was not done by private right, but by the common right which other free peoples also enjoy on the sea.[27]

He acknowledged that this common right might be limited by an agreement about its exercise (so that one nation might agree not to police part of the sea which another nation was willing to patrol), but (my italics) '*this agreement does bind those who are parties to it, but it has no binding force on other nations, nor does it make the delimited area of the sea the private property of any one. It merely constitutes a personal right between contracting parties,*' (p. 35). In other words, jurisdictional sovereignty at sea is critically different from jurisdictional sovereignty on land, and the two could not be casually equated as had been customary among the civil lawyers. Neither Grotius nor any other seventeenth-century jurist would have said that the sovereignty of (say) Venice over the terra firma was the consequence of a 'personal right between contracting parties' which any other nation that had not been a party to the agreement might ignore; by claiming this about Venice's rights over the Adriatic, Grotius was making a very radical move, which took him close (as he acknowledged) to the position of Vazquez. The basis of the idea seems to have been a sense that even the Romans could not, as matter of sheer practicality, enforce their will on the high seas in a consistent and effective fashion—because of the size and unmanageable character of the sea, it was always possible for other people to slip through it unmolested and to fish in it. Giving naval jurisdiction to the Romans thus involved some people promising not to attempt to exercise any rival control over users of the sea, rather than (as it would be on land) the recognition of both a right and a capacity on the part of the Romans to do so against the wishes of anyone else.

[26] Ibid. 26. [27] Ibid. 35.

The extreme originality of his view is not often recognized, and indeed most modern histories of the law of the sea misrepresent both Grotius's position and that of his predecessors. It was widely imagined, particularly at the beginning of this century by historians such as Fulton, that the freedom of the seas in its Grotian form was an ancient doctrine which merely needed restating against some novel opponents.[28] But as we saw in Chapter 2, the almost universal view before Grotius was that states could claim jurisdiction over their neighbouring waters, and even over the ocean itself, against all other states; and that jurisdiction, while it might not allow the ruler actually to ban traffic and fishing, could permit him to regulate them in such a manner that they were virtually banned. Among the major jurists, only Vazquez had hitherto questioned this view, albeit in a somewhat elusive fashion; though, as we shall see in Chapter 4, English sailors in the last decades of the century had begun to oppose it with formidable effect. Grotius's novel view of the matter rested on his equally novel assimilation of states and individuals, for there were in general no specifically *political* rights in Grotius's theory. If an individual could not own something, he could not give his rights in it to a state; and since 'every right comes to the state from private individuals', a state could not have political control over unownable territory.

Grotius had to establish one other minor, but still interesting principle in *De Indis* before he had completed his defence of Dutch commercial activity in the East. Anxiety among Dutch Protestants about the conduct of the India companies was not confined to unhappiness about their military activities; probably more influential among the bulk of the Protestant population was a belief that Christians ought not to make treaties with non-Christians. This was an important issue because the techniques the companies used, once they had run the Portuguese blockade, included signing preferential trading agreements with the native rulers and inciting them to break any understandings they had earlier had with the Portuguese. Heemskerk himself made such agreements, and as early as 1601 the King of Bali wrote to the 'King of Holland' pledging mutual loyalty.[29] The capture of the Portuguese

[28] See Thomas Wemyss Fulton, *The Sovereignty of the Sea* (Edinburgh, 1911). This was also the principal point of James Brown Scott's publishing programme for the Carnegie Endowment.

[29] See the fascinating documents in J. E. Heeres ed., *Corpus Diplomaticum Neerlando-Indicum*, I (*Bijdragen tot de Taal-, Land- en Volkenhunde van Nederlandsh-Indië*, VII. 3 (1907)). Heemskerk's treaty with ruler of Banda is p. 11 and the letter to the King of Holland is p. 15.

carrack itself was an incident in a war carried on by Heemskerk notionally on behalf of the Sultan of Johore, who wanted to trade directly with the Dutch and break the Portuguese embargo; moreover, Grotius himself had been involved in the treaty negotiations with the Sultan which began in 1602 and ended with a trading agreement in 1606 covering the modern site of Singapore. Conventional Catholic theology, including Aquinas, had usually held that binding treaties could be made with infidels, and the Portuguese had duly followed suit.[30] But Protestants, influenced particularly by the censure of the Kings of Judah in I Kings for doing just this, were inclined to say that no treaty should be made with an infidel. The humanist Protestant theologian Peter Martyr argued this in the mid-sixteenth century, and as we have seen, the humanist Protestant jurist Gentili followed him in his discussion of whether a Christian should promise armed assistance to an infidel under a treaty.

> Either a Christian joins arms with an infidel against another infidel or against a Christian. Against infidels the Maccabees did this and the kings of Judah, and in modern times the Portuguese. And such an alliance does not seem to me lawful . . . Therefore it is lawful neither to lend aid to infidels nor to accept aid from them against other infidels. And if it is not lawful to do this against infidels, how much less will it be allowed to do it against the faithful? . . . In this case I agree with a most learned theologian of our generation [Peter Martyr] who says that it is never right to make an alliance with infidels, although peace may be made and kept with them . . . It is characteristic of infidel barbarians to burn, pillage, and destroy. It is their way to use unfair wiles, to fight with poison, to wage a merciless war, at any rate to inflict slavery, which has been abolished in all Christian warfare. Hence I do not approve the treaty of the King of France with the Turks, because of which once so many thousands of men, boys, and women were captured and led off into everlasting and intolerable servitude. Moreover, you cannot trust the infidels. For although the impious oath of an infidel may be accepted, yet what trust can be put in an unbeliever?[31]

Grotius responded to this by applying the principles he had outlined at the beginning of *De Indis*, and in particular the principle that in nature we may punish other men who breach the laws of inoffensiveness and abstinence. According to him, the Portuguese had breached

[30] See the treaties collected in J. F. Judice Biker ed., *Colecção de Tratados e Concertos de pazes que o Estado da India Portugueza fez com os Reis e Senhores con quem teve relações nas partes da Asia e Africa Oriental desde o principio da conquista até ae fin do seculo XVIII*, I (Lisbon, 1881).

[31] *De Iure Belli Libri Tres*, ed. Coleman Phillipson, trans. John C. Rolfe (Carnegie Endowment, Oxford University Press, 1933), II, 401–2.

these laws by seeking to prevent the Sultan of Johore from trading with the Dutch.

Do we perhaps believe that we have nothing in common with persons who have not accepted the Christian faith? Such a belief would be very far removed from the pious doctrine of Augustine, who declares (in his interpretation of the precept of Our Lord whereby we are bidden to love our neighbours) that the term '*neighbours*' obviously includes *every human being* . . . Accordingly, not only is it universally admitted that the protection of infidels from injury (even from injury by Christians) is never unjust, but it is furthermore maintained, by authorities who have examined this particular point [including Vitoria], that alliances and treaties with infidels may in many cases be justly contracted for the purpose of defending one's own rights, too. Such a course of action was adopted (so we are told) by Abraham, Isaac, David, Solomon, and the Maccabees.

In any case, it is certain that the cause of the King of Johore was exceedingly just. For what could be more inequitable than a prohibition imposed by a mercantile people upon a free king to prevent him from carrying on trade with another people? And what would constitute interference both with the law of nations and with the distinct jurisdictions of different princes, if such a prohibition does not?[32]

De Iure Belli ac Pacis: Sociability

During the period between 1609 and 1613 Grotius returned on a couple of occasions to the themes of *Mare Liberum*. Both times it was to defend the Dutch against English accusations that they were now insisting on a Portuguese-style *dominium maris* in the Far East, and on each occasion he insisted that the treaties which the Dutch had struck with the local rulers entitled the company to monopoly trading privileges without violating the general principles of *Mare Liberum*. As we have just seen, the original draft of the *De Indis* included a full defence of such treaties, so Grotius's repeated claim that they were not inconsistent with *Mare Liberum* was justifiable—though it was greeted with understandable scepticism by his opponents.[33] Along with his master Oldenbarnevelt,

[32] *De Iure Praedae Commentarius*, I, p. 315.

[33] One of these occasions was the Colonial Conference of 1613 at London, where Grotius drafted many of the position papers for the Dutch delegates. A sardonic English diplomat noted in the margin of one of them, which claimed that 'we think it very honest to defend oppressed people', 'against their wills'. G. N. Clark and W. J. M. Eysinga, *The Colonial Conferences Between England and the Netherlands in 1613 and 1615*, *Bibliotheca Visseriana Dissertationum Ius Internationale Illustrantium*, 15 and 17 (Leiden, 1940 and 1951) (quotation from 17, p. 133). See also F. De Pauw, *Grotius and the Law of the Sea*,

he fell from power in 1618 as part of the coup by the Statholder and the Calvinists against the religiously liberal republicans who had been running the United Provinces; Oldenbarnevelt was executed and Grotius narrowly escaped death, being imprisoned for life in Loevestein Castle. He escaped in 1612 and fled to France, where he became a pensioner of the King of France, and later (1634) Ambassador of the Crown of Sweden at the French court. It was in this time of exile that he wrote and published *De Iure Belli ac Pacis* (1625), which became the most authoritative statement of his political theory. In many ways his fundamental arguments remained as they had been in his earlier works; but he developed them in some new ways which were to prove both influential and controversial for the rest of the century.

It is important to remember that although he was to remain an exile for most of the rest of his life, in 1625 he did not know that this was to be the case: indeed, in that very year the old Statholder died and was succeeded by his brother Frederick Henry, with whom Grotius had remained on good terms since 1621, and whose succession he had always expected would make his return easier. Grotius had provided some diplomatic help to Frederick Henry in Paris, as he had done also to the East India Company, with whose directors he kept in close contact. So we must not read *De Iure Belli ac Pacis* as the work of a hostile and bitter exile; rather, it was in part a contribution to rehabilitating himself with the Dutch government. The opposition to Oldenbarnevelt had also been the party which most supported the continuation of war with Spain, particularly over the Indies; Grotius had always tried to distance himself from Oldenbarnevelt's peace policy,[34] and *De Iure Belli ac Pacis* reminded his audience that he was still an enthusiast for war around the globe. He was indeed a most improbable figure to be the tutelary deity of the Peace Palace at The Hague.

Most of the substantive theory of the *De Iure Belli ac Pacis* was in fact an expansion of the arguments of *De Indis*, with, in particular, a crucial role being played throughout the work by the analogy between states and natural individuals. For all the complexity and nuanced character of

trans. P. J. Arthern (Université de Bruxelles, 1965). The other occasion was Grotius's unpublished reply to Welwood's *An Abridgement of all Sea-Lawes* (London, 1613), entitled *Defensio Capitis Quinti Maris Liberi* (first printed in Samuel Muller, *Mare Clausum. Bijdrage tot de Geschiedenis der Rivaliteit van Engeland en Nederland in de Zeventiende Eeuw* (Amsterdam, 1872), 331–61).

[34] Grotius, *Briefwisseling*, II, ed. P. C. Molhuysen (The Hague, 1936), 20.

the book, this is the simple message which its readers received and which was so important to the later seventeenth century. And the state which Grotius used as the analogue for a natural individual was still the sovereign state of the *De Indis*:

That is called Supreme, whose Acts are not subject to another's Power,[35] so that they cannot be made void by any other human Will. When I say, by any other, I exclude the Sovereign himself, who may change his own Will, as also his Successor, who enjoys the same Right, and consequently, has the same Power, and no other. Let us then see what this Sovereign may have for its Subject. The Subject then is either common or proper: As the Body is the common Subject of Sight, the eye the proper; so the common Subject of Supreme Power is the State [*civitas*]; which I have before called a perfect Society of Men[36] . . . [S]everal States may be linked together in a most strict Alliance, and make a Compound, as *Strabo* more than once calls it; and yet each of them continue to be a perfect State . . .[37] The State then is, in the Sense I have just mentioned, the common Subject of Sovereignty. The proper Subject is one or more Persons, according to the Laws and Customs of each Nation. (I. 3. 7)[38]

Here, though (interestingly) the term *civitas* has replaced the term *respublica* to describe the initial subect of sovereignty, the basic idea is still the same, with the social pact creating a sovereign body which can then exercise its sovereignty through a magistrate (though Grotius now, famously, was less prepared to treat the magistrate as expendable by the *civitas*—see I. 3. 8).

However, unfortunately for his later readers, Grotius did not make it anything like as clear as he had done in his earlier work what the theoretical foundations of his argument were. But it should be said that they were somewhat clearer in the first edition than in subsequent editions, since one of the things which has confused commentators on the book is that Grotius introduced some marked changes into the second edition, which he produced in what we shall see were special circumstances, in 1631.[39] It is worth bearing in mind that Hobbes and

[35] *Summa autem illa dicitur cujus actus alterius juri non subsunt*—that is, 'Power' is *jus*, *moral* power.

[36] This is a reference to I. 1. 14: 'The State is a compleat Body of free Persons, associated together to enjoy peacably their Rights, and for their common Benefit.'

[37] This is, of course, a defence of Grotius's concept of the federated republics of the United Provinces.

[38] *The Rights of War and Peace, in Three Books* (London, 1738), 63–4.

[39] For some reason, subsequent students of Grotius have been uninterested in these changes; all modern editions of the *De Iure Belli ac Pacis* have simply used the text of the 1642 or 1646 editions; which themselves simply reproduced in large part the 1631 edition.

the other early readers of Grotius may well have read the 1625 edition.

In the *De Iure Belli ac Pacis*, the principal discussion of self-interest and sociability comes in the *Prolegomena*. It follows immediately a famous passage in which Grotius summarizes Carneades's scepticism about a universal morality and proclaims his own intention to refute it. The first edition reads in full at this point (using my own translation, as no translation of the first edition exists):

When he [Carneades] undertook the critique of justice (which is my particular subject at the moment), he found no argument more powerful than this: men have established *jura* according to their own interests [*pro utilitate*], which vary with different customs, and often at different times with the same people: so there is no natural *jus*: all men and the other animals are impelled by nature to seek their own interests: so either there is no justice, or if there is such a thing, it is the greatest foolishness, since pursuing the good of others harms oneself. We should not accept the truth in all circumstances of what this philosopher says, nor of what a poet said in imitation—'never by nature can wrong be split from right'. For though man is an animal, he is one of a special kind, further removed from the rest than each of the other species are from one another—for which there is testimony from many actions unique to the human species. Among the things which are unique to man is the desire for society [*appetitus societatis*], that is for community with those who belong to his species—though not a community of any kind, but one at peace, and with a rational order [*pro sui intellectus modo ordinatae*]. Therefore, when it is said that nature drives each animal to seek its own interests, we can say that this is true of the other animals, *and of man before he comes to the use of that which is special to men* [my italics] [*antequam ad usum eius, quod homini proprium est, pervenerit*] . . . This care for society in accordance with the human intellect, which we have roughly sketched, is the source of *jus*, properly so called, to which belong abstaining from another's possessions, restoring anything which belongs to another (or the profit from it), being obliged to keep promises, giving compensation for culpable damage, and incurring human punishment.[40]

A particularly interesting feature of this passage is the remark which I have emphasized—'when it is said that nature drives each animal to seek its own interests, we can say that this is true of the other animals, *and of man before he comes to the use of that which is special to men*'. Read in the context of the theory which we know he had drafted in *De Indis*, this part of the *Prolegomena* does not sound radically different from his

[40] *De Iure Belli ac Pacis* (Paris, 1625) sig ã vj. (The later division of the *Prolegomena* into numbered paragraphs does not occur in this edition; the passage was later numbered 5–8.)

original work: Grotius was arguing against the sceptic (in the person of Carneades) who believed that there were *no* universal principles of justice, but he was not willing—yet—to deny that in some sense self-interest was a primary principle for human beings, nor to give a richer account of human natural society than he had done in *De Indis*.

It is true that he spoke eloquently about the fundamental human desire for society with other human beings, and it is also true that instead of applauding Horace for his Epicurean or sceptical sentiments, he was now cautiously critical:

> What not Carneades alone but others as well have said, 'expediency might perhaps be called the mother of justice and equity', is not true, if we speak accurately: for human nature itself is the mother of natural law, for it drives us to seek a common society [*societatem mutuam*] even if there is no shortage of resources . . . But expediency [*utilitas*] is annexed to the natural law.[41]

But on the central question of what the character of this natural common society might be, he reiterated in the clearest fashion his original idea about the distinction between corrective and distributive justice, and the assimilation of the former but not the latter to the notion of universal justice.

He now said that corrective justice dealt with rights 'strictly so called', whereas distributive justice dealt with what was customarily termed 'imperfect' rights, or claims upon other people for their assistance, which, he insisted (against, he recognized, the conventional view) was not really part of the system of natural right. To distributive justice, he wrote,

> belongs a prudent Management in the gratuitous Distribution of Things that properly belong to each particular Person or Society [*coetus*], so as to prefer sometimes one of greater before one of less Merit, a Relation before a Stranger, a poor man before one that is rich, and that according as each Man's Actions, and the Nature of the Thing require; which many both of the Ancients and Moderns take to be a part of Right properly and strictly so called; when notwithstanding that Right, properly speaking, has a quite different Nature, since it consists in leaving others in quiet Possession of what is already their own, or in doing for them what in Strictness they may demand.[42]

And Grotius nowhere in the body of the book used imperfect rights to explicate the relationships of states, or persons in a state of nature. His approach to them was made particularly clear at II. 22. 16:

[41] *Prolegomena*, 16, my translation.
[42] *The Rights of War and Peace, in Three Books*, p. xviii (*Prolegomena*, 10).

If a Man owes another any Thing, not in strictness of Justice but by some other Virtue, suppose Liberality, Gratitude, Compassion, or Charity, he cannot be sued for it in any Court of Judicature, neither can War be made upon him on that Account; for to either of these it is not sufficient, that that which is demanded ought for some moral reason to be performed, but besides it is requisite that we should have some Right to it, such a Right as both divine and human Laws do sometimes give us to those Things which are due by other Virtues; and when that is so, there arises a new Obligation which belongs to Justice. But when this is wanting, the War on that Account is unjust, as was that of the *Romans* against the King of *Cyprus*, for his Ingratitude.

So a careful reader of the first edition of *De Iure Belli ac Pacis* might well get a sense of Grotius's governing idea which was not far removed from the sense they would have got from reading the manuscript *De Indis*. Their task would have been rendered rather harder by the second edition of the work, however, for the remark in the *Prolegomena* about men being in some way primarily self-interested, and the comparison between man and the other animals, was replaced by the following passage in the second edition.

Among the things which are unique to man is the desire for society, that is for community with those who belong to his species—though not a community of any kind, but one at peace, and with a rational order: a desire which the Stoics call *oikeosis*. Therefore, when it is said that nature drives each animal to seek its own interests, this ought not to be allowed as a universal truth.

And Grotius now referred to man's possession of 'a conspicuous desire for society, together with speech, an instrument for that desire which is unique among animals'.

Grotius produced the second edition of the book at a very delicate period in his life, in December 1631. This was the period in which he was trying extremely hard to move back to the United Provinces, and indeed had returned incognito to live there three months earlier. But after only six months' residence he gave up any hope of being allowed officially to return to the United Provinces and left for Hamburg, never to return in life to his native land. It is clear that the alterations to the text of *De Iure Belli ac Pacis* were part of a campaign to make Grotius's views appear more acceptable to the Aristotelian, Calvinist culture of his opponents within the United Provinces.

Exactly the same purpose can be seen in the other changes which he introduced, notably into the discussion of the role of God in the foundation of the natural law. This is a subject whose full treatment is impossible here; but, briefly, I would argue that in this area also the 1625 edition was more like *De Indis* than the 1631 edition was to be. *De Indis* argued that the laws of nature are based on the will of God—'*What God has shown to be His Will, that is law*. This axiom points directly to the cause of law, and is rightly laid down as a primary principle' (p. 8). But Grotius argued that the *content* of the laws of nature was then to be sought in a consideration of the character of the natural world, and in particular the fundamental principles upon which all creatures seem to act, above all the principle of self-preservation (p. 9). This claim, that the *legal character* of the law comes from the assumption that God has created the natural order, but our knowledge of its content comes simply from our observation of the facts of the material universe, is broadly what Grotius says in the first edition of *De Iure Belli ac Pacis* (for example, that the *ius naturale* is 'a dictate of right reason, indicating of any act whether it possesses moral turpitude or moral necessity, from its congruity or incongruity with rational nature itself, and consequently whether it was forbidden or permitted by God the author of nature').[43]

But in 1631 Grotius attempted to make divine law a basis for natural law in a more direct fashion, unmediated by an examination of the material world. The very first sentence of the *Prolegomena* included the claim in 1625 that

> the law which adjudicates between different peoples, or between the rulers of peoples, whether proceeding from nature itself or introduced by custom and tacit agreement, has been handled by few writers, and not by anyone hitherto in a systematic and comprehensive fashion.

In 1631, this read

> the law which adjudicates between different peoples, or between the rulers of peoples, whether proceeding from nature itself, *or established by divine laws* [my italics], or introduced by custom and tacit agreement, has been handled by few writers, and not by anyone hitherto in a systematic and comprehensive fashion.

Similarly, immediately after his explication of his famous claim that the natural law would govern man 'even though we should assume that

[43] I. 1. 10 (my trans). Barbeyrac inserted at his own initiative the words 'and social' (*ac sociali*) after the word 'rational' in this passage (*The Rights of War and Peace, in Three Books* (9, n. 2)—from my perspective, a revealing attempt to make Grotius more of a theorist of sociability than in fact he was).

there is no God' (*Prolegomena*, 11), Grotius in 1625 continued that the natural law

> despite the fact that it stems by necessity from internal principles of man, can rightly be ascribed to God, since he willed that such principles should exist in us: in which sense Chrysippus and the Stoics said that the origin of *jus* was not to be sought anywhere but in Jove himself; it can probably be said that the Latins took the word *jus* from the name of Jove. Among men, our parents are like Gods, to whom is due not an infinite but a proper obedience.

In 1631 this limited claim was greatly expanded. First, the phrase 'by necessity' was dropped; then Grotius inserted after 'the name of Jove' the following long passage.

> It should be added that God has made these same principles more conspicuous by giving laws, even to those whose powers of reasoning are feeble: and he has forbidden those powerful impulses which attend to the interests of both ourselves and others from straying into the wrong courses,[44] by strictly restraining the more vehement of them and by coercing them in both their ends and their means. Moreover sacred history, besides that part which consists of precepts, greatly excites our social feeling, since it teaches us that all men are sprung from the same first parents; so that in this sense too we can truthfully say what Florentinus said in another sense, that there is a kinship established among us by nature: and as a consequence that it is wrong for one man to plot against another.

Revealingly, this last passage also includes a more strident claim about human sociability than he had put forward in 1625. There can be no question but that the first edition of *De Iure Belli ac Pacis* was far more dismissive of the role of God in natural law than the subsequent editions: in 1625 God (in some ways) played merely the same role that he was to play in Hobbes's work, that of the maker of a universe which included creatures endowed with the appropriate natural 'principles' or feelings. In 1631 his status as *law-giver*, whose laws were apparent to his subjects *as* his laws, was stressed for the first time, setting in train a long-standing puzzle for the interpretation of Grotius's ideas.

[44] This is a translation of the sentence *& in diversa trahentes impetus, qui nobis ipsis, quique aliis consulunt, vagari vetuit*, which appears in all the editions seen through the press by Grotius. Since the time of Barbeyrac, it has been customary to suppose that this should read *male consulunt*, but that seems to me to be a misrepresentation of what Grotius was saying. His point was that our self-interested and benevolent impulses did in principle keep us on the right road, though they might (as he claimed in 1631) need some sort of control by God to make sure that they did so.

It is important to stress, however, that all these changes did not affect the body of the book: the actual theory which Grotius put forward about the principles of natural human relations, and international relations, remained unaltered between the two editions. The consequence was that a theory about minimal natural sociability, based on a general view of the role of self-interest in the natural world, appeared to later readers to be based instead on a different view, and one which was closer to traditional notions of both human sociability and divine law. Nevertheless, the extent to which early readers of Grotius saw something disturbing in his account of sociability and self-interest should not be underestimated. I shall have more to say about this in Chapter 5; here, I will simply observe that it became to a degree a commonplace in late seventeenth-century Germany that Grotius had failed to refute Carneades because his own basic idea was the same, and that there was at bottom little to choose between Grotius and Hobbes. This line of criticism culminated in the marvellous observations of Rousseau in *Emile* which I quoted in the Introduction

> When I hear Grotius praised to the skies and Hobbes covered with execration, I see how far sensible men read or understand these two authors. The truth is that their principles are exactly the same: they only differ in their expression. They also differ in their method. Hobbes relies on sophisms, and Grotius on the poets; all the rest is the same.[45]

De Iure Belli ac Pacis: Native Peoples

In addition to this carefully judged reworking of the fundamental theory he had put forward in *De Indis*, Grotius in *De Iure Belli* both expanded his ideas in certain areas, and modified them in others. The most striking matter about which he was now much more explicit was the principle of international punishment. In *De Indis* he had briefly registered his agreement with the conventional humanist view, found for instance in Gentili, that barbarians or natural slaves might rightfully be appropriated by civilized peoples. In *De Iure Belli ac Pacis*, he was much more eloquent on the subject.

> Kings, and those who are invested with a Power equal to that of Kings, have a Right to exact Punishments, not only for Injuries committed against themselves, or their Subjects, but likewise, for those which do not peculiarly con-

[45] Rousseau, *Political Writings*, ed. C. E. Vaughan (Oxford University Press, 1915), II, 147.

cern them, but which are, in any Persons whatsoever, grievous Violations of the Law of Nature or Nations. For the Liberty of consulting the Benefit of human Society, by Punishments, which at first, as we have seen, was in every particular Person, does now, since Civil Societies, and Courts of Justice, have been instituted, reside in those who are possessed of the supreme power . . . And upon this account it is, that Hercules is so highly extolled by the Antients, for having freed the Earth of Antaeus, Busiris, Diomedes, and such like Tyrants, Whose Countries, says Seneca of him, he passed over, not with an ambitious Design of gaining them for himself, but for the Sake of vindicating the Cause of the Oppressed . . . For the same Reason we make no Doubt, but War may be justly undertaken against those who are inhuman to their Parents . . . [against those who kill Strangers that come to dwell amongst them] [a sentence found only in the 1625 edition] . . . ; against those who eat human Flesh . . . ; and against those who practise Piracy . . . And so far we follow the Opinion of Innocentius, and others, who hold that War is lawful against those who offend against Nature; which is contrary to the Opinion of Victoria, Vasquez, Azorius, Molina, and others, who seem to require, towards making a War just, that he who undertakes it be injured in himself, or in his State, or that he has some Jurisdiction over the Person against whom the War is made. For they assert, that the Power of Punishing is properly an Effect of Civil Jurisdiction; whereas our Opinion is, that it proceeds from the Law of Nature . . . (II. 20. 40)

It is remarkable—and, I think, completely unrecognized by modern scholars—that Grotius specifically aligned himself with Innocent IV and against Vitoria on this crucial issue. The idea that foreign rulers can punish tyrants, cannibals, pirates, those who kill settlers, and those who are inhuman to their parents neatly legitimated a great deal of European action against native peoples around the world, and was disconcertingly close to the extreme pre-Vitorian arguments used by the Spaniards in America (though it is worth noting that Grotius praised 'the Incha's, Kings of Peru' who 'obtained an Empire, of all we read of, excepting their Religion, the justest') (p. 438 n. 9). The central reason why Grotius had developed his argument in this direction was, I think, that the Dutch had begun to change the character of their activity in the non-European world since his earlier works, and in particular had begun to annex territory.

In 1604 and 1609 Grotius had been entirely concerned with the question of the sea, and in both the *De Indis* and *Mare Liberum* he had assumed that land should be owned and politically controlled in a traditional fashion. This was no doubt (at least in part) because at that time the East India Company was concerned purely to force trade and capital on the native rulers, and had not yet any thoughts of colonial occupation. But from 1612 onwards its mind turned to planting colonists in the East Indies, and it was from 1619 onwards (spurred on by increasing English and French competition in the East, and indeed by armed conflict with the English) that the company began forcibly to annex native territory (hitherto all forts and factories had been set up by agreement with native rulers).[46] At more or less the same time Dutch policy in the West suffered the same transformation, under the same spur of competition from England and France (see the next chapter). The first Dutch settlements in North America were very like its factories in the East—Fort Orange, the present-day Albany, established in 1614 near the limit of navigation on the Hudson River, deep into the fur-producing area, was not at first the centre of a substantial agricultural colony. After the foundation in 1621 of a West Indies Company, however, policy in North America changed: the company was charged under its charter with advancing 'the peopling of those fruitful and unsettled parts'.[47] Two substantial settlements were fairly quickly established, one in Guiana and the other centred on Manhattan Island at the bottom of the route up the Hudson (New Netherlands). From 1628 the company also controlled a major colony, New Holland, in North-East Brazil.

These recent activities focused Grotius's attention on the implications of his general theory of property for the occupation and ownership of uncultivated land; and he perceived that if the sea could not be owned by the men who hunted over it, neither presumably could the land. In II. 2 of *De Iure Belli ac Pacis* he listed a number of qualifications on men's right to enjoy ownership over terrestrial objects, which together represent a formidable set of constraints on property in land. The alleged owners of a territory must always permit free passage over it, both of persons and goods; must allow any strangers the right to build temporary accommodation on the seashore; must permit exiles to settle (all of these again rights which the Spaniards and other Europeans had pleaded against native peoples); and, in particular, must allow anyone to possess things which are of no use to the owners. This is a right (he argued II. 2. 11) based on

[46] George Masselman, *The Cradle of Colonialism* (New Haven, 1963) 297, 390 ff.
[47] E. B. O'Callaghan, *History of New Netherland* (2nd edn., New York, 1855), I, 104.

innocent Profit; when I seek my own Advantage, without damaging anyone else. *Why slould we not,* says Cicero, *when we can do it without any Detriment to ourselves, let others share in those Things that may be beneficial to them who receive them, and no inconvenience to us who give them. Seneca* therefore denies that it is any Favour, properly so called, to permit a Man to light a Fire by ours. And we read in *Plutarch . . . 'Tis an impious Thing for those who have eat sufficiently, to throw away the remaining Victuals; or for those who have had Water enough, to stop up or hide the Spring; or for those who themselves have had the Advantage of them, to destroy the Sea or Land Marks; but we ought to leave them for the Use and Service of them, who, after us, shall want them.*

Seneca's remark is important in Grotius's general argument, for he too wished to emphasize that it is not a *favour*, that is, it does not belong to the sphere of distributive justice and imperfect right, the *locus* of 'benefits'. There is no ownership in things which are of no use to their owners, and therefore other people have a *perfect* right to occupy them.

Drawing on Gentili, though characteristically without acknowledgement, Grotius argued (II. 2. 17) that it followed from this that

if there be any waste or barren Land within our Dominions, that also is to be given to Strangers, at their Request, or may be lawfully possessed by them, because whatever remains uncultivated, is not to be esteemed a Property, only so far as concerns Jurisdiction [*imperium*], which always continues the Right of the ancient People. And *Servius* remarks, that seven hundred Acres of bad unmanured Land were granted to the *Trojans*, by the original *Latins*: So we read in *Dion Prusaensis* [i.e. Dio Chrysostom] . . . that *They commit no Crime who cultivate and manure the untilled Part of a Country*. Thus the *Ansibarians formerly cried* [in a quotation from Tacitus's *Annals*] that *As the Gods have Heaven, so the Earth was given to Mankind, and what is possessed by none, belongs to every one. And then looking up to the Sun and Stars as if present, and within hearing, they asked them, whether they could bear to look upon those uninhabited Lands, and whether they would not rather pour in the Sea upon those who hindered others to settle on them.*

He made the connection between his account of common ownership and the American situation (and the prehistory of Europe) clear in II. 2—'the Right common to all Men'

must have continued till now, had Men persisted in their primitive Simplicity, or lived together in perfect Friendship. A Confirmation of the first of these is the Account we have of some People of *America*, who by the extraordinary Simplicity of their Manners, have without the least Inconvenience observed the same Method of Living for many Ages . . . *Horace*, speaking of the *Scythians* and the *Getae*, represents their Way of living in the following Manner, that *they lived in the Fields, and drew their moveable Huts with Waggons*, whenever they changed Place, that *they did not divide their Lands by Acres*. (II. 2. 2 and n. 3)

Grotius's ideas about cultivating land should be associated with an equally striking passage in his *De Veritate Religionis Christianae*, composed in Loevestein and first published (in Dutch) in 1622, in which he praised Christianity for being the religion which most clearly recognized the moral truth that

our natural needs are satisfied with only a few things, which may be easily had without great labour or cost. As for what God has granted us in addition, we are commanded not to throw it into the sea (as some Philosophers foolishly asserted), nor to leave it unproductive (*inutile*), nor to waste it, but to use it to meet the needs (*inopiam*) of other men, either by giving it away, or by lending it to those who ask; as is appropriate for those who believe themselves to be not owners (*dominos*) of these things, but representatives or stewards (*procuratores ac dispensatores*) of God the Father.[48]

The assimilation of a Christian moral vision to that of the religions of antiquity is absolutely characteristic of Grotius.

As we have just seen, part of Grotius's argument over this question turned on a distinction between *property* and *jurisdiction*—there is a general natural right to possess any waste land, but one must defer to the local political authorities, assuming they are willing to let one settle. If they are not, of course, then the situation is different, for the local authorities will have violated a principle of the law of nature and may be punished by war waged against them. This distinction between property and jurisdiction was, as we have seen, a standard feature of earlier theories about the law of the sea, but was expressly ruled out, at least in its orthodox form, by Grotius in the *Mare Liberum*. In *De Iure Belli ac Pacis*, however, he went into more detail about his own current view of the distinction. Thus, he remarked

as to what belongs properly to no Body, there are two Things which one may take Possession of, Jurisdiction, and the Right of Property, as it stands distinguished from Jurisdiction . . . Jurisdiction is commonly exercised on two Subjects, the one primary, *viz*. Persons, and that alone is sometimes sufficient, as in an Army of Men, Women, and Children, that are going in quest of some new

[48] Grotius, *Opera Omnia Theologica* (London, 1679), III, 43 (II. 14). The last sentence is a reference to 1 Tim. 6: 17, 18.

Plantations; the other secundary [*sic*], *viz.* the Place, which is called *Territory* . . . (II. 3. 4)

This distinction between primary and secondary senses of jurisdiction was the key to his argument. Essentially, Grotius understood by jurisdiction a special and stable right to police people—the kind of right exercised over the personnel of an army or a fleet at sea by the general or admiral. Armies could come to enjoy an equally stable and effective right to command anyone who entered into a certain area of land, and they could then be said to possess jurisdiction over territory; this right should be distinguished from the kind of right which he had allowed to the Romans over the Mediterranean in *Mare Liberum*, since that right (he had argued) was enforceable only against other nations who recognized it and had agreed to it. Only along coasts, he now accepted, could jurisdiction of this territorial kind be exercised.

The Jurisdiction or Sovereignty over a Part of the Sea is acquired, in my Opinion, as all other Sorts of Jurisdiction; that is, as we said before, in Regard to Persons, and in Regard to Territory. In Regard to Persons, as when a Fleet, which is a Sea-Army, is Kept in any Part of the Sea: In Regard to Territory, as when those that sail on the Coasts of a Country may be compelled from the Land, for then it is just the same as if they were actually upon the Land. (II. 3. 13)

So jurisdiction is a right over people, not over things, though it is a right which may be exercised over all people who come into certain areas of the world's surface, where such a comprehensive control is feasible. So while the Romans could not possess jurisdiction, in this sense, over the Mediterranean, the King of the Algonquins could possess it over the New Netherlands, despite the fact that in neither case was the actual material of the earth's surface owned by anyone. However, the key point for Grotius was that jurisdictional rights could not be pleaded as a justification for stopping free passage or the occupation of waste: since both these activities are entirely legitimate, no local authorities could have rights over people in their territory which would extend to preventing them from behaving in this way. This view of colonization and passage across the sea in fact fitted rather neatly into the actual Dutch practices during the 1620s: as the famous purchase of Manhattan Island in 1626 illustrates, the Dutch were in general fairly anxious to ensure that what they took to be local political authorities were agreeable to the removal of land from their jurisdiction. Indeed, the rules of the West India Company for New Netherlands, drawn up in 1629, specified that 'whoever shall settle any colony out of the limits of the Manhattes' Island, shall be obliged to satisfy the Indians for the land they shall settle upon'.[49] But it is not at all clear that Grotius's distinction between jursidiction and property was a satisfactory one, and if it were to fail, then either a more ruthless colonization or no colonization at all would be the consequence. As we shall see in the next chapter, the English determinedly took the former course.

As I have already suggested, the view taken of Grotius in the conventional histories of international law badly misrepresents his real position. Far from being an heir to the tradition of Vitoria and Suarez, as was assumed by writers at the beginning of this century, he was in fact an heir to the tradition Vitoria most mistrusted, that of humanist jurisprudence. The account of states' rights in international affairs from which Grotius's general theory took its start was in most respects modelled on that of jurists such as Gentili; the one significant respect in which Grotius differed from Gentili was over the question of treaties with non-Christians. As a consequence, Grotius endorsed for a state the most far-reaching set of rights to make war which were available in the contemporary repertoire. In particular, he accepted a strong version of an international right to punish, and to appropriate territory which was not being used properly by indigenous peoples. Since, as I have stressed, his general theory then involved him in attributing comparable rights to *private* individuals, he equipped the modern liberal rights theories which he had launched with a far-reaching account of what agents can do to one another, both in a state of nature and in the international arena. In the following chapters, we shall see how his successors reacted to the often brutal implications of his ideas.

[49] E. B. O'Callaghan, *History of New Netherland*, I, p. 119.

4

THOMAS HOBBES

Elizabethan Ideas on Colonization

If one way of viewing Grotius, as we saw in the previous chapter, is that he put into the form of a modern rights theory the ideas about war found in writers like Gentili, then just the same kind of claim can be made about Hobbes. As I said in the Introduction, Hobbes was the most clear-headed exponent of the new ideas, and the intellectual relationship between him and Grotius was much closer than many eighteenth-century writers were willing to admit—with the striking exception of Rousseau. In this chapter, I want to show how Hobbes can be read in this way, and how his ideas grew in part out of an English debate about war and colonization, in which Gentili was both intellectually and personally a commanding presence.

Just as in the case of France which we looked at in Chapter 1, the English began their colonial activity as part of their struggle against Spain at home. Successful action against Spain in Europe gave rise to the hope of supplanting it in the world as a whole, a hope articulated particularly well, for example, by Walter Ralegh in his *History of the World* (1614), with its suggestive account of the rise of great empires and their overthrow by small but valiant nations which went on to achieve new world hegemonies. But the English took a very different path from the French when it came to justifying the occupation of the lands of native peoples. It is, I think, safe to say that seventeenth-century English writers took the most uninhibited and non-legalist approach to these matters of all contemporary theorists; and it may well be that the disconcerting but historic consequence of this was that in the end the English were the most successful of all these rival nations at constructing a world empire.

Already under Elizabeth we can see that the preferred justifications for the English resembled much more the literature of secular *raison d'état* than was ever the case in France or Spain. The first English colonial expeditions, those of Humphrey Gilbert to the territory south of Acadia in 1583 and Richard Grenville on behalf of Ralegh to Virginia in 1585, were defended by their friend Richard Hakluyt in a lengthy and systematic *Discourse of Western Planting* of 1584. The most striking thing about this work, and the various other documents associated with it, is that Hakluyt on the whole completely eschewed any religious justification for colonization (revealingly, even the appointment of two preachers for the expedition was tacked on at the end of the *Discourse* as one of the 'thinges forgotten').[1] This remained a distinctive feature of the English approach throughout the period. The first charter of the Virginia Company in 1606 did say that the colony would serve 'in propagating of Christian Religion to such People, as yet live in Darkness and miserable Ignorance of the true Knowledge and Worship of God', but it was rather unusual in being so French in character—the patent given to Robert Heath in 1629 for an abortive colony in Carolina, which was the model for most of the mid-century foundation documents, said nothing about the conversion of the Indians.

Instead of religion, Hakluyt insisted on two principles. One was that the English should deal with the native peoples as the Portuguese and Dutch were dealing with the inhabitants of the East Indies, that is, they should liberate them from Spanish tyranny and construct informal empires by aiding one nation against another, in best *raison d'état* manner. He put this clearly in his call for a settlement in Virginia: after the first English 'factory' had been settled there,

> Yf our nacion doe not make any Conqueste there but onlye use trafique and chaunge of Comodyties by meane [= because] the Countrye is not so mightie a nacion as ether Fraunce or Spayne, they shall not dare to offer us any anoye but suche as we maye easylie revenge with sufficient Chastisement to the unarmed people there.
>
> Yf they will not suffer us to have any Comodyties of theres without Conqueste which doeth require long tyme, yet may we maynteyn our firste voyadges by the Sea fishinge on the Coastes there . . .
>
> Yf we fynde any kinges readye to defende their Tirratoryes by warre and the Counytrye populous desieringe to expell us that seeke but juste and lawfull Traffique, then by reason the Ryvers be lardge and deepe and we lordes of navigacion, and they without shippinge,[2] we armed and they naked, and at

[1] *The Original Writings & Correspondence of the Two Richard Hakluyts*, II ed. E. G. R. Taylor (London, 1935; Hakluyt Society Series, II (77), 324).

[2] A shortened version of the same tract reads succinctly at this place, 'we are lords of navigation, and they are not' (*The Original Writings & Correspondence of the Two Richard*

continuall warres one with another, we maye by the ayde of those Ryvars joyne with this kinge here or with that king there at our pleasure and soe with a fewe men be revenged of any wronge offered by them and consequentlie maye yf we will conquere fortefye and plante in soyles moste sweete, most pleasaunte, moste fertill and strounge. And in the ende to bringe them all in subjection or scyvillitie for yt is well knowen they have bynne contented to submytte them selves and all that which they possesse to suche as hathe defended them againste there Enemyes speciallie againste the caniballes.[3]

The second principle was that there should be absolute freedom of navigation even in waters notionally claimed by Spain. In the late sixteenth century the English had become the most vociferous advocates of open seas, going well beyond traditional juristic thinking on the matter and defending the kind of incursions into other nations' jurisdictions which Grotius was later to justify more systematically. In the early part of Elizabeth's reign, English lawyers had still accepted the traditional view that states can command the sea off their coasts: a dispute with Portugal about access to the African littoral in the 1560s turned (as Selden later rightly observed) on the question of how extensive Portugal's African possessions were, rather than on the issue of *dominium maris* as such.[4] But twenty years later this had changed, as the English began to think of themselves as 'lords of navigation'. Thus the diplomat and juridical writer Robert Beale defended the Elizabethan government's incursions into Spanish waters in the following vigorous terms in a conference of 1580:

[The Queen] understood not, why hers and other Princes Subiects, should be barred from the Indies, which she could not perswade her selfe the Spaniard had any rightfull title to the the Bishop of *Romes* donation, in whom she acknowledged no prerogative, much lesse authority in such causes, that he should binde Princes which owe him no obedience . . . nor yet by any other title than that the Spaniards had arrived here and there, built Cottages, and given names to a River or a Cape; which things cannot purchase any proprietie.

Hakluyts, p. 329). 'We have got / The Maxim gun, and they have not' (Hilaire Belloc, *The Modern Traveller*, pt. 6).

[3] *The Original Writings & Correspondence of the Two Richard Hakluyts*, p. 342.

[4] The papers for this dispute are in BL Cottonian MSS Nero B.I. Portuguese translations of the documents are to be found in M. de Santaren, ed., *Quadro Elementar das Relações Politicas e Diplomaticas de Portugal com as Diversas Potencias do Mundo*, XV (Paris, 1854), pp. 128–339. For the English position, see e.g. the Privy Council letter p. 174. The Portuguese ambassador took the view that 'all the provinces of Ethiopia recognise the supremacy and sovereignty of the Crown of Portugal' (p. 158). Selden's observation upon this material (which he will have seen in Cotton's library) is in his *Opera Omnia*, II col. 1243.

So as this donation of that which is anothers, which in right is nothing worth, and this imaginary propriety, cannot let, but that other Princes may trade in those Countries, and without breach of the Law of Nations, transport Colonies thither, where the *Spaniards* inhabite not, forasmuch as prescription without possession is little worth, and may also freely navigate that vast Ocean, seeing the use of the Sea and Ayre is common to all. Neither can any title to the Ocean belong to any people, or private man; forasmuch as neither Nature, nor regard of the publicke use permitteth any possession thereof.[5]

By the end of the reign, the English had also worked out a fairly coherent position in their perennial dealings with the rulers of Denmark over the Northern seas, which allowed greater freedom than the traditional civil lawyers permitted, but which also ruled out the kind of maritime anarchy which Vazquez envisaged. The instructions given to the English delegates to a conference with the Danes in 1602 contain the essential English view, which was to become the standard position in later international law.

Sometimes in Speech *Denmark* claymeth Propertie in that Sea as lying between *Norway* and *Island*, both sides in the Dominions of oure loving Brother *the King*, supposing thereby that for the Propertie of a whole Sea, it is sufficient to have the Banckes on both sides as in Rivers; Whereunto you may answere, that though Propertie of Sea in some small distance from the Coast, maie yeild some Oversight and Jurisdiction, yet use not Princes to forbid Passage or Fishing, as is well seen in our Seas of England and Ireland, and in the Adriaticke Sea of the *Venetians*, where We in ours, and they in theirs have Propertie of Command; and yet neither We in ours, nor they in theirs, offer to forbid Fishing, much lesse Passage to Ships of Merchandize, the which by Law of Nations cannot be forbidden ordinarilie, neither is it to be allowed that Propertie of Sea in whatsoever distance is consequent to the Banks, as it hapneth in small Rivers; For then by like reason the half of every Sea should be appropriated to the next Bank, as it hapneth in small Rivers where the Banks are proper to divers Men, whereby it would follow that noe Sea were common, the Banks on every side being in the Propertie of one or other . . .[6]

[5] William Camden, *Annals, or, The Historie of the Most Renowned and Victorious Princesse Elizabeth* (London, 1635), 225. For the Latin text, see Thomas Hearne's edn., *Annales Rerum Anglicarum et Hibernicarum* (n.p. 1717), 359–60. It is a conjecture that this is the speech by Robert Beale referred to in *Calendar of State Papers Foreign 1579–1580*, p. 463, but it so fits Beale's known interests and capacities that I think there can be little doubt. For Beale, see *Dictionary of National Biography*, s. n.

[6] T. Rymer, *Foedera*, VII. 2 (The Hague, 1742), 28–9. For a discussion of the English position, though one which overstresses the readiness of the English (but not the Scots) before this date to allow the freedom of the seas, see Thomas Wemyss Fulton, *The Sovereignty of the Sea*, pp. 57–117.

Hakluyt himself came to realize that some Continental jurists were saying very similar things, and by 1598 he was citing Vazquez in further notes urging an American plantation on the government.[7] Almost as soon as Grotius's *Mare Liberum* appeared, in 1609, he produced a manuscript translation of it.[8]

Under the government of James I and Charles I, however, Hakluyt's views came to be replaced by a set of ideas deriving in most cases from the teachings of Gentili. On the issue of free navigation, the English largely abandoned their earlier view and began to defend a stringent version of maritime protectionism, while on the issue of colonialism, they enthusiastically accepted Gentili's and Grotius's ideas about the moral rights of cultivators. In both cases, the specific conclusions could be argued for in terms of a view of moral agency which was essentially that found in the new natural law writers, and which Hobbes was to develop and systematize.

John Selden

Gentili had always been sceptical about the Elizabethan claims for free navigation, remaining loyal to the basic civil law theory that jurisdiction could be claimed even on the high seas, though he conceded (as was usual, and as we have just seen the English delegates conceded for the Narrow Seas) that a sovereign could not rightfully deny peaceful passage through his maritime dominions. In *De Iure Belli* he wrote

> there is jurisdiction even over the deep; otherwise no magistrate will punish crimes committed at sea. But there is also a magistracy at sea. Such a magistracy belongs to the law of nations and its jurisdiction also; therefore must necessarily be everywhere where they are needed. Furthermore, as regards magistracy and jurisdiction that is evident, and is good law, that very many things are put in the hands of the sovereign on the sea as well as on the land; and these no one who sails the sea will evade. The sovereign himself will bring war upon himself, if he refuses the sea to others; and those will be justified in making war who are refused a privilege of nature.[9]

In a later work (written while he was acting as a permanently-retained advocate for the King of Spain before the Admiralty Court in

[7] *The Original Writhings & Correspondence of the Two Richard Hakluyts*, p. 425; the 'Spanish lawiers' referred to are clearly (from the examples cited) substantially Vazquez.

[8] Ibid. 497–9.

[9] *De Iure Belli Libri Tres*, ed. Coleman Phillipson, trans. John C. Rolfe (Carnegie Endowment, Oxford University Press, 1933), II, 92.

England, dealing mainly with cases which had arisen as a result of armed conflict between Spain and the United Provinces in or near English waters) he drew out the implications of this view. 'The word territory' applies 'equally to land and to water', and Britain controlled the seas all round its coast—'the southern coast of Ireland extends towards Spain; the western, towards the Indian realms of Spain'. 'Let the Dutch, let everyone enjoy the use of the sea,' argued Gentili, 'but without violating the jurisdiction of another nation . . . Let them remember that other things, once undefined, are defined today, and that the distinction made by the law of nations, of eminent domains and jurisdictions, should be most scrupulously observed.'[10] It is significant that although (as we saw in the first chapter) Hakluyt consulted his Oxford colleague about the juridical basis of colonization, he eschewed both Gentili's use of the 'Utopian' argument for annexation and Gentili's sympathy for monopolistic maritime jurisdictions.

But both of these views, and much else of Gentili's approach to war, became more acceptable in England in the course of the next few years. By the accession of James VI to the English throne, Spain had ceased to be seen as such a threat to England; increasingly, it was the astonishing rise of their former allies the Dutch that alarmed the English government, though it was a long time before a wider public opinion caught up. This shift in emphasis brought with it a general change in royal policy about maritime jurisdiction. The attack on Spain had required open seas: the attack on the Dutch required closed seas, for it was Dutch exploitation of allegedly English waters which had become a central issue. In particular, James had decided to tax the Dutch herring fleet of some 2,000 vessels, accompanied by an armed naval squadron, which from June to January every year moved from the Shetlands to the Kent coast, extracting vast quantities of fish—the fleet represented the most profitable enterprise in the whole Dutch economy (and it was, interestingly, run by the 'College of the Great Fishery' based at Delft, Grotius's home town).[11] As part of this campaign, a Scot, William Welwood, published in 1613 and 1615 a couple of works on the *dominium maris* in which he went even further than Gentili in opposition to the

[10] *Hispanicae Advocationis Libri Duo*, ed. and trans. Frank Frost Abbott (Carnegie Endowment, New York, 1921), II 35 and 38.

[11] George Edmundson, *Anglo-Dutch Rivalry During the First Half of the Seventeenth Century* (Oxford, 1911), 160.

Dutch view. According to Welwood, the doctrine of natural *communio universalis rerum* was 'redolent of the anabaptists',[12] and he insisted that Scripture showed clearly that the whole world had always been in a state of ownership—first by Adam, and then by Noah and his descendants after the Flood.

The earth, by the infinite multiplication of mankind, beeing largely replenished, and therefore of necessitie thus divided, and things upon the earth not sufficient for the necessaries and desires of man in every region, followed of force the use of trading upon the seas . . . For the which . . . the waters became divisible, and requiring a partition in like manner with the earth.

And he answered Grotius's point about free passage by denying that this made any difference between land and sea—'since passage upon land through all Regions Christian, is this day so indifferently permitted to all of all Nations, even to Turkes, Iewes, Pagans, not being professed enimies'.[13] Welwood's actual arguments were pretty shoddy, as Grotius pointed out in a reply which he drafted but never published;[14] but his reluctance to use the distinction between jurisdiction and ownership, and his insistence upon the universality of private property, even over the sea, pointed the way for the most sophisticated English response to the Dutch, that of John Selden.

Selden was the nearest English equivalent to Grotius: another formidable humanist with a deep interest in the history of his country's political institutions, and a good instinct about the shape of modern political theory. The parallels are sometimes remarkable—for example, both Selden and Grotius independently, but at the same time, in the first decade of the century, came to the conclusion that the ancient form of government right across Northern Europe had been neither patriarchal monarchy nor elective kingship, but aristocracy. Both also participated in the general attempt, the story of which I have told elsewhere, to find a post-sceptical moral theory: in the major political writings of each of them, the figure of the sceptic Carneades is prominent as the opponent who must be defeated if politics and ethics are to

[12] William Welwood, *De Dominio Maris* ('Cosmopoli', 1615), 1–2. This incorporated part of his *An Abridgement of all Sea-Lawes* (London, 1613), to which Grotius had replied in his *Defensio Capitis Quinti Maris Liberi*; see Samuel Muller, *Mare Clausum. Bijdrage tot de Geschiedenis der Rivaliteit van Engeland en Nederland in de Zeventiende Eeuw* (Amsterdam, 1872), 331–61.

[13] Samuel Muller, *Mare Clausum. Bijdrage tot de Geschiedenis der Rivaliteit van Engeland en Nederland in de Zeventiende Eeuw* (Amsterdam, 1872), 324–5.

[14] Ibid. 331–61.

be properly founded.[15] So the idea of recruiting Selden to answer Grotius's *Mare Liberum* was an ingenious one.

Selden wrote the first draft of his answer to Grotius (he said himself) not at anyone's request but *ex liberrimo studiorum meorum more* at the same time as his *History of Tythes*, that is in 1616–17.[16] After the furore caused by his anti-clerical remarks in the *History of Tythes*, he saw the work as a way to win back royal favour. It was almost printed in 1618, but was pulled back from the press at the last minute; James told Selden that it was because he was afraid of offending the King of Denmark,[17] though it may also have been because he did not want to push the negotiations with the Dutch over the herring fleet to an open rupture. The project then lay, Selden said, 'among my neglected and scattered papers' until it was revived in the mid-1630s, at a time of great tension and indeed armed conflict between the two countries.[18] Charles's government had decided by 1635 that the United Provinces were without question a greater threat to England than Spain, and it committed itself to an extensive series of pro-Spanish measures, including a treaty in May 1635 by which the English promised to assist the Spaniards with a naval force against the Dutch, and an agreement to mint Spanish silver in the Tower of London into coins to pay the Spanish army in Flanders. In December 1635 Selden's treatise, rewritten and given the title *Mare Clausum*, was published as effectively an official statement of the English government view;[19] its appearance was a dramatic illustration of the extremism of Charles's government compared with that of his father. At the same time, of course, the government began to levy a new tax to pay for naval activity against the Dutch—the notorious 'Ship Money'. When the tax was tested in court in 1637–8, *Mare Clausum* was quoted in the government's defence.[20]

Selden's fundamental idea in *Mare Clausum* (as James Tully has pointed out)[21] was that the original community of property which

[15] See *Philosophy and Government 1572–1651* (Cambridge University Press, 1993).

[16] *Opera Omnia* ed. David Wilkins (London, 1726), II, col. 1421.

[17] Ibid., col. 1425. [18] Ibid. 1181.

[19] Secretary of State John Coke seems to have been principally responsible for its publication—see the letter from Sir Kenelm Digby congratulating him on doing so in August 1635, which speaks of the book as going on apace in the press. H. M. C. Cooper MSS, II p. 90.

[20] *A Complete Collection of State Trials . . .*, ed. T. B. Howell (London, 1809–26), III, col. 928, 1023.

[21] James Tully, *A Discourse of Property: John Locke and his Adversaries* (Cambridge University Press, 1980), 77–9, 91–2.

Grotius and most other writers had taken to be a negative community—the natural right of anyone to take what they needed from the unowned natural world—was better understood as a positive community. All men originally were co-owners of the whole world, in the same sense that English villagers or townspeople might be co-owners of their local common. There was thus never a time when every bit of the earth's surface was not owned by someone: at first (if Scripture was to be believed) by one man, namely Adam, then after the Flood by several men collectively, namely Noah's sons.[22] In arguing this, Selden was ingeniously using a key weak spot in Grotius's *Mare Liberum*: for in chapter V, Grotius had remarked that in the beginning, 'God had not given all things to this individual or to that, but to the entire human race, and thus a number of persons, as it were en masse, were not debarred from being owners [*domini*] of the same thing, which is quite contradictory to our modern meaning of ownership [*dominium*]. For it now implies private property [*proprietatem*], a thing which no one then had.'[23] As the example of the English commons shows, it was far from the case that the modern notion of ownership precluded collective ownership, and it was reasonable for Selden to ask why, if the human race was taken to be the owner of the world, this was not true ownership.

On this view of the matter, all derogation from positive communal ownership had to be by formal agreement among the owners: there must therefore at some point have been agreements that some territory should be possessed by named individuals, and other territory should by acquired by (for example) occupation; as Selden forcefully pointed out, there is no obvious reason why first occupation should give the occupier rights against anyone else who might want the territory, if no prior convention in the matter is to be presumed (and indeed Grotius had in effect admitted the force of convention in his discussion of occupation).[24]

With this argument, Selden was quickly able to establish at least the theoretical possibility of owning the sea in the same way as the land, and he followed this up with a laborious historical demonstration that

[22] *Opera Omnia*, coll. 1195–8.

[23] *The Freedom of the Seas, or, The Right which Belongs to the Dutch to Take Part in the East Indian Trade*, ed. J. B. Scott, trans. R. Van D. Magoffin (New York, 1916), 24, trans. corrected by me.

[24] *Opera Omnia*, coll. 1197–8.

the Kings of England did indeed own the neighbouring seas, including the whole of the Atlantic Ocean. But the full significance of what he had done with this idea about natural positive community has, I think, seldom been recognized, and it may have taken a little while to sink into Selden's own mind. The picture he had drawn was of men who collectively owned their world, like (as I have said) English commoners. And like English commoners, they had to make arrangements about the exercise of their ownership rights, in order not to conflict—common rights in England were governed by a complicated network of agreements and traditions about how much wood each commoner could take, and so on. But Selden's insight was that these agreements were ways of limiting an original commonality of ownership: before any such arrangements were made, it would be true to say that all the commoners owned all the land. What he had done, in other words, was to put before the English public the disconcerting notion of a right of all men to all things as the fundamental natural right over the material world.

There is no doubt that Selden came to recognize what he had done, even if he did not realize it fully at first. This is clear from the work he published only four years later, his *De Iure Naturali et Gentium iuxta Disciplinam Ebraeorum*. The *De Iure Naturali* is a notoriously peculiar work, for it sought to provide a theory of the law of nature based purely on Jewish traditions, both in the Bible and in the Talmud. But again, there was an ingenious point to it. Like Grotius, Selden was searching for a theory of natural law which would be acceptable at all times and places, irrespective of the superstructure of social conventions and laws; it had therefore to be minimalist in character, and compatible with whatever beliefs and practices were to be found around the world. By looking at the Hebrew, and general oriental, ideas about fundamental morality, Selden provided a complex set of beliefs which could be set alongside those of Christian Europe and act as a new check on any proposal about the natural minimal morality. And what Selden found in that tradition (he claimed) was an even more exiguous and therefore even more fundamental account of man's moral life than Grotius had provided; this foundational character was, he claimed, not a coincidence, for the Jews had preserved traditions about the life of the earliest men which had been lost among the Christians.

The most striking aspects of his theory were contained in Book VI of the work, on questions of property and war. He reasserted the ideas of

Mare Clausum about property, insisting that originally all men had owned the world collectively, as a grant from God. All forms of private property had then come in by agreement, including rights to occupy unoccupied land, and so on. But Selden then traced out in some detail the Hebrew and other ancient oriental ideas about warfare, and concluded startlingly that it was the general belief among all these peoples that 'neither precedent injury nor safety were nececessary for war, but extending empire was a good enough reason'.[25] He also pointed out that this view extended to war made against these people—the Jews (for example) accepted the legitimacy of the Roman conquest of Israel (this is the theme of chapter 17). As he said, this was strikingly different from the views of Christians, such as Augustine (whom he quoted);[26] but the clear point of his argument was that making war simply for territorial aggrandizement was compatible with the basic law of nature—any greater restraint, like the principles of private property, must have come in as a result of agreement between people to respect one another's territory. He outlined in chapter 13 of Book VI the kind of agreement which the Hebrews characteristically made in order to have peace with their neighbours; but if no such agreement had taken place, he implied, warfare was a perfectly legitimate condition. The original 'right of all men to all things' was associated in Selden's argument with a right to make war for whatever reason the belligerent party thought fit.

Selden's account of the rights of war, though recognizably in a tradition stemming from Gentili and the other sixteenth-century humanists, was thus the most extreme defence of war for aggrandizement which had yet been presented by any European theorist. In principle, it could have legitimated European activity in the New World extremely easily, but it is a striking fact that Selden did not himself apply it systematically to that issue. He was a shareholder in the Virginia Company, down to the time of its dissolution in 1624, and may have been quite active in its affairs,[27] but he seems to have had surprisingly little interest in the theoretical issues raised by the company's presence in North America. In *Mare Clausum*, he criticized the Vitorian argument that the interruption of trade justified warfare by the Spanish against the Indians, and sympathized with Molina's claim that no people ought

[25] *Opera Omnia*, I, col. 664 (ch. 13). [26] *Opera Omnia*, I, col. 660.

[27] See Noel Malcolm, 'Hobbes, Sandys and the Virginia Company', *Historical Journal*, 24 (1981), 306.

to trade with strangers unless they were driven to do so out of necessity, or had already made some treaty with them.[28] He also endorsed the argument that as much unoccupied land can be claimed 'as one might hope to use, and up to any designated boundary';[29] but his preferred defence of the English colonies in North America was the letter patent issued to Sebastian Cabot by Henry VII which entitled him to acquire lands 'not yet known'. This presumably fitted rather better with the ideas about warfare which he was to develop in *De Iure Naturali*, since there were by definition no treaty commitments between the English and the inhabitants of unknown lands.

The Occupation of the Wilderness

But other writers were willing to take up the burden of defending the occupation of the New World, and in particular to utilize extensively the 'Utopian' or Gentilian defence of the expropriation of waste land. This became an urgent issue after 1607, when the first permanent colonists arrived in Virginia under the aegis of the newly formed Virginia Company. This settlement was followed by others in some of the West Indian islands, and eventually by the succesful colonization of New England from 1620 onwards. Though much larger than the population of trading posts or factories, the numbers of people involved down to the 1630s were small: in 1635 there were still only 5,000 people in Virginia, partly because of the horrifying death-rate (at one time nearly three-quarters of the population were dying within five years of landing in America).[30] But even an enterprise on this scale was significant: the largest English towns outside London at the same date, for comparative purposes, were Norwich with around 15,000 inhabitants, Bristol (12,000), and York (11,000).[31]

A number of recent American historians (notably Francis Jennings and Robert A. Williams jun.)[32] have emphasized that this colonial enterprise should properly be seen not as a 'settlement' but as a *conquest*, analogous to the Conquest of Mexico, or indeed, the Norman Con-

[28] *Opera Omnia*, II, col. 1252. [29] Ibid., col. 1406.

[30] Richard Lee Morton, *Colonial Virginia* (Chapel Hill, NC, 1960), I, 130 and 88.

[31] Figures from Peter Clark and Paul Slack, *English Towns in Transition 1500–1700*, (Oxford University Press, 1976), 83.

[32] Francis Jennings, *The Invasion of America* (Chapel Hill, NC, 1975); Robert A. Williams jun., *The American Indian in Western Legal Thought: The Discourse of Conquest* (Oxford University Press, New York, 1990).

quest of England, in which the native peoples were overcome by superior military force. There is much truch in this; but it is also the case that from the colonists' point of view, too ready an admission that they were involved in conquering the new land carried many dangers *vis-à-vis* the home government. From the late seventeenth century onwards, it was clear to jurists that there was an important difference beween settlement on unoccupied land and military conquest: the former meant that the settlers carried with them the laws of their home country, whereas the latter meant that the laws of war and conquest applied to the territory.[33] This distinction may not have been as clear-cut in the early seventeenth century, but even so there is little doubt that the settlers did not wish to admit to the English Crown that America had been taken by conquest, for that would have implied much greater *royal* authority over their activities.

Precisely this issue was indeed raised in the Parliament of 1621, when Secretary of State Sir George Calvert remarked, 'Newe Conquests are to be ordered by the Will of the Conquerour. Virginia is not anex't to the Crowne of England And therefore not subiect to the Lawes of this House'.[34] The Company's spokesman, Sir Edwin Sandys (a former pupil of Gentili, as it happens)[35] denied this, but avoided getting involved in a theoretical debate; instead, he insisted on the terms of the first Virginia Charter, which had decreed that lands in the colony were to be held in socage as of the manor of East Greenwich,

[33] Holt's judgement on Jamaica in 1694, in the case of Blankard *vs.* Galdy: William Salkeld, *Reports of Cases Adjudged in the Court of King's Bench . . . from the First Year of King William and Queen Mary, to the Tenth Year of Queen Anne* (London, 1795), II, 411–12; *The English Reports*, 91, 356–7. It should be observed that while Holt may have taken Jamaica to have been conquered from the Spanish rather than from its indigenous inhabitants, he elsewhere described Virginia as 'being a conquered country' in his famous judgement in Smith *vs.* Brown and Cooper 1706 decreeing that 'as soon as a negro comes into *England*, he becomes free . . . [but] the laws of *England* do not extend to *Virginia*, being a conquered country their law is what the king pleases . . . (Salkeld, *Reports*, 666–7, *The English Reports*, 91, 566–7). The dilemma pointed up by Holt's judgement was of course fundamental to early American history: if the laws of England applied, slavery was impossible, while if they did not, the king had absolute power. It should also be noted that in Blankard *vs.* Galdy, Holt went on to say that 'in the case of an infidel country, their laws by conquest do not entirely cease, but only such as are against the law of God; and that in such cases where the laws are rejected or silent, the conquered country shall be governed according to the rule of natural equity'—which raises an interesting question about his view of the status of aboriginal laws in Virginia and elsewhere.

[34] *Commons Debates in 1621*, ed. Wallace Notestein, Frances Helen Relf, and Hartley Simpson (New Haven, 1935), IV, 256; Conrad Russell, *Parliaments and English Politics 1621–1629* (Oxford University Press, 1979), 94.

[35] See Gentili, *De Iure Belli*, ed. Thomas Erskine Holland (Oxford, 1877) xv.

and which therefore implied that at least English land law governed the colonists.[36]

The dangers of the conquest theory are well illustrated by one of the best expressions of it, in Sir Edward Coke's famous report on Calvin's case (the case was heard in 1606, but Coke's *Seventh Reports* with his summary of the arguments of himself and the other judges in the Exchequer Chamber was first published in 1608). In the course of a general discussion about who counts as an alien,[37] Coke drew a distinction between a 'temporarie alien, that being an enemie, may be a friend, or being a friend may be an enemie.'

> A perpetuall enemie (though there be no warres by fire and sword between them) cannot maintaine any action, or get any thing within this Realme. All Infidels are in law *perpetui inimici*, perpetual enemies (for the law presumes not that they will be converted, that being *remota potentia*, a remote possibilitie) for between them, as with the devils, whose subjects they be, and the Christian, there is perpetual hostility, and can be no peace . . .
>
> And upon this ground there is a diversitie between a Conquest of a kingdome of a Christian King, and the Conquest of a kingdome of an Infidell: for if a King come to a Christian kingdome by conquest, seeing that he hath *vitae & necis potestatem*, he may at his pleasure alter and change the Lawes of that kingdome, but untill he doth make an alteration of those lawes, the ancient lawes of that kingdome remaine. But if a Christian King should conquere a kingdom of an Infidel, and bring them under his subjection, there *ipso facto* the lawes of the Infidel are abrogated, for that they be not only against Christianitie, but against the law of God and nature, contained in the Decalogue. And in that case, until certaine lawes be established amongst them, the King by himself and such Judges as he shall appoint, shall judge them and their causes, according to naturall equitie, in such sort as Kings in ancient time did within their kingdomes, before any certaine municipall lawes were given.[38]

This aggressive account of war against infidels (going, as we have seen, well beyond anything which was commonly said in the Middle Ages) is probably derived from humanist sources (which Coke, con-

[36] *Commons Debates in 1621*, II, 321. As Robert Williams has pointed out, such evasiveness about the theoretical issues involved was absolutely characteristic of the managers of the company, who formally decided against issuing any defence of their first plantation. Robert A. Williams jun., *The American Indian in Western Legal Thought: The Discourse of Conquest*, pp. 202–4.

[37] The issue in Calvin's case was whether a Scotsman born after the Union of the Crowns could inherit property in England.

[38] Edward Coke, *La Septieme Part des Reports* (Lindon, 1671), 17.

trary to his popular reputation, had studied quite closely).[39] But it is far from clear that it was generally accepted as the basis for the English colonies. More to their taste was Gentili's argument, derived from *Utopia*, that uncultivated land was unoccupied and might simply be appropriated. Already in 1609 this was being argued about Virginia, in a sermon for the Company:

> Some affirme, and it is likely to be true, that these Savages have no particular proprietie in any part or parcell of that Countrey, but only a general residencie there, as wild beasts have in the forest, for they range and wander up and downe the Countrey, without any law or government, being led only by their own lusts and sensualitie, there is not *meum et tuum* amongst them: so that if the whole lande should bee taken from them, there is not a man that can complaine of any particular wrong done unto him.[40]

Though Gray did not make this clear, the implication of the More-Gentili theory of occupation to which he was referring (as Grotius later understood) was that the occupiers acquired rights only over the *land* and not, at least initially and directly, over the native *inhabitants*; on the conquest theory, however, rights over the inhabitants were the essence of the occupation. In general (though the matter is often very obscure) the English colonists seem to have assumed that English law did not apply to the Indians, and that the aboriginal nations remained in some sense independent, unless (as in Massachusetts in 1644) they clearly placed themselves under the government of the English; though since they were treated as the equivalent of fleets on the sea—that is, as exclusively or largely bands of individuals rather than owners of territory—their independence did not add up to much when it came to controlling and organizing the lands of the colony.[41] Grotius, of course, had made the point that not only did the colonists not have political control over the aboriginals, but strictly speaking the aboriginals had control over the colonists: though possessing a complete right to occupy the land, colonists ought to acknowledge some kind of *imperium* in the local ruler. The force of this idea, though often muted

[39] See e.g. his library catalogue, ed. W. O. Hassall (New Haven, 1950).

[40] Robert Gray, *A Good Speed to Virginia* (London, 1609), sig. C3v–C4; though Gray went on to say that in fact the Indians were willing to part with their land. Earlier (sig. C2) he had said that 'we are warrented by this direction of *Ioshua* [Joshua 17 : 14, his text] to destroy wilfull and convicted Idolaters, rather then to let them live, if by no other meanes they can be reclaimed.'

[41] See James Axtell, *The Invasion Within: The Contest of Cultures in Colonial North America* (Oxford University Press, New York, 1985), 220.

in practice, is illustrated by the vague attempts of English colonists in this period to reassure public opinion in England that the native rulers had been indemnified in some way for the colonies.[42]

The discussion of the Virginian colony in the early years of the century was followed by a great burst of writing in England in the early 1620s about the moral basis for the new colonies of that decade. Again, the More–Gentili (and, we can now say, Grotian) theory was central: thus John Donne, in a sermon to the Virginia Company in November 1622, while saying that 'your principall ende is . . . to gaine Soules to the glory of GOD' gave equal prominence to the claim that

In the Law of Nature and Nations, a Land never inhabited, by any, or utterly derelicted and immemorially abandoned by the former Inhabitants, becomes theirs that will possesse it. So also is it, if the inhabitants doe not in some measure fill the Land, so as the Land may bring foorth her increase for the use of men: for as a man doth not become proprietary of the Sea, because he hath two or three Boats, fishing in it, soo neither does a man become Lord of a maine Continent, becausee hee hath two or three Cottages in the Skirts thereof. That rule which passeth through all *Municipal Lawes* in particular States, *Interest reipublicae ut quis re sua bene utatur, The State must take order, that every man improove that which he hath, for the best advantage of that State*, passeth also through the Law of *Nations*, which is to all the world, as the *Municipall* Law is to a particular State, *Interest mundo, The whole world, all Mankinde must take care, that all places be emprov'd, as farre as may be, to the best advantage of Mankinde in generall.*[43]

The same argument had been used about the settlement in Massachusetts the previous year by Robert Cushman, one of the Pilgrim Fathers, in his *Reasons and considerations touching the lawfulness of removing out of England into parts of America*,[44] and was to be used most influentially by Samuel Purchas in the 1625 edition of *Purchases Pilgrimage*:

as men, we have a naturall right to replenish the whole earth: so that if any Countrey be not possessed by other men, . . . every man by Law of Nature and Humanitie hath right of Plantation . . . And if a country be inhabited in some parts thereof, other parts remaining unpeopled, the same reason giveth liberty to other men which want convenient habitation to seat themselves.[45]

[42] See e.g. *Chronicles of the Pilgrim Fathers of the Colony of Plymouth*, ed. Alexander Young (Boston, 1844), 259, n. 3.

[43] *The Sermons of John Donne*, IV, ed. George R. Potter and Evelyn M. Simpson (University of California Press, Berkeley, 1959), 274.

[44] *Chronicles of the Pilgrim Fathers of the Colony of Plymouth*, ed. Alexander Young (Boston, 1844), 239–53.

[45] *Hakluytus Posthumus or, Purchas his Pilgrimes* (London, 1625), IV, 1809 ff.

Purchas was also explicitly critical of the view that there might be a religious justification for the settlement.

The prevalence of this particular line of argument among the first settlers and their English supporters is also illustrated by the fact that during the 1630s, it was the principal point in debate in the first and most important controversy within English North America about the legitimacy of the settlements, that between John Cotton and Roger Williams in Massachusetts during the mid-1630s. This was, in effect, the English equivalent of the debate between Las Casas and Sepulveda. In it, Williams insisted that the settlers could have no title to their lands by royal grant, since the country 'belonged to the native Indians'.

It was answered to him, first, That it was neither the Kings intendement, nor the English Planters to take possession of the Countrey by murther of the Natives, or by robbery: but either to take possession of the voyd places of the Countrey by the Law of Nature, (for *Vacuum Domicilium cedit occupanti*:) or if we tooke any Lands from the Natives, it was by way of purchase, and free consent.[46]

In reply, Williams made an extremely apposite and difficult point.

This answer did not satisfie Mr. Williams, who pleaded, the Natives, though they did not, nor could subdue the Countrey, (but left it *vacuum Domicilium*) yet they hunted all the Countrey over, and for the expedition of their hunting voyages, they burnt up all the underwoods in the Countrey, once or twice a yeare, and therefore as Noble men in England possessed great Parkes, and the King, great Forrests in England onely for their game, and no man might lawfully invade their Propriety: So might the Natives challenge the like Propriety of the Countrey here.[47]

The similarity between the parks of England and the landscape of parts of North America was indeed often remarked upon by the first settlers. Cotton's reply was unavoidably rather feeble, making such observations as that the king and nobility in England 'employed their Parkes, and Forrests, not for hunting onely, but for Timber, and for the nourishment of tame beasts, as well as wild, and also for habitation to sundry Tenants'. The only passage in it which came from the heart was the outburst that 'we did not conceive that it is a just Title to so vast a Continent, to make no other improvement of millions of Acres in it. but onely to burne it up for pastime'[48]—a passage which (as Axtell has

[46] Roger Williams, *The Complete Writings* (New York, 1963), 46.
[47] Ibid. 46–7. [48] Ibid. 47.

noted about similar remarks of a later date) conveyed the deeply-rooted English sense that hunting must be merely a 'pastime', and that the Indian way of life was really one of incurable frivolity.[49]

Hobbes: Introduction

It is in part against this background of debate about war and colonization, I think, that we should read the work of the greatest English political theorist of the period, Thomas Hobbes. Hobbes may have attended Gentili's lectures at Oxford, and his early life after graduating was spent in the household of a family which was heavily involved in military matters: the Earl of Newcastle, cousin to Hobbes's employer the Earl of Devonshire, became the leading Royalist general in the Civil War, and at various times Hobbes worked closely with him. But perhaps the first direct influence on Hobbes's thinking about these matters came from his association with Francis Bacon.[50]

I have already quoted Bacon on the need for pre-emptive strikes, and for his endorsement of the view ascribed by Plato to Clinias in *The Laws* that 'humanity is in a condition of public war of every man against every man';[51] both remarks came from a treatise which Bacon wrote in

[49] See the remark on the 'Gentlemany Diversions of Hunting and Fishing' practised by the Indians. James Axtell, *The Invasion Within: The Contest of Cultures in Colonial North America*, p. 158.

[50] For a brief account of this, but the most accurate hitherto, see Noel Malcolm, 'A Summary Biography of Hobbes', in *The Cambridge Companion to Hobbes*, ed. Tom Sorell (Cambridge University Press, 1996), 18. Hobbes was certainly working with Bacon from 1619, and Malcolm thinks that his acquaintance began in 1617–18, when an Italian translation of the *Essayes* was undertaken, probably with Hobbes's help. See also V. Gabrieli, 'Bacone, la riforma e Roma nella versione hobbesiana d'un carteggio di Fulgenzio Micanzio', *The English Miscellany*, 8 (1957), 215; Hobbes, *Correspondence*, ed. Noel Malcolm (Oxford University Press, 1994), 628–9. Important and unpublished manuscripts of Bacon are still at Chatsworth, the home of the Cavendish family, where they were presumably brought during this period of association between Hobbes and Bacon. See Peter Beal, *Index of English Literary Manuscripts 1450–1625* I (London, 1980), 48–9, and Graham Rees and Christopher Upton, *Francis Bacon's Natural Philosophy: A New Source. A Transcript of Manuscript Hardwick 72A with Translation and Commentary* (British Society for the History of Science Monograph 5, Chalfont St Giles, 1984), 8. They include a version of the *Tractatus de Justitia Universali . . . Per Aphorismos* which is part of Book VIII of the *De Augmentis Scientiarum*, published in 1623. Hobbes may well have worked on the *De Augmentis*, as it was put into its final Latin form by 'Mr. Herbert [George Herbert] and some others, who were esteemed Masters in the *Roman* Eloquence'—which seems an apt description of Hobbes. [Thomas Tenison], *Baconiana* (London, 1679), 24. See John Aubrey, *Brief Lives*, ed. A. Clark (Oxford, 1898), I. 331 for remarks about Hobbes as translator of Bacon, particularly the essay *Of the True Greatness of Kingdomes and Estates*, which appears in its Latin form as part of the *De Augmentis*.

[51] *The Letters and the Life*, VII, ed. James Spedding (London, 1874), 477–8.

1624 urging Prince Charles, James I's son, to reopen war with Spain. Bacon had long been an advocate of war, going back to his time as a supporter and counsellor of the Earl of Essex at the end of Elizabeth's reign, when the Earl was the principal opponent of peace with Spain.[52] Bacon's 1624 treatise is in effect a complete analysis of the issues involved in pre-emptive strikes on the grounds of fear, and it includes a full discussion of the ancient texts which supported their legitimacy, pointing out (*inter alia*) that Thucydides said 'that the true cause of that war was the overgrowing greatness of the Athenians, and the fear that the Lacedaemonians stood in thereby; and doth not doubt to call it, a necessity imposed upon the Lacedaemonians of a war'.

The early 1620s were the years when Hobbes was close to Bacon, and a number of early works by Hobbes grew out of this association.[53] Indeed, given the striking resemblance in almost every particular between the sentiments of Bacon's *Considerations Touching a War with Spain*, and the views which Hobbes expressed in his later works, it is hard not to believe that Hobbes actually drafted the treatise for his master. The work includes *inter alia* a notable plea for the right of self-preservation even if the agent had endangered himself by his own unjust conduct, which goes well beyond what was commonly believed even by advocates of war.[54]

> An offensive war is made, which is unjust in the aggressor; the prosecution and race of the war carrieth the defendant to assail and invade the ancient and indubitate patrimony of the first aggressor, who is now turned defendant; shall he sit down, and not put himself in defence? Or if he be dispossessed, shall he not make a war for the recovery? No man is so poor of judgement as will affirm it.[55]

[52] See my *Philosophy and Government 1572–1651*, pp. 105–8.

[53] These probably include his translation of Thucydides, which was published in 1629; in the preface to the translation he recorded that his enthusiasm for Thucydides had led him to undertake the project some time earlier, but 'after I had finished it, it lay long by me: and other reasons taking place, my desire to communicate it ceased'. Richard Schlatter, ed., *Hobbes's Thucydides* (Rutgers University Press, New Brunswick NJ, 1975), 8. They also include three discourses, and particularly the long *Discourse upon the Beginning of Tacitus*, which appeared in the volume *Horae Subsecivae* of 1620. For the convincing attribution of these discourses to Hobbes, see Noel B. Reynolds and John L. Hilton, 'Thomas Hobbes and Authorship of *Horae Subsecivae*', *History of Political Thought*, XIV (1993), 361–80.

[54] Though see Gentili's remarks on this subject, *De Iure Belli*, p. 59 (and Chapter 1).

[55] Bacon, *The Letters and the Life*, VII, pp. 471–2. The last sentence is particularly Hobbesian, both in tone and sentiment; for parallels, and for their significance, see my 'Hobbes's Moral Philosophy', in *The Cambridge Companion to Hobbes*, ed. Tom Sorell (Cambridge University Press, 1996), 200.

Not only was Hobbes, through Bacon, involved in the campaign for a war with Spain in the early 1620s, he was also heavily involved in the colonizing project; indeed, he was a landowner in Virginia, at least technically, as Noel Malcolm discovered ten years ago. In June 1622 his principal employer, Lord Cavendish, who had been involved in the Virginia Company for at least ten years,[56] transferred one of his shares of land there to Hobbes, who was acting at the time as his secretary. This was part of an attempt by Cavendish to pack the court of the company with supporters during a bitter struggle over the future of the company, which culminated in its dissolution by royal fiat in 1624. Hobbes attended the court regularly during the last two years of the company, and seems to have been particularly interested in the affairs of Bermuda, run by the Somers Island Company (effectively a subsidiary of the Virginia Company). Support for the Virginia Company shaded, of course, naturally into support for a war with Spain, since Spain was Virginia's great commercial rival.

If Hobbes's hypersensitivity to the character and importance of warfare dated from these experiences in the 1620s, in the following decade he was able to refine his thoughts about the issues involved through his involvement in the politics of Ship Money; indeed, I have argued elsewhere that it was the Ship Money case which inspired his fundamental political idea, that there must be a common source of judgement not only of what is right and wrong, but also of what is 'profitable or unprofitable'—he was very conscious that the issue at stake in the legal arguments over Ship Money was the question of who had the right to judge when the country was in danger or not.[57] He read Selden's *Mare Clausum* with great interest as soon as it came out.[58] and he may be presumed to have read *De Iure Naturali* with comparable attention. His concern with these matters was signalled clearly in the dedicatory letter to *De Cive* of November 1641, which reported the origin of his political philosophical project (I have also given elsewhere some reasons for

[56] His father, Lord Cavendish, appears as one of the adventurers in the company in its Third Charter of 1612, while in the same year 'Sir William Cavendish' was nominated by the company to the King's Council on Virginia; this was presumably Hobbes's pupil and friend, who himself became Lord Cavendish when his father became Earl of Devonshire in 1618. *The Three Charters of the Virginia Company of London with Seven Related Documents; 1606–1621*, ed. Samuel M. Bemiss (Williamsburg, Va., 1957), 80 and 85.

[57] *Philosophy and Government 1572–1651*, p. 313.

[58] Hobbes, *Correspondence*, ed. Noel Malcolm (Oxford University Press, 1994), 30–2.

supposing that the general philosophical project he describes in this letter was far advanced by 1640, and that the English *Elements of Law*, his first generally circulated work on political philosophy, was derived from it).

When I turned my thoughts to the inquiry into natural justice, I was alerted by the very name of justice (by which is meant a constant will to give every man *his right*) to ask first how it is that anyone ever spoke of something as *his own* rather than *another's*; and when it was clear that it did not originate in nature but in human agreement (for human beings have distributed what nature had placed in common), I was led from there to another question, namely, for whose benefit and under what necessity, when all things belonged to all men, the preferred that each man should have things that belonged to himself alone. And I saw that war and every kind of calamity must necessarily follow from community in things, as men came into violent conflict over their use.[59]

Hobbes's basic assumption about this original community of goods was consistently the same as Selden's, namely that before an agreement of some kind, each man could claim a right to all things; it was in this sense, he said, that '*natura dedit omnia omnibus*'. He differed from Selden largely in the greater single-mindedness with which he based this right on the principle of self-preservation, though as we saw in the previous chapter, this principle was central for this entire modern natural law tradition of thinking about post-sceptical politics. In general, he adopted most of the essential features of this tradition, as I have outlined them: thus, above all, he accepted both the Grotian assimilation of individuals to sovereign states, and the claim that all political rights must therefore come to the magistrate from the citizens. 'The precepts [of the law of nature and the right of nations] are the same: but because commonwealths once instituted take on the personal qualities of men, what we call a *natural law* in speaking of the duties of individual men is called the *right of Nations*, when applied to whole commonwealths, peoples or nations' (*De Cive*, XIV, 4).[60] He could equally well have said, like all the writers in this tradition, that individuals heuristically took on the characteristics of sovereign states.

[59] Hobbes, *On the Citizen*, ed. Richard Tuck and Michael Silverthorne (Cambridge University Press, 1998), 5–6; *De Cive. The Latin Version*, ed. Howard Warrender (Oxford University Press, 1983), 75 (*Epistola Dedicatoria*, 9).

[60] Hobbes, *On the Citizen*, p. 156; *De Cive. The Latin Version*, p. 208.

Hobbes: Fear as the Basis for War

What Hobbes did within this tradition (as I have argued in a number of works)[61] has, however, often been misunderstood, and was misunderstood already in the eighteenth century—Montesquieu, for example, remarked that 'Hobbes gives men first the desire to subjugate one another, but this is not reasonable. The idea of empire and domination is so complex and depends on so many other ideas, that it would not be the one they would first have . . .'.[62] In fact, Hobbes was clear that this was not so: the Preface to *De Cive* (the work which was most accessible to a continental audience in the seventeenth and eighteenth centuries) says plainly that his theory rests on a first principle

well known to all men by experience and which everyone admits, that men's natural Disposition is such that if they are not restrained by fear of a common power, they will distrust and fear each other, and each man rightly may, and necessarily will, look out for himself from his own resources . . . Some object that if we admit this principle, it follows directly not only that all Men are evil (which perhaps, though harsh, should be conceded, since it is clearly said in holy Scripture), but also (and this cannot be conceded without impiety) that they are evil by nature. However it does not follow from this Principle that men are evil by nature. For we cannot tell the good and the bad apart, hence even if there were fewer evil men than good men, good, decent people would still be saddled with the constant need to watch, distrust, anticipate, and get the better of others, and to protect themselves by all possible means.[63]

In other words, men are fundamentally self-protective, and only secondarily aggressive—it is the fear of an attack by a possible enemy which leads us to perform a pre-emptive strike on him, and not, strictly speaking, the desire to destroy him.

Hobbes said the same in *De Cive*, I. 4:

In the state of nature there is in all men a will to do harm, but not for the same reason or with equal culpability. One man practises the equality of nature, and allows others everything which he allows himself; this is the mark of a modest man, one who has a true estimate of his own capacities. Another, supposing himself superior to others, wants to be allowed everything, and demands more

[61] See in particular *Philosophy and Government 1572–1651*; *Hobbes* (Pastmasters, Oxford University Press, 1988); Hobbes, *Leviathan* (2nd edn., Cambridge University Press, 1996); and Hobbes, *On the Citizen*.

[62] *The Spirit of the Laws*, ed. Anne Cohler, Basia Miller, and Harold Stone (Cambridge University Press, 1989), 6.

[63] Hobbes, *On the Citizen*, pp. 10–11; *De Cive. The Latin Version*, p. 80.

honour for himself than others have; that is the sign of an aggressive character. In his case, the will to do harm derives from vainglory [*inane gloria*] and overvaluation of his strength. For the first man, it derives from the need to defend his property and liberty against the other.[64]

But even the man with an 'aggressive character' owes his aggression not to an innate disposition, but to his fear of other people: in the first part of the *Elements of Law* (1640) Hobbes produced a systematic account of the passions as the 'pleasure men have, or displeasure from the signs of honour or dishonour done to them', where 'honour' is the conception that the man who is honoured 'hath the odds or excess of power above him that contendeth or compareth himself' (I. 8. 5,8). Glory in particular is the conception of our own power 'above the power of him that contendeth with us', and vainglory is the 'fiction (which also is imagination) of actions done by ourselves, which never were done' (I. 9. 1). So there is no such person, on Hobbes's account, as the man who is simply and spontaneously aggressive—even the destructive passions arise from measuring ourselves against other people in order to be confident of our own power over them, and consequently confident of our security from their attacks.

The prime source of the conflicts of the state of nature, for Hobbes, is thus epistemic in character: it is the differing judgements which people make about their own relative power, and about all other matters of importance to them. These judgements need not, strictly speaking, be driven by self-interest *at all*, since they may arise simply from the fact that there is no objective standard of truth. He put this very clearly in a passage at the end of the *Elements*:

In the state of nature, where every man is his own judge, and differeth from other concerning the names and appellations of things, and from those differences arise quarrels, and breach of peace; it was necessary there should be a common measure of all things that might fall in controversy; as for example: of what is to be called right, what good, what virtue, what much, what little, what *meum* and *tuum*, what a pound, what a quart, &c. For in these things private judgements may differ, and beget controversy. This common measure, some say, is right reason: with whom I should consent, if there were any such thing to be found or known *in rerum natura*. But commonly they that call for right reason to decide any controversy, do mean their own. But this is certain, seeing right reason is not existent, the reason of some man, or men, must supply the place thereof; and that man, or men, is he or they, that have the sovereign

[64] Hobbes, *On the Citizen*, p. 26; *De Cive. The Latin Version*, p. 93.

power . . . ; and consequently the civil laws are to all subjects the measures of their actions, whereby to determine, whether they be right or wrong, profitable or unprofitable, virtuous or vicious; and by them the use and definition of all names not agreed upon, and tending to controversy, shall be established. As for example, upon the occasion of some strange and deformed birth, it shall not be decided by Aristotle, or the philosophers, whether the same be a man or no, but by the laws. (II. 10. 8)

Hobbes's men are primarily fearful rather than aggressive creatures, who are led into conflict by their differing judgements about what will protect them. This can sometimes correspond to real conflicts over resources, but in general Hobbes was loath to use this as an explanation of conflict—it appears only last on the list of possible reasons in *De Cive*, after 'vainglory' and doctrinal conflict (I. 4–6), and Hobbes consistently argued that there was not in fact any shortage of basic resources for all men, but merely a dispute over their allocation.

Hobbes: Minimal Sociability

Moreover, men's fear of one another exists alongside an—albeit mimimal—sense of mutual respect. Hobbes explained the basis of the 'right of nature', the right to act on one's own judgement about what will conduce to one's preservation, in something like the following terms in all his works (this passage is from the *Elements of Law*): 'It is not against reason that a man doth all he can to preserve his own body and limbs, both from death and pain. And that which is not against reason, men call RIGHT, or *jus*, or blameless liberty of using our own natural power and ability' (I. 14. 6). In other works, men respect in one another their intention to protect their body, and will not *blame* anybody who does so. As I have argued elsewhere,[65] this universal recognition by all men of the blamelessness of self-preservation is the practical foundation for Hobbes's moral theory: his confidence that his theory was of general applicability rested on his confidence that all men displayed this fundamental moral agreement.[66]

Although this is seldom observed about Hobbes, mutual respect of

[65] See in particular my 'Hobbes's Moral Philosophy' in *The Cambridge Companion to Hobbes*, ed. Tom Sorell (Cambridge University Press, 1996), pp. 175–207.

[66] Hobbes does ascribe rights to animals also: in *De Cive*, VIII. 10 he says that an animal may kill a man by natural right. But that whole paragraph draws an interesting parallel between our treatment of men and of animals, implying that to some extent they may be admitted into the circle of beings whom we minimally respect; though animals cannot of course reciprocate by describing our conduct as based on rights.

this kind requires some degree of fellow-feeling—men who call one another's 'blameless liberty' a 'right' are not treating one another simply as material for exploitation. There is in Hobbes a rather conventional set of assumptions, broadly of the modified Epicurean kind we saw in the early Grotius, about the mutual recognition human beings accord one another. These assumptions repeatedly come out in his remarks about the origin of speech, for example in Chapter IV of *Leviathan*. There, he explained the origin of language first as due to our need to record our own thoughts and experiences for our future use, but then (since such an account plainly cannot capture the *communicative* function of language) 'when many use the same words, to signifie (by their connexion and order,) one to another, what they conceive, or think of each matter; and also what they desire, feare, or have any other passion for'. The point of this, he continued, is

to shew to others that knowledge which we have attained; which is, to Counsell, and Teach one another . . . to make known to others our wills, and purposes, that we may have the mutuall help of one another . . . [and] to pleasure and delight our selves, and others, by playing with our words, for pleasure or ornament, innocently.[67]

This interest in 'mutuall help', and the capacity provided by language to secure it, are features of the state of nature—that is, they do not require a sovereign and civil society to be manifested, though they do require them to be *secured*. This has puzzled some readers of Hobbes: surely language is a conventional matter, and surely an inability to make agreements, including the tacit conventions which uphold a language, is a defining characteristic of the state of nature?

But in fact, as is quite well known, Hobbes was surprisingly equivocal on this issue; indeed, the first draft of the *Elements of Law* included the straightforward claim that 'Of the law of nature also it is: that entering into peace every man be allowed those rights which he hath acquired by the covenants of others.'[68] No conventions or covenants are *secure* in the state of nature, since at any time they may be trumped by the force of the right of self-preservation and private judgement; but in the absence of such disruption they can maintain a weak existence.

[67] *Leviathan*, ed. Richard Tuck (Cambridge University Press, 1991), 25 (p. 13 of the original edition). See also *The Elements of Law*, ed. Ferdinand Toennies (London, 1889), 23 (I. 5. 4).

[68] *The Elements of Law*, p. 89 n. For a comment on this, see Maurice Goldsmith's Introduction to the 1969 reprint of Toennies's edn., p. xi.

In the case of language, we can say (with Hobbes) that it is always vulnerable to epistemic conflict in certain key areas—'one man calleth *Wisdome*, what another calleth *feare*; and one *cruelty*, what another *justice*; one *prodigality*, what another *magnanimity*; and one *gravity*, what another *stupidity*, &c.' (*Leviathan*, p. 31)—and that these are the areas which give rise to physical conflict in the state of nature; but in other areas a more placid relationship between natural men is possible. And one such area is of particularly great importance, namely the mutual recognition by natural men of the meanings they attach to the description of self-protective conduct: as we have seen, were it not the case that there was already agreement on the proposition that self-preservation is a *right*, Hobbes's solution to the conflict over other propositions would not work.

Hobbes never supposed that even quite a high degree of mutual aid was impossible in the absence of a sovereign. For example, in the eloquent and striking passage of *De Cive* where he set out his case against the natural sociability of man, he accepted that one could have ordinary interactions motivated by a desire for mutual assistance.

For if man naturally loved his fellow-man, loved him, I mean, as his fellow-man, there is no reason why everyone would not love everyone equally as equally men; or why every man would rather seek the company of men whose society is more prestigious and useful to him than to others. By nature, then, we are not looking for friends but for honour or advantage [*commodum*] from them. This is what we are primarily after; friends are secondary. Men's purpose in seeking each other's company may be inferred from what they do once they meet. If they meet to do business, everyone is looking for profit not for friendship. If the reason is public affairs, a kind of political relationship develops, which holds more mutual fear than love; it is sometimes the occasion of faction, but never of good-will. If they meet for entertainment and fun, everyone usually takes most pleasure in the kind of amusing incident from which (such is the nature of the ridiculous) he may come away with a better idea of himself in comparison with someone else's embarrassment or weakness. Even if this is sometimes harmless and inoffensive, it is still evident that what they primarily enjoy is their own glory and not society . . . Every voluntary encounter [*congressus*] is a product either of mutual need or of the pursuit of glory; hence when people meet, what they are anxious to get is either an advantage for themselves [*commodum*] or what is called εὐδοκιμεῖν, which is reputation and honour among their companions. (I. 2)[69]

[69] Hobbes, *On the Citizen*, pp. 22–3; *De Cive. The Latin Version*, pp. 90–1.

Intense self-interest, in nature, did not preclude a degree of joint action and communication, though it might be a very precarious business.[70]

This view of man's natural state does not seem to me to be so far removed from the view which Grotius had put forward both in his early and unpublished work, and even in *De Iure Belli ac Pacis*. Grotius too supposed that natural man was primarily concerned with his own preservation, and secondarily with avoiding injuring other people; such principles as benevolence came only with the creation of a civil society, for only then would people be inclined actually to help one another rather than merely refrain from unnecesarily injuring them. The difference between Grotius and Hobbes was simply that Hobbes recognized that this minimal natural morality was not sufficient to prevent conflict, since there is no objective criterion for determining what is necessary for our preservation. Hobbes need not be seen as differing from Grotius over ethical matters, strictly understood, *at all*; his very different conclusions can all follow solely from a disagreement about the material conditions for the application of the ethical principles.

Hobbes: The State of Nature

A full description of the state of nature was clearly at the heart of Hobbes's work; indeed, he was the first person to coin the term, though it is clear that Grotius's theory in fact involved such a notion. As we saw in the Introduction, the state of nature is a key element in modern rights theories, as is the issue of whether it is hypothetical in character or not. Hobbes addressed this question both in the footnotes he added to the second edition of *De Cive* in 1647, and in Leviathan itself, and he gave the fullest answer in *Leviathan*.

> It may peradventure be thought, there was never such a time, nor condition of warre as this; and I believe it was never generally so, over all the world: but there are many places, where they live so now. For the savage people in many places of America, except the government of small Families, the concord

[70] This is true for *De Cive*; it should be said, however, that in *Leviathan* Hobbes took a more pessimistic view of the practical possibility of such interaction. 'Men have no pleasure (but on the contrary a great deale of griefe) in keeping company, where there is no power able to overawe them all. For every man looketh that his companion should value him, at the same rate he sets upon himselfe: And upon all signes of contempt, or undervaluing, naturally endeavours, as far as he dares (which amongst them that have no common power to keep them in quiet, is far enough to make them destroy each other,) to extort a greater value from his contemners, by dommage; and from others, by the example' (p. 88, p. 61 of the original edn.).

whereof dependeth on natural lust, have no government at all; and live at this day in that brutish manner . . . But though there had never been any time, wherein particular men were in a condition of warre one against another; yet in all times, Kings, and Persons of Soveraigne authority, because of their Independency, are in continuall jealousies, and in the state and posture of Gladiators . . . But because they uphold thereby, the Industry of their Subjects; there does not follow from it, that misery, which accompanies the Liberty of particular men.[71]

This same passage in the Latin *Leviathan* adds another, interesting example: 'But someone might say, there never was a War of all against all. Surely Cain would not have killed his brother Abel out of jealousy, he would not have dared to perform such a deed, if a common power to punish crimes had then existed?'[72] This additional example was probably the result of a fascinating correspondence which he conducted in the 1650s with a young French admirer, François Peleau, which Noel Malcolm discovered at Chatsworth. We do not possess Hobbes's side of the correspondence, but from Peleau's letters we can tell what he said in answer to a query on precisely this question. Peleau wrote in November 1656 that

I am being hounded [by opponents of Hobbes] with syllogisms designed to prove to me that the state of nature in the strict sense (such as you show it to be in your Politics) has never existed in the world. It is no use if I say that this state existed before there were any towns, cities, or republics in the world, before there were even any pacts or agreements between men. I have argued that this state still exists in America; that savages wage a war of all against all among themselves; that after the death of Noah, his three sons, Shem, Japhet, and Ham, could, if they had wanted to, have waged a war of that kind; and that this state of nature is therefore possible. But they maintain that there have always been families in the world, and that since families are little kingdoms, they exclude the state of nature . . . Please enlighten me on this.[73]

In January 1657 he wrote again.

The examples you give of soldiers who serve in different places and masons who work under different architects fail, in my view, to illustrate accurately enough the state of nature. For these are wars of each against each only

[71] *Leviathan*, ed. Richard Tuck, p. 90 (p. 63 original edn.); see also Hobbes, *On the Citizen*, pp. 24–5; *De Cive. The Latin Version*, pp. 92–3 (nn. to I. 2).

[72] *Opera Philosophica, quae Latine scripsit, Omnia* (Amsterdam 1668) *Leviathan* p. 65 (sig.kkk).

[73] *Correspondence*, pp. 331–2.

successively and at different times; whereas the one I was discussing was at one and the same time.

Having meditated a little on the subject, I found that, in my opinion, there is now and has always been a war of minds, so far as opinions and feelings are concerned, and that this war is exactly like the state of nature. For example: doesn't it often happen among the members of a single parliament that each man, having a different view and being convinced that he is right, obstinately maintains his view against each of his colleagues? So that there is a war of minds, waged by each against each. Similarly, in philosophy there are so many teachers of doctrines, and so many different sects. Each thinks he has found the truth, and imagines that each and every one of the others is wrong; he treats them all as adversaries and opponents. And in the same way, in religion each sect claims to be the true church, and treats all the others as heretics. These, more or less, are the examples which I think illustrate your state of nature as purely as possible.

Besides, I think there has been a state of nature in the civil state. This proposition does seem absurd and self-contradictory; but, I promise, you will soon admit that it is not without plausibility. For as you know, Sir, in the Republic of Sparta anyone was permitted to steal whatever he might take: in that republic, therefore, all the citizens had an equal right to all things.[74]

The state of nature for Hobbes, and for an acute contemporary reader like Peleau, was thus not straightforwardly or wholly hypothetical: there were empirical examples of what he meant. The examples Hobbes committed himself to in print were exactly those in the Grotian tradition, namely the Americans, the Scythians or their equivalents, and the modern state system. He signalled this graphically on the title page of *De Cive* (which, like the title page of *Leviathan*, was specially drawn for him and carefully thought out). It contrasts the states of *Libertas* and *Dominium*: *Dominium* is the settled agricultural landscape of Europe, with peasants cutting the corn (and a city depicted only rather vaguely in the background—agriculture is the central theme), while *Libertas* is the life of the American Indian, with sporadic crops, hunting, and savagery. *Libertas* is personified as an Indian in a grass skirt, while *Dominium* is a sovereign judge in a toga. The representation of the Indian way of life is based on John White's famous drawings of the Roanokes of Virginia, as reproduced in Theodor De Bry's *America* of 1590 (together with Hariot's reports on the Virginia Indians).[75] In the

[74] Ibid. 424.

[75] For a discussion of these pictures, see M. M. Goldsmith, 'Picturing Hobbes's Politics?', *Journal of the Warburg and Courtauld Institutes*, 44 (1981), 232–7.

text of *De Cive* he remarked of the state of nature that 'the present century presents an example of this in the Americans. Past centuries show us nations, now civilized and flourishing, whose inhabitants then were few, savage, short lived, poor and mean, and lacked all the comforts and amenities of life which *peace* and society afford.'[76] Unfortunately, we cannot tell from Hobbes's correspondence with Peleau just what was in his mind when he suggested the other examples, of mercenaries and masons, though it may be (interestingly) that he had something like a free market in labour in mind.

In addition to adopting the Grotian accounts of the natural life of men as equivalent to an international order, and the American Indians as users rather than owners of their land, Hobbes endorsed the More–Gentili–Grotius theory of colonization (though this has rather seldom been noticed). As he remarked in *Leviathan*,

> The multitude of poor, and yet strong people still encreasing, they are to be transported into Countries not sufficiently inhabited: where neverthelesse, they are not to exterminate those they find there; but constrain them to inhabit closer together, and not range a great deal of ground, to snatch what they find; but to court each little Plot with art and labour, to give them their sustenance in due season. And when all the world is overcharged with Inhabitants, then the last remedy of all is Warre; which provideth for every man, by Victory, or Death. (*Leviathan*, p. 239)[77]

So, seen from the perspective of the issues I have been discussing in this book, Hobbes is (as I suggested from a different perspective in *Philosophy and Government*)[78] the culmination of a humanist tradition—in this case, the tradition of thinking about war which I sketched in Chapter 1 and of which I used Gentili as the prime example. Just as Hobbes saw more deeply than any of his contemporaries into the philosophical implications of the Tacitist, reason-of-state tradition, so he saw more deeply into the implications of the account of war among the humanist jurists and their successors; and in particular, into the consequences of the claim that fear, whether objectively justified or not, was a legitimate basis for aggressive war. His philosophical enter-

[76] Hobbes, *On the Citizen*, ed. Richard Tuck and Michael Silverthorne (Cambridge University Press, 1998), 30; *De Cive. The Latin Version*, ed. Howard Warrender (Oxford University Press, 1983), 96 (I. 13). See also *Leviathan*, ed. Richard Tuck (Cambridge University Press, 1991), 89 (p. 63 original edition); *The Elements of Law*, ed. Ferdinand Toennies (London, 1889), 73 (I. 14. 12).

[77] *Leviathan*, ed. Richard Tuck p. 239 (p. 181 original edn.).

[78] *Philosophy and Government 1572–1651*, pp. 346–8.

prise was an attempt to show why the idea of objective criteria for establishing the justification of a fear was chimerical; but many of his predecessors had divined that no objective criteria could be given, and they had been prepared to accept the moral consequences, even if they failed to see them through to the end. As we shall see in subsequent chapters, Hobbes's ideas remained for many of his contemporaries the *reductio ad absurdum* of the tradition running from the Romans through Gentili to Grotius, and separating him from the more acceptable figures in that tradition became a constant concern of writers in the late seventeenth and eighteenth centuries—until Rousseau and Kant (as I argue in Chapter 5) simply gave up the struggle, and accepted him as the most penetrating writer on these issues.

5

SAMUEL PUFENDORF

There was an obvious and deep problem about Hobbes's political theory, seen from the perspective of international relations. Hobbes insisted repeatedly that his state of nature was modelled on the relationship between states, but the plainest fact about that relationship was that it had not ended with all states submitting to a common sovereign, nor was it likely to do so. If the imaginative force of the state of nature depended on its plausibility as a picture of states as much as individuals—and the central argument of these lectures is that this was indeed the case for all writers in this tradition—then Hobbes's theory seemed to be clearly and immediately refuted.

Hobbes himself addressed this problem in the passage from *Leviathan* which I have already quoted.

> But though there had never been any time, wherein particular men were in a condition of warre one against another; yet in all times, Kings, and Persons of Soveraigne authority, because of their Independency, are in continuall jealousies, and in the state and posture of Gladiators . . . But because they uphold thereby, the Industry of their Subjects; there does not follow from it, that misery, which accompanies the Liberty of particular men.[1]

This is an interesting passage in many ways, with its stress on upholding *industry* as the key duty of the sovereign; it implies that despite the analogy between the state of nature and the world of nation states, one is not to expect the same kind of reasoning from the individuals in each case. The state of war would persist in the international realm, and even if it seemed at any one time to be at peace, this was an illusion:

> For as the nature of Foule weather, lyeth not in a showre or two of rain; but in an inclination thereto of many dayes together: So the nature of War, consisteth

[1] *Leviathan*, ed. Richard Tuck (Cambridge University Press, 1991), 90 (p. 63 original edn.).

not in actuall fighting; but in the known disposition thereto, during all the time there is no assurance to the contrary.[2]

But until the mid-eighteenth century, this authentically Hobbesian view was unpopular; as we shall see in the final chapter, it was the great achievement of Rousseau to have revived it, along with much else that was authentically Hobbesian.

Almost as unpopular was what one might term a naive Hobbesianism, that the state of war among nations would lead to an international Leviathan. The most striking example of this view is the Abbé de Saint-Pierre, whose *Projet Pour Rendre la Paix Perpétuelle en Europe*, written in the last years of the War of the Spanish Succession, depicted Europe as the Hobbesian state of nature in which sovereigns had to resort to force to achieve their ends, and in which neither temporary alliances nor the balance of power were of any effect in stopping conflict. 'Ever since there have been Sovereigns in the world, War has not ended, claims have not ceased and conflicts have not been resolved except by the fall and ruin of Sovereign Houses and by the overthrow of their States.'[3] De Saint-Pierre proposed that these embattled sovereigns should submit to a common government which would in turn help to secure them in their own position *vis-à-vis* their subjects.[4] De Saint-Pierre's later reputation was often as a utopian visionary, and indeed he was (as Rousseau pointed out) extremely naïve about the processes whereby the warring states of Europe could unite; but he did at least draw one straightforward conclusion from Hobbes.

Much the most popular view was, however, the one put before the public with great success by Samuel Pufendorf, in the first philosophically serious discussions of Hobbes's ideas.[5] This was that the international realm was a persuasive *refutation* of Hobbes's concept of the

[2] Ibid. 88–9.

[3] Claude Irenée Castel de Saint-Pierre, *Projet Pour Rendre La Paix Perpétuelle en Europe*, ed. Simone Goyard-Fabre (Corpus des Oeuvres de Philosophie en Langue Française, Fayard, Paris, 1986), 25.

[4] See e.g. his remarks at pp. 40–1.

[5] For the details of Pufendorf's life, see the introduction to his *On the Duty of Man and Citizen*, ed. James Tully, trans. Michael Silverthorne (Cambridge University Press, 1991) and the introductions to the Carnegie Endowment edns. of his works—*Elementorum Jurisprudentiae Universalis Libri Duo*, ed. Hans Wehberg, trans. William Abbott Oldfather and Edwin H. Zeydel (Carnegie Endowment for International Peace, Oxford University Press, 1931) and *De Jure Naturae et Gentium Libri Octo*, ed. Walter Simons, trans. C. H. and W. A. Oldfather (Oxford University Press, 1934).

state of nature: nations could and often did live in peace with one another without the necessity of a common power over them, and the same could be said about individuals in a state of nature. Hobbes's attempt to differentiate between the circumstances of the two kinds of agent was unnecessary, since men were to a sufficient degree naturally sociable. Pufendorf used this idea as a central part of his general enterprise, which was to call into question Hobbes's characterization of the state of nature, and thereby to undermine Hobbes's political theory. This was an extremely subtle enterprise, however, the subtlety of which led him to be branded as himself a Hobbesian by many German Aristotelians.

It also led him to redefine Grotius's programme, in a way which was to prove very influential for the eighteenth century. Although most recent historians (including myself fifteen years ago)[6] have followed the lead of the late seventeenth- and early eighteenth-century writers such as Jean Barbeyrac, and have stressed the similarities between Grotius and Pufendorf, I now think we were very wrong to have done so: in fact, Pufendorf was using some of Grotius's theoretical assumptions in order to undermine the practical implications of the Dutchman's ideas for the international realm—particularly where those ideas resembled those of Hobbes. Pufendorf was in general very keen to separate Grotius and Hobbes, against (as we have already seen) the views of many contemporaries.

The political world which Pufendorf inhabited, it is also clear in retrospect, was peculiarly well suited to serve as the background to such a critique; for Pufendorf lived in the group of European states which felt themselves most at risk from the kind of militarist and imperialist expansion in which the Dutch and English writers gloried. Although he was born (in 1632) in Chemnitz in Saxony, the son of a Lutheran minister, he followed his elder brother into the service of the Swedish crown. It must be remembered that in the aftermath of the Thirty Years War, Sweden had become a German state, with possessions on the south side of the Baltic; many Protestant Germans turned to the Swedes as a source of employment, and as a guarantor of freedom from encroachment by other states on the delicate balance drawn up at the Peace Conferences in Westphalia.

In the last years of Queen Christina's reign, Pufendorf's elder

[6] In *Natural Rights Theories* (Cambridge University Press, 1979).

brother Isaiah became an adviser and diplomat for the Swedes in Germany; he eventually became Chancellor of the Swedish possessions of Bremen and Verden. Samuel followed his example: his first post after graduating from Jena was the standard humanist one of tutor to the sons of a great Swedish nobleman, who was acting as ambassador in Denmark. Pufendorf found himself caught up in the war between Denmark and Sweden in 1658–9, and was imprisoned in Copenhagen; he used the time (as Grotius had used his imprisonment in Loevestein) to write a work of general political theory, his *Elementa Jurisprudentiae Universalis*, which was published in 1660.

To understand the point of this work, and (as we shall see) the acclaim with which it was greeted in parts of Germany, we have to consider the political role of Sweden in the late 1650s and 1660s. The international stance of the Swedish crown had undergone a remarkable shift since the great days of Gustavus Adolphus. In the early seventeenth century, the Swedes modelled themselves very much on the Dutch, and behaved with what seemed to contemporaries to be a similar ruthlessness: thus, for example, the Swedes insisted on freedom of the seas through the Sound and into the Baltic (a position taken up, of course, in opposition to the crown of Demark, which controlled the Sound in the early seventeenth century). In 1640, indeed, the Swedes and the Dutch formally allied to secure the free navigation of both the Baltic and the North Sea. The employment of Grotius as ambassador in Paris by Sweden from 1633 onwards was a straightforward expression of this interest: the most famous advocate of the *Mare Liberum* was put to work defending Sweden's rights to a free passage through the Sound. At the same time, Sweden was involved in the same kind of colonial expansion as the Dutch: they settled the colony of New Sweden (in what is now Delaware) in 1638, next to the Dutch colony of New Holland, and similarly planted settlements in West Africa among the forts and factories of the Dutch West African Company.

But by 1658 this had changed. The Danes won the Dutch away from a Swedish alliance in 1649 by offering them free passage through the Sound, and the Sweden became (understandably) very anxious about the prospect of the great economic power of the Baltic, as the Dutch were, in alliance with the other Scandinavian kingdom. The rulers of Sweden looked for ways of breaking this commercial stranglehold on them, a search which culminated in the wars of Charles X in the late 1650s against both the Danes and the Brandenburg-Prussians; Prussia, which was clearly a rising power after the Treaty of Westphalia, was fairly consistently in alliance with the Dutch during the 1650s and 1660s. The Dutch put a great deal of investment into Prussia and, like the Swedes when in alliance with the Dutch, the Prussians in the 1650s began to think about colonial activities, contemplating the creation of a Brandenburg colony on the coast of Coromandel.

By brilliant military tactics of the kind the Swedes had so often displayed, Charles X found himself (for a time) master of both sides of the Sound, and of an increased territory on the southern shore of the Baltic. He therefore argued in his war with Denmark that the *dominium maris Baltici* had now passed to Sweden, and indeed the Second Danish War, during which Pufendorf was imprisoned by the Danes, was an attempt to make good this claim. At the same time, the Swedish colonial enterprise had been destroyed by the Dutch: New Sweden was forcibly occupied by the Dutch of New Holland in 1656, after (revealingly) an argument between the two communities over the Dutch right to settle waste land within the boundaries of New Sweden—the Dutch were treating their fellow Europeans exactly as they had treated the American Indians. In terms of geopolitics, therefore, the Swedes had come to represent the most determined and articulate spokesmen against everything for which the Dutch (and by extension the other great commercial powers, such as the English) stood. They were at the head of a clutch of German states which feared both the Dutch and the Prussians as well as their traditional enemy the Habsburgs; an example of this was the alliance of the Rheinbund, signed on the day the Second Danish War broke out, between Sweden and a number of these smaller states, including both Protestant Brunswick-Luneburg and Catholic Mainz.

German Critics of Grotius

Many theorists moving in these political circles in the 1650s were unhappy about Grotius and the English writers, and they tended to focus their unhappiness on three things. The first was, of course, the theoretical foundations of Grotius and Hobbes, and in particular their anti-Aristotelianism and apparent atheism. Aristotelianism remained much stronger in Germany than elsewhere in Europe, and it provided the backbone for the professional courses in which the administrative class of the German states were trained. But the Aristotelians' hostility to

Grotius and Hobbes was as much a hostility to their particular conclusions as to the foundations of their theories—as is shown, indeed, by the different response accorded the equally anti-Aristotelian Pufendorf. Thus the second object of criticism in their theories was the account of property, including Grotius's ideas about the sea; while the third object was the doctrine that individuals or states could punish other people or nations without having political authority over them.

All these points were stressed by the first of the German critiques of Grotius, Johannes Felden's *Annotata* of 1653, dedicated to his rulers the Dukes of Brunswick-Luneburg. As a loyal Aristotelian, he was critical on general philosophical grounds both of Grotius's notion of a general human society, and of the priority which he accorded to self-interest. On the former, he said (sig. A2^r), 'if the state [*civitas*] is a perfect society, as Aristotle has established . . . it is pointless to use the society of nations [*societas gentium*] in order to investigate it . . . If what Aristotle says about civil society is true, the society of nations is not natural, so natural law is not to be looked for in it.'[7] While on the latter he remarked (acutely) that when Grotius praised Cicero for making self-preservation 'the first impression of nature', he was speaking 'more oratorically than philosophically' [*haec potius Oratoria sunt, quam Philosophica*] (p. 24). As a corollary of these criticisms, he described as 'an inane subtlety' (p. 105) the idea that one state might punish another for breach of natural law. Since he was a citizen of a state which had almost been destroyed by a war fought in order (originally) to punish heresy, it is not surprising that Felden was strongly opposed to admitting any principle of this kind into international relations.

He was also a citizen of a state which stood in an extremely complex relationship to other states, and whose sovereignty (as a member of the German Empire, even in the era after the Treaty of Westphalia) seemed very different from the model used by Grotius or Hobbes. Here again, Felden spotted the unusual character of Grotius's ideas (he seems not to have read Hobbes). Rehearsing the Aristotelian categories of 'despotic' or 'civil' government, he remarked: 'If a sovereign is, as Grotius defines it, one "whose Acts are not subject to another's Power, [so that they cannot be made void by any other human Will]", then I say that none of these rulers is sovereign, however they govern.' A despot's acts 'can be made void as unjust by the will of his subjects',

[7] Ioannes à Felden, *Annotata in Hug. Grotium De Iure Belli et Pacis* (Amsterdam, 1653), sig. A2^r.

while in civil government the sovereign's acts could be made void by the citizens if he exceeded his legal powers (p. 50). Instead Felden urged that the laws of any state are sovereign and determine the allocation of rights, which can include the fragmentation of 'sovereign' powers among different bodies.

When it came to Grotius's theory of property, Felden was not entirely opposed to its general character; but he was anxious to deduce from it the possibility of *dominium* over the sea. He argued (pp. 96 ff) that among the uses which men might reasonably make of the sea, fishing and the control of navigation might both give rise to full property rights in the oceans; as Grotius's follower Dirck Graswinckel pointed out in a defence of his master against Felden the following year,[8] Felden's intention seemed to be largely to vindicate tolls charged upon ships sailing through water controlled by a particular state—that is, the question of the Sound again. Felden was also critical of Grotius's remarks about colonization, arguing that any people were perfectly entitled to exclude foreigners from their territories for whatever reason (p. 105).

As I said, Felden, writing in 1653, seems not to have not to have been aware of Hobbes's work; but another Protestant Aristotelian, Caspar Ziegler of Wittenberg, writing thirteen years later, spotted the similarities between Grotius's ideas and Hobbes's. As he said, 'I do not know whether Grotius is very far from what Thomas Hobbes teaches, that injustice to men presupposes human laws, of which there are none in the state of nature.' Grotius, Ziegler argued, did not say expressly that the 'unique dictate of nature' is to seek one's own interest, but the practical consequence of his insistence on the need for survival was much the same.[9] John Adam Osiander also attacked Grotius's narrow account of human natural sociability in his *Observationes* of 1671, while in England during the 1650s and 1660s it was to some extent a commonplace that Grotius and Hobbes resembled one another.[10] The connection drawn in these years between Grotius and the most threatening

[8] Theodor Graswinckel, *Stricturae ad Censuram Ioannis à Felden . . . ad Libros Hugonis Grotii De Iure Belli ac Pacis* (Amsterdam, 1654), 103.

[9] C. Ziegler, *In Hugonis Grotii De Iure Belli ac Pacis Libros Notae & Animadversiones* (Wittenberg, 1666), 71–2.

[10] See e.g. Roger Coke, *A Survey of the Politicks of Mr. Thomas White, Mr. Thomas Hobbs, and Mr. Hugo Grotius* (London, 1662); and Sir Robert Filmer's, 'Observations Concerning the Originall of Government', in his *Patriarch and Other Writings*, ed. Johann P. Sommerville (Cambridge University Press, 1991).

modern political theorist is in striking contrast to the view of him put forward later in the century, and it was largely owing to Pufendorf that the interpretation of Grotius shifted in this fashion.[11]

The fundamental similarity between Pufendorf's concerns and those of the German Aristotelians is illustrated by the fact that we can find very similar arguments, though presented with much greater theoretical sophistication, in Pufendorf's *Elementa*; the reception of the work also illustrates that it appealed to the same audience as Felden's. Baron Boineburg, the chief minister of Mainz and the Metternich figure behind the creation of the Rheinbund, hailed Pufendorf as the man who could create the new Christian theory of natural law which was now needed, and he put him in touch with Johannes Boecler (himself a critic of Grotius, who dedicated his partial critique of the *De Iure Belli* to Boineburg in 1663)[12] and Herman Conring, the leading jurist of Protestant Germany, and a recent publicist for the Swedish cause in the war against Prussia in 1656.[13] At about the same time the Elector Palatine, another figure in this nexus of small states looking to Sweden for some protection, gave Pufendorf a chair at the University of Heidelberg, where he remained until 1670 when he returned to Sweden, first as professor at Lund and then as royal historiographer and a privy councillor at Stockholm. It was while at Lund that he published, in 1672, his major work of political theory, a much-expanded version of the *Elementa* entitled *De Iure Naturali et Gentium*.[14] As we shall see later, however, the Revocation of the Edict of Nantes in 1685 stimulated Pufendorf to a change in his political attitudes, and the following year he migrated from Sweden, where Charles XI had proved a rather feeble opponent of Louis XIV's France, to Prussia, to take up the post of

[11] Though Heinrich von Cocceji could still argue at the end of the century that Grotius had quite failed to refute Carneades since his own theory (whatever he might have said) depended as much on utility as his opponent's did. Grotius, *De Iure Bell ac Pacis Libri Tres, cum . . . Commentariis Henr. L.B. de Cocceii . . . Insertis quoque Observationibus Samuelis L.B. de Cocceii Henrici filii* (Lausanne, 1751), 43, 45. His son, however, dissociated himself from his father's out-of-date views in his observations on his father's commentary.

[12] *In Hugonis Grotii Jus Belli et Pacis* (Giessen, 1687), the first edn. was 1663.

[13] The best account of this episode is in the unpublished Ph.D. thesis of Dr Timothy Hochstrasser, 'Natural Law Theory, its Historiography and Development in the French and German Enlightenment, c.1670–1780' (Cambridge, 1989). See also F. Palladini, 'Le Dure Letteri di Pufendorf al Barone di Boineburg', *Nouvelles de la Republique des Lettres*, 1 (1984).

[14] This was itself enlarged and issued as a second edn. in 1684; the differences between the two edns. are sometimes significant, but (as I argue below) I think that Pufendorf's basic ideas remained broadly consistent during his time in Sweden.

adviser and historiographer to the Great Elector. He died in Berlin in 1694.

Pufendorf as Critic of Hobbes

The basic idea in both the *Elementa* and the *De Iure Naturali* was that Grotius's and Hobbes's theories about the conversion of interests into rights could be used as the basis for a quite different set of political conclusions. Pufendorf's theory began with what appeared to be the strongly anti-realist claim that all moral qualities are 'imputed' to things or 'imposed' on them by agents, who are in some sense free to describe things in whatever way they choose—any action can be described as 'right' or 'wrong', depending on the will of the agents who determine the matter. These agents are principally human beings,[15] though God should also be reckoned a free agent with the capacity to assign arbitrarily chosen moral values to persons, events, or things. I said just now that agents are 'in some sense' free, and it was Pufendorf's qualification to this freedom which is important. He did not make it absolutely clear anywhere, and recent historians of philosophy have found it as a consequence difficult to assess his theory; but we can see what he meant from a striking passage in Book I of *De Iure Naturali*, where he was talking about the 'imposition' which produces 'moral persons', that is people or entities with specific rights and duties.

> Men sometimes frame a kind of Shadows, or Images of *moral Persons*, for the representing of them in Sport and Jest. Whence it comes to pass, that the Term of *Person* hath been peculiarly challeng'd by the Stage. The essence of a *feigned Person*, consists in this, that the Habit, Gesture, and Speech of another *real Person* be handsomely express'd: Thus the whole Procedure bears only a Countenance of Mirth, and whatever such a fictitious Actor says or does leaves no *moral Effect* behind it, and is valu'd only according to the Dexterity and Artifice of the Performance . . . But the *Imposition* which produceth true *moral Persons*, is allow'd no such Liberty; but ought always to presuppose such Qualities, as may contribute to the solid Use, and real Benefit of human Life: And he that in constituting Persons hath not a Regard to these Endowments, is to be esteem'd an extravagant Buffoon, and a vain Insulter over Mankind. Thus *Caligula* might have made a *Consul* of the most wicked, or of the most senseless Wretch in *Rome*, provided the Man had been a free Citizen, and could at least have perform'd the common and formal Part of that Office: But to

[15] *The Law of Nature and Nations*, trans. Basil Kennet (5th edn., London, 1749), 3 (I. 1. 3).

design his Horse *Incitatus* the same Honour, was a Pitch of Madness, and of insipid Raillery.[16]

The fundamental idea here is thus rather close to Hobbes (who is clearly being alluded to throughout the discussion of persons), and yet at the same time profoundly critical of him. According to Pufendorf, men and other agents use an arbitrary moral language; but the practical point of the language is to advance their individual interests by getting them to do something profitable collectively, and unless it succeeds in doing so it counts as 'empty' or 'vain'. The point of a language containing 'moral entities' was that men should not 'pass their Lives like Beasts, without Culture and without Rule; but that they and their Actions should be moderated by settled Maxims and Principles; which could not be effected without the Application of such Terms and Notions'.[17] Pufendorf also talked about 'the polishing and the methodizing of a common Life'. Although our moral language thus reflects our interests, it does not directly reflect our personal interest, as Hobbes had thought; instead, if used properly, it always refers to whatever will in some way advance a collective interest, or aid in the construction of patterns of social life that would be impossible for 'brutes'.

For Pufendorf, we can therefore say, all moral language resembled the regulated and policed language which Hobbes looked to the sovereign to provide—the entirely subjective language Hobbes had postulated in the state of nature ('where every man is his own judge, and differeth from other concerning the names and appellations of things, and from those differences arise quarrels, and breach of peace')[18] was vain or 'trifling'. Pufendorf indeed used the latter term to describe Hobbes's account of natural rights.[19] But he was only able to dismiss the radically subjective account of natural morality by imposing a sovereign on men in the state of nature, responsible for controlling the basic ethical terminology, namely God.

Altho' the Usefulness and Expediency of [natural moral rules] be clearly apparent, yet this bare Consideration could never bring so strong a Tie on Mens Minds, but that they would recede from these Rules, whenever a Man was pleas'd either to neglect his own Advantage, or to pursue it by some different Means, which he judg'd more proper, and more likely to succeed . . . It is

[16] Ibid. 9 (I. 1. 15). [17] Ibid. 3 (I. 1. 3).

[18] *The Elements of Law*, ed. Ferdinand Toennies (London, 1889), 188 (II. 10. 8).

[19] *The Law of Nature and Nations*, p. 267 (III. 5. 3).

therefore . . . to be concluded, and to be maintain'd, that the Obligation of *natural Law* proceeds from GOD himself.[20]

The fact that even in the state of nature we all call the same things by the same moral names is thus assured by our belief that a sovereign God has declared what is to count as profitable for us; it is strictly parallel to the belief of the citizen in the Hobbesian commonwealth that 'the civil laws are to all subjects the measures of their actions, whereby to determine, whether they be right or wrong, profitable or unprofitable, virtuous or vicious . . .'[21]

The parallels between Pufendorf's state of nature and Hobbes's civil society go even further, however. Hobbes, it will be remembered, always insisted on the savagery of the state of nature, governed by nothing more than the bare search for self-preservation; civil society, on the other hand, displayed the arts and culture of peace (including, of course, above all agriculture). Pufendorf denied this, arguing that a state of nature (which he took to be actual and not hypothetical, and represented both by early men and by the modern international order—a view which he attributed to Hobbes also) could be a state of peace and self-improvement, since the men concerned would be led by God to seek a wider range of 'utilities' than mere self-preservation. And he made his prime motive for claiming this perfectly clear when he remarked

Hobbes is the more inexcusable for maintaining that the natural State cannot be remov'd and broken up, but by letting in the Sovereignty of another, and by uniting in the same Commonwealth: For that those Commonwealths, how distinct soever, which are allied by Friendship and by Leagues, should still continue in a State of mutual War, is a Contradiction evident to the common Sense of Mankind.[22]

Here we have the observation that international affairs are themselves the best refutation of Hobbes; and indeed we might say that, for Pufendorf, the successful attempt by the Germans to reconstruct a decent and pacific life in Germany on the basis of precisely such alliances and leagues between states was a key vindication of his own anti-Hobbesianism. As one might expect, he was always much more cautious than either Grotius or Hobbes about the nature of state sover-

[20] *The Law of Nature and Nations*, 141 (II. 3. 20).
[21] *The Elements of Law*, p. 188 (II. 10. 8).
[22] *The Law of Nature and Nations*, p. 110 (II. 2. 8).

eignty, arguing from an early date that it was a mistake to squeeze the constitution of the German Empire into the straightjacket of conventional political classifications: the empire was an 'irregular system', neither monarchy, aristocracy, nor democracy, and most closely resembling an 'unequal federation' in which the emperor was the senior partner (like the alliance between the Romans and the Latins).[23] When Pufendorf discussed such federations in his *De Iure Naturae et Gentium*, he described them in markedly unGrotian terms as submitting 'certain Parts of the Sovereignty to mutual direction', and, in a pointed reference to Grotius's own fate in the United Provinces, he asked 'How that State can entirely preserve its Liberty, the Subjects of which are liable to be arraign'd under another Government, and to be punished upon Conviction?'[24] This willingness to accept a much more fluid account of sovereignty sharply distinguishes Pufendorf from Grotius and Hobbes, and matches very neatly his general unhappiness about the picture of sovereign individuals found in the other two authors.

It has recently been argued by a number of scholars that Pufendorf's anti-Hobbesianism in *De Iure Naturae et Gentium* masked a fundamental agreement with Hobbes's account of men as basically self-interested beings; Pufendorf's theory of sociability, on this account, was a 'utilitarian' theory, that is, it depicted social life as pragmatically necessary for self-interested beings, rather than as springing from some intrinsic and first-order set of human wants.[25] A generous notion of pragmatic necessity would be quite hard to distinguish from an idea of inherent sociability; but in fact Pufendorf at one point does seem to have attempted such a distinction, and to have denied that his theory was utilitarian in this sense.

Although another Person hath done me neither Good nor Hurt, and though he hath nothing in him to raise either my Fear or my Love, yet Nature obliges me

[23] 'Severinus de Monzambano', *De Statu Imperii Germanici . . . Liber Unus* (Geneva, 1667), 158–9. This is an important analysis of the constitution and political interests of the German Empire produced by Pufendorf in the guise of an Italian Catholic commentator on German affairs.

[24] *The Law of Nature and Nations*, p. 683 (VII. 5. 18). Grotius and Oldenbarnevelt were tried by an irregular court authorized by the States General, and not by the High Court of Holland. For the discussions about jurisdiction and the revolutionary nature of the court, see Jan den Tex, *Oldenbarnevelt* (Cambridge University Press, 1973), 648–50.

[25] See in particular Fiammetta Palladini, *Samuel Pufendorf Discepolo di Hobbes* (Bologna, 1990); and Istvan Hont, 'The language of sociability and commerce: Samuel Pufendorf and the foundations of Smith's 'Four Stages' theory', in A. Pagden ed., *Languages of Political Theory in Early-Modern Europe* (Cambridge University Press, 1986), 271–316.

to esteem even such a one as my Kinsman and my Equal; which Reason alone (had we no others) were sufficient to enforce the Practice of a friendly Society and Correspondence amongst Men. And upon this Consideration, supposing there was a Nation in the World maintaining Peace and Justice amongst themselves, and of such mighty Strength as to be formidable to all others, and so not restrain'd from hurting them by the Fear of a like Return; yet should this Nation or People assault, drive, kill, or drag into slavery their weaker Neighbours, as often as they thought convenient, we should pronounce them actually guilty of a Breach of the Law of Nature. And yet (as we suppose) these People might *preserve* themselves, whether they allowed any Rights to others, or not.[26]

It would be hard to imagine a clearer denial of Hobbes's fundamental beliefs than this, and it would seem difficult in the light of this passage to argue that Pufendorf believed that sociability arose straightforwardly from man's 'imbecillity'. The powerful rogue nation in this example is condemned by a moral language which has as its ultimate sovereign, as I have said, a deity who wished men to lead a decent common life, and it is the presence of this deity in Pufendorf which in the end (and with all due allowance for his subtlety of mind) makes the difference between him and Hobbes.

Pufendorf as Critic of Grotius I

Sociability

Pufendorf's assault on the Hobbesian state of nature led him back to a new interpretation of Grotius. As we have just seen, the first German readers such as Felden were conscious of the distinction between Grotius's 'human society' and civil society, a distinction manifest in *De Iure Belli ac Pacis* largely through Grotius's discussion of distributive justice. They lacked, of course, what we possess, the early manuscripts of Grotius, in which he made clear that mutual aid and respect for the claims of the needy were solely the product of life in civil society; but (like Hobbes) they had nevertheless divined the essential character of Grotius's idea. Pufendorf, however, cited Grotius's account of human

[26] *The Law of Nature and Nations*, p. 137 (II. 3. 16), the section where Pufendorf directly deals with Hobbes's idea of unsociability. It should be pointed out that this passage is present in the first edn. of *De Iure Naturae* as well as subsequent edns.—Palladini has rightly stressed the significance of the changes which Pufendorf introduced into the second edn. under the influence of Cumberland, but in this area his criticism of Hobbes goes back to the beginning.

sociability as the basis for his own very different theory of the state of nature, in which distributive justice and imperfect rights played an important role. Book III, chapter III of *De Iure Naturali* contains the key discussion of Pufendorf's theory: it begins with the resounding sentiment that

> It is but a poor Thing not to have hurt another, or not to have robb'd him of his just Esteem: This negative Kindness to a Man will barely hinder him from having any fair Reason to hate, but can give him little Encouragement to love us. To knit Mens Minds more strongly together, it is necessary to add to this Forbearance of mutual Evil, the real Practice of mutual Good.

While Grotius had firmly excluded from the domain of the law of nature such virtues as *gratitude*, Pufendorf insisted that gratitude was clearly entailed by the natural obligation to provide mutual aid, though it is true 'that from every Transgression of the Law of *Nature*, it does not presently follow, that there must lie an *Action* (or the Resemblance of an *Action*) against a Man in *Nature's Court*' (III. 3. 17)—there may be a variety of practical reasons why no punishment should be visited upon such an offender. He explained what he had in mind in I. 7. 7, where he discussed the difference between *perfect* and *imperfect* rights:

> That some Things should be thus *due* to us *perfectly*, and others *imperfectly*, the Reason amongst those who live in a State of natural Liberty is, the great Diversity of Precepts in Nature's Laws, of which some conduce to the very Being, others only to the well-being of Society: And therefore, since there's less Necessity of performing these latter than the former, Reason shews that the former may be requir'd and executed by more severe Courses and Means; whereas, in regard to the latter, it is mere Folly to apply a Remedy more grievous than the Disease.

Similarly, when he discussed Grotius's concept of distributive justice in Book I, he stated plainly that 'when . . . we exhibit to another either Actions, or Things, due to him only by *imperfect* Right, or when we exercise towards another, Actions not coming under the Head of strict Commerce, we are said to have observ'd *general*, or *universal Justice*' (I. 7. 8). Grotius had of course denied that the considerations which gave rise to imperfect rights were part of 'Right, properly speaking', and he had not envisaged the vague boundary between perfect and imperfect rights which Pufendorf proposed.

The point of Pufendorf's insistence that the law of nature includes mutual aid as well as mutual forbearance comes out most clearly in

III. 3, the chapter on 'the common[27] duties of humanity'—though the point was not what one might naively have expected. One might have supposed that a natural duty to help one another would lead (for example) to an obligation to share one's possessions with the needy, such as one had (on Grotius's account) in civil society. To some extent, Pufendorf asserted that this was so, but there was an important qualification in practice. III. 3 consists of a methodical discussion of the examples which Grotius had given of the limits on private property, including the right of free passage across another's territory and (most tellingly) the right to settle on land which was not being properly used by its alleged owners.

Grotius, it will be remembered, had argued that these rights followed not from anything like charity,[28] but from the original and intrinsic limitations on the acquisition of private property in material objects, so that (for example) American Indians who claimed property rights in their hunting grounds were simply mistaken. Pufendorf dissented from this, arguing instead that the rights—in so far as they *were* rights—were the corollary of the duties upon men in a state of nature to help one another. But circumstances might well be such that the requirement of mutual aid would not give rise to perfect rights of the Grotian type: for example, it might be an act of 'humanity' to grant foreigners their request to settle among us, but

> since whatever we bestow upon such Petitioners, we may justly reckon a Matter of free Bounty in us, hence it follows, that they are not presently to lay Hands on what they please, nor to fix themselves, as it were, by some Right, in any Spot of Waste-ground they find among us; but that they ought to rest satisfied with the Station and Privileges we assign them.[29]

So the natural obligation of mutual aid could turn out in practice to *restrict* the kinds of rights which natural agents could claim against on another. By making the distinction between perfect and imperfect rights a fluid one, and by treating the state of nature as more like a civil society, Pufendorf was able to produce a theory which restrained the aggressive conduct of men in the state of nature.

[27] Or 'mutual'—the English translation of Barbeyrac's edn. uses both terms to translate Pufendorf's *promiscuus*.

[28] 'That Sentiment is not founded on what some alledge, that the Proprietor is obliged by the Rules of Charity to give of his Substance to those that want it; but on this, that the Property of Goods is supposed to have been established with this favourable Exception, that in such Cases one might enter again upon the Rights of the primitive Community . . .' (*De Iure Belli ac Pacis* II. 2. 6).

[29] *The Law of Nature and Nations*, p. 253 (III. 3. 10).

Pufendorf as Critic of Grotius II

Property

The same approach, leading to precisely the same conclusion, can be seen in his general discussion of property rights, and in his criticism of the narrowness of the idea of 'use' which Grotius had employed. As we saw in Chapter 3, Grotius's theory was that there is a fundamental natural right to possess bits of the material world which are useful for our personal consumption—the wild animal we have caught or the fruit we have picked; and that this natural right by extension develops into fully fledged property in anything where private property rights are necessary to produce commodities. Pufendorf attacked this idea at its heart. In both the *Elementa* and *De Iure Naturali* he began by making a clear distinction between *negative* and *positive* community of goods, and insisting that in nature there was strictly speaking only the former, in which goods were not owned by anyone in particular. So far he was in agreement with Grotius, and opposed (as we have seen) to Selden; but he then argued that if negative community was to be taken seriously, it must mean that even goods picked for personal consumption were not owned, and that they could legitimately be snatched from the mouth of the prospective consumer. This would obviously be unsatisfactory, so 'we apprehend the first Agreement, that Man made about this Point, to have been, that what any Person had seiz'd out of the common Store of Things, or out of the Fruits of them, with design to apply to his private Occasions, none else should rob him of'.[30] But Pufendorf's point was that even this right must have been *agreed*, as must (he asserted) the equally 'natural'-looking right to occupy territory as yet unoccupied. All property, even of the minimal sort Grotius had supposed to be natural, was artificial or contractual—again, there was no sharp distinction between a state of nature and a civil society. To put it another way (a way Pufendorf himself also put it), God did not determine what was to be owned by anyone, but instead left the imputation of property terms such as *meum* and *tuum* entirely to human beings. They were therefore free to use the language of property in any way they thought fit, consonant with the general end of advancing a 'polished' common life.

With this argument, Pufendorf neatly avoided the implications of Grotius's theory, that all property must bear some relationship to the

[30] Ibid. 367 (IV. 4. 5).

fundamental and natural human needs to consume the fruits of the earth. Instead, property could always be legitimated by a much wider set of human wants, comparable to the wants which would be taken seriously by a civil society. These ideas are found already in the *Elementa* applied to the central question of the seas—almost the first substantive part of the *Elementa* was concerned with this issue. Pufendorf made the principal plank in his argument the claim that the sea can be privately utitized in ways which Grotius had not conceded—so that control of neighbouring waters both for fishing and for defence could legitimately be claimed by a nation, and the Romans had been entitled 'to prevent any ships whatsoever of outsiders from passing through the straits at Gades'[31]—a fairly clear allusion to the problem of the Sound. Moreover, Pufendorf assumed that control of this kind *was* property, albeit (possibly) 'eminent' *dominium*, i.e. property rights enjoyed by a state rather than an individual. He had no interest in making the distinction between property and jurisdiction which Gentili and Grotius had employed. But if by no stretch of the imagination could private ownership of the sea provide any kind of benefit, then Pufendorf agreed with Grotius that it could not be owned. He argued that this was likely to be true of the great oceans, which could not be policed effectively by any one nation, and whose ownership could therefore not be defended on the grounds of protection, or of any other non-trivial good. Moreover, no one could claim to occupy the sea as it were vacant land: to such a claim

we answer, That Men have, indeed, a Privilege of making waste Places their own, by first seizing upon them: But they are always to remember, that GOD gave the World not to this nor to that Man, but to [the] human Race in general; as, likewise, that all Men are, by Nature, equal. Wherefore, that tacit Convention between the first Introducers of *Property*, assigning the Right of those Things which did not fall under their prime Division, to the Persons who should first take Possession of them, can, by no Means, be extended to such an Object, which, if one should hold alone, he might oppress all others with most unjust Slavery, or might intercept some most important Advantages, which would otherwise accrue to all Nations in common. Inasmuch as such a Case could not enter into the Imagination of those primitive Divisors.[32]

[31] *Elementorum Jurisprudentiae Universalis Libri Duo*, ed. Hans Wehberg, trans. William Abbott Oldfather and Edwin H. Zeydel (Carnegie Endowment for International Peace, Oxford University Press, 1931), II, 28.

[32] *The Law of Nature and Nations*, pp. 383–4 (IV. 5. 9).

Pufendorf was therefore critical of the Spaniards in the East Indies, and endorsed at least that part of Grotius's *Mare Liberum*.[33]

The implication of this argument about the sea, however, was that what counted as 'waste' was far from straightforward: states might reasonably claim property rights in an area of the world's surface which they could not actually cultivate, if it was necessary for their defence or if they wished to hunt (that is, fish) over it. Applied to the land, this same argument thus prohibited the kind of forcible dispossession of the Indians which Grotius's theory legitimated, and again Pufendorf drew this conclusion. In the *Elementa*, he made the point using an argument which did not entirely square with his general premisses:

It was by title of occupation alone, if you remove from consideration the concession on the part of God, that the first man received his authority over all things, and he needed no further title, because there existed no one whose right could stand in his way. And he acquired dominion over all things none the less because he was unable by an act to take possession of all things, and apply them to his own use. For it is sufficient that, while he took possession physically of some portion of things, he included others in his intent, and was going to take possession of them when need of them arose; just as he who entered merely one apartment of a palace, has occupied the whole.[34]

But in the later work, Pufendorf put forward the same conclusion on a more satisfactory basis, dealing explicitly with Grotius's argument in II. 2 of *De Iure Bulli ac Pacis*. Pufendorf argued in *De Iure Naturali et Gentium*, first, that the apparently 'natural' principle that vacant land should belong to 'him who, before others, took bodily Possession of it' (IV. 6. 2) was really conventional, though a very early convention of the whole human race; and second, that part of this convention (it might be presumed) was an important distinction between occupancy by a single individual and occupancy by a group of people.

In Relation to the Occupancy of Immoveables, especially of Lands, we are carefully to observe and distinguish, whether it be made by one Person only, or by many in Conjunction. One Man is then adjudged to be the Occupant of Land, when he tills and manures it, or when he encloseth it with settled Boundaries and Limits: Yet still with this Proviso, that he grasp at no more than what, upon a fair Account, seems tenable to one Family, however enlarged and multiplied. Should one Man, for Instance, be, with his Wife, cast upon a desert

[33] See also *Do Iure Naturali et Gentium*, IV. 5. 5.

[34] *Elementorum Jurisprudentiae Universalis Libri Duo*, II, 36.

Island, sufficient to maintain Myriads of People; he could not, without intolerable Arrogance, challenge the whole Island to himself upon the Right of Occupancy, and endeavour to repulse those who should land on a different part of the shore. But when any number of Men jointly possess themselves of a Tract of Land, this Occupancy is wont to be made either *by the Whole*, or *by Parcels*. The former happens, when Men in an united Body seize on some desolate Region, encompassed with certain Bounds, either by Nature, or by human Appointment . . . Nor is it necessary that all things which are first occupied in this general Way, should be afterwards divided amongst particular and distinct Proprietors. Therefore, if in a Region thus possessed, any thing should be found, which is not ascertained to a private Owner, it must not presently be looked upon as *void* and *waste*, so that any one Person may seize it as his *Peculiar*; but we must suppose it to belong to the whole People.[35]

Since Pufendorf did not in this passage, any more than in his discussion of the sea, distinguish between jurisdiction and property, his point is quite clear: the waste lands in a territory occupied by a people are owned by the people collectively, and may be disposed of in all sorts of ways. It is not the case that the principle by which property is acquired is different from that by which jurisdiction is acquired, and that foreigners may claim a natural right to occupy the vacant territory, as long as they submit to the political authority of the local people.

Pufendorf as Critic of Grotius III

International Punishment

On the basis of very unAristotelian metatheory of ethics, therefore, Pufendorf had arrived at the same conclusions as the North German Aristotelians about property rights in the sea and in the waste lands of the world. We can see the same process at work in the other principal area with which they were concerned, the issue of whether one state or nation can punish another for breach of the natural law. Pufendorf was very critical of Grotius for arguing that the right to punish was a natural right possessed by all men: as he said in the *Elementa*, all that a natural man could do was *retaliate*, that is, use force against someone who had actually injured *him* (though once embarked on the course of retaliation, he could use any violence necessary to force compensation out of the aggressor).

[35] *The Law of Nature and Nations*, pp. 386–8 (IV. 6. 3–4).

When a man unjustly hurts a second person, unless he hurt me indirectly at the same time, or unless I myself am under obligation to defend that other person against unjust violence, there does not come to me the right of bringing force to bear upon the first person, as long, indeed, as he shows no evidences of a hostile mind towards me.[36]

Both in the *Elementa* and in the *De Iure Naturae et Gentium* Pufendorf justified this argument by claiming that part of the *meaning* of punishment was that it must be 'threatened before, and . . . inflicted after the Crime is known',[37] and he turned to Hobbes for support (albeit of a rather ambiguous kind) for this position, for Hobbes, as Pufendorf pointed out, had also defined punishment as something necessarily administered by a superior (VIII. 3. 7). Pufendorf was, however, forced to admit that Hobbes elsewhere asserted that the right of civil punishment came to the sovereign from the citizens' natural rights to defend themselves—'to which it may be answer'd, that the Right of Punishing is different from the Right of Self-preservation: and, by the Exercise of it upon Subjects, we can never understand what a State of Nature allowed, where there is no Subjection'.[38]

According to Pufendorf, this fact about the meaning of punishment, that it had to be threatened in advance of the sanction being applied, meant that it could only be administered by someone who had agreed political authority over other men, in a situation where established laws could be recognized by subjects and acted upon in a methodical way by the sovereign. Grotius's idea that we could have a natural right to punish any other men for breaches of the laws of nature was therefore quite false. Pufendorf fully recognized the practical implications of this position for the colonial enterprises, and in the second edition of *De Iure Naturali* (1684) he quoted as a representative of the standard humanist view (and also, as he understood, Grotius's view also) a passage from Francis Bacon:

My Lord *Bacon* . . . gives this a sufficient Reason for making War upon the *Americans*, which I must confess I cannot agree with him in: 'That they were to be look'd upon as People proscribed by the Law of Nature, inasmuch as they had a barbarous Custom of sacrificing Men, and feeding upon Man's Flesh.' For it ought to be distinctly considered, whether Christian Princes have sufficient

[36] *Elementorum Jurisprudentiae Universalis Libri Duo*, II, 252.

[37] *The Law of Nature and Nations*, p. 769 (VIII. 3. 7).

[38] Ibid. 761 (VIII. 3. 1).

Licence given them to invade those *Indians*, as People proscribed by Nature, only because they made Man's Flesh their common Food? Or because they eat the Bodies of Persons of their own Religion? Or, because they devoured Strangers and Foreigners? And then again it nust be ask'd, whether those Strangers they are said to kill and eat, come as Enemies and Robbers, or as innocent Guests and Travellers, or as forc'd by Stress of Weather? For this last Case only, not any of the others, can give any Prince a *Right of War* against them; and this to those Princes only, whose Subjects have been used with that Inhumanity by them.[39]

But Pufendorf no doubt also had in mind the experiences of Germany during the Thirty Years War, and the continued involvement during that conflict of non-German powers whose chief interest was in a religious crusade of one kind or another. His repeated concern at this time was that war should only be made by states which had been directly injured by other states, or which were in clear and explicit alliance with the injured parties, and that the laboriously constructed legal arrangements achieved in Westphalia should be a secure basis for peace in Germany, and should not be disrupted by international adventuring of the Dutch, French, or Spanish kind. As he said (in another passage added in the second edition), it was primarily allies or acknowledged friends whom we could legitimately help, and while 'the common *Affinity* and publick *Relations* of Mankind' might sometimes 'be sufficient Motives to us to undertake the Defence of a Person manifestly injured and abused; especially since it may easily be made our own Interest to do it',

we are not to imagine that every Man, even they who live in the *Liberty of Nature*, hath a Right to correct and punish with War any Person who hath done another an Injury, barely upon Pretence that common Good requires, that such as oppress the Innocent ought not to escape Punishment, and that what toucheth one ought to affect all. For otherwise, since the Party we suppose to be unjustly invaded, is not deprived of the Liberty of using *equal* Force to repel his Enemy, whom he never injured; the Consequence *then* would be, that, instead of one *War*, the World must suffer the Miseries of two. Besides, it is, also, contrary to the natural *Equality* of Mankind, for a Man to force himself upon the World for a *Judge*, and *Decider* of *Controversies*. Not to say what

[39] *The Law of Nature and Nations*, 840 (VIII. 6. 5.). The passage from Bacon (as Barbeyrac observed) is from his dialogue *An Advertisement Touching an Holy War*, which was written at about the time Bacon was associating with Hobbes, and which Hobbes may have translated into Latin—Bacon himself arranged for its translation, though it first appeared after his death in *Operum Moralium et Civium Tomus*, ed. W. Rawley (London, 1638); see sig. $A3^r$–$A3^v$.

dangerous Abuses this Liberty might be perverted to, and that any Man might make War upon any Man upon such a Pretence. The Wrong therefore another Man suffers is not Reason sufficient to engage me in his Quarrel, unless he calls me particularly to his Assistance; so that whatever I undertake to do, is not to be charged upon me, but upon the Person who desires my Help.[40]

Consequently, he allowed that Grotius might have been right about intervention in support of the subjects of a foreign ruler, when they requested it, and when they were clearly suffering such 'insupportable Tyranny and Cruelties' that they would themselves be entitled to take up arms against their government.[41]

In II. 5. 6 Pufendorf carefully discussed the related question of pre-emptive strikes against a state which was threatening its neighbours by its power. Against Gentili, he insisted that 'although such a mighty Neighbour hath shewn himself to have the Will of hurting as well as the Power, he doth not yet give me directly a just Cause of setting upon him, because he doth not yet express this ill Will towards me in particular'. This was so even if the over-mighty neighbour was already attacking other nations, unless 'I may happen to be united by a more peculiar Obligation to the injur'd Person'—that is, in some stable alliance with the victim. Only if there was clear evidence that the aggressive state possessed a 'real Design' to attack us, were we entitled to strike first.

These arguments of Pufendorf implied a highly restrictive attitude to both the European colonial expansion, and the internecine wars of the continent itself; but there was one area of warfare where his account of natural sociability *did* allow a general right of intervention and punishment. In his discussion of 'esteen' (VIII. 4), he urged that pirates and robbers in general deserved no esteem—that is, no basic moral respect.

Neither will whole *States* and *Commonwealths* deserve better *Rank*, when they are not content to acquiesce in the Enjoyment of their own *Rights* at *home*, but invade and ravage the rest of the World, without regard to *Faith* or *Compacts* to the contrary . . . Now, the Effects that attend Men under such a *Loss* of *Esteem*, are generally such as these; that, unless they leave off their *unjust* and *bloody*

[40] *The Law of Nature and Nations*, p. 847 (VIII. 6. 14).

[41] In his *De Officio Hominis et Civis Juxta Legem Naturalem* of 1673, which is in most respects simply an abridgement of his *De Iure Naturali et Gentium*, Pufendorf added to the list of legitimate cases for intervention 'kinship alone' (*sola communis cognatio*). II. 16. 11; for translation, see the edn. by James Tully and Michael Silverthorne (Cambridge University Press, 1991).

Way of *Life*, it will be necessary for other Men to shew them no more Mercy, than they do to Beasts of Prey.[42]

It is not entirely clear what kind of state he had in mind in these remarks: in the same passage, he expressly denied that this applied to people such as the inhabitants of the Barbary Coast, who

> are so partial, as to be just in the Observation of *Compacts* with some particular *Allies*, but to *all other* their Neighbours, or at least to certain *Nations*, shew little Regard in the Observation of the *Law of Nature* . . . their Credit, it is evident, must very much sink, but it would be too severe to deny them every Degree of *Esteem*.

Presumably he was thinking of instances such as the Mongols, or the Turks in their early incursions into Christendom.

These remarks were not sufficient to counteract the strong case against intervention which Pufendorf had made in *De Iure Naturali et Gentium*, and his views in that work were to be bitterly criticized a few years later (as we shall see in the next chapter) by his otherwise loyal editor the Huguenot exile Jean Barbeyrac, on the grounds that they precluded the kind of war against France in defence of the Protestant religion which Barbeyrac believed to be necessary. But in fact Pufendorf himself had already begun to modify his views in the works which he produced in the anxious years after Louis XIV's revocation of the Edict of Nantes. As we saw from the brief sketch of Pufendorf's life at the beginning of this chapter, after the publication of *De Iure Naturali et Gentium* and *De Officio Hominis et Civis* in 1672 and 1673, Pufendorf's intellectual energies were largely expended on works of history and political policy. While he had begun to produce books of this kind during the years he was working on natural jurisprudence—notably the work on the German Empire published under the name of 'Severino do Monzambano'—from 1677 onwards his employment as historiographer and adviser, first in Sweden and then in Prussia, led him to concentrate almost entirely on this type of book. In the process, his awareness of the role of national interest in global politics led him to be increasingly sympathetic to the construction of coalitions aimed at checking and—if necessary—making war on the threats to European stability, and in particular on the French.

[42] *The Law of Nature and Nations*, p. 802 (VIII. 4. 5).

During his time in Sweden, he consistently opposed the policy of alliance with France, urging (as he put it in 1679) that

> now that *France* is arriv'd at so high a degree of Power that it huffs all the States of *Europe*, and pretends to prescribe 'em Laws, Sweden is oblig'd, in Consideration of the publick good, which consists in preserving the Ballance of *Europe*, not to assist *France* in the vast designs that she forms every day.[43]

Or, as he put it the following year, the chief interest of Sweden was 'to Confederate her self with those Protestants who have the same Aims with her self, *To maintain the Peace of Westphalia*.'[44] But the Revocation of the Edict of Nantes in 1685 brought home to him that merely maintaining the Peace of Westphalia and the balance of Europe was not enough: Protestantism itself was now threatened, and the persecution of their co-religionists within France was a ground for intervention by the Protestant powers. He urged this in a series of striking and eloquent works produced in the last years of his life, after his migration to Prussia in the year following the Revocation—a migration no doubt prompted by the relative feebleness of the Swedish government in the face of the new threat, and by the Great Elector's energetic marshalling of European powers against France.

The clearest statement of his new view came in his *De Habitu Religionis Christianae ad Vitam Civilem* of 1687, translated into English as *Of the Nature, and Qualification of Religion, in Reference to Civil Society* (London, 1698).

> That Prince therefore who does trouble his faithful Subjects for no other reason, but because they cannot conform to his Opinion (especially if they can maintain theirs out of the Holy Scriptures) commits and Act of Injustice; Nay, I cannot see how he can with Justice force them out of his Territories . . . All true Christians therefore ought couragiously to oppose the Threats and Attempts of this Beast [a reference to Revelations 18: 3], committing the rest to Divine Providence.[45]

He concluded, ominously, that faced with the example of such inhuman persecution, princes and free peoples who have thrown off the

[43] *The History of Popedom*, trans. J. C. (London, 1691), 200. This is a translation of the *Historische und Politische Beschreibung der Geistlichen Monarchie des Stuhls zu Rom* by 'Basilius Hyperta' (Hamburg, 1679).

[44] *A Discourse upon the Alliances between Sweden and France* (London, 1709), 52. The discourse was written in 1680.

[45] *Of the Nature, and Qualification of Religion, in Reference to Civil Society*, trans. J. Crull (London, 1698), 153, 155.

Roman yoke 'will know what to do without any advice from me, if they are not dim-witted'.[46] Similarly, in a work from these years on Protestant unity, he attacked the French Calvinist Jurieu for proposing *Christian* unity, and instead urged an association of Protestants to 'defend the common Cause against the Papists'.[47] In a work produced right at the end of his life, he applied these notions to the freedom of the sea, arguing that the northern nations which were neutral in the war of the Grand Alliance between William III (ruler of both the United Provinces and England) and Louis XIV, should recognize that he cause of Protestantism hung on the outcome. The defeat of *insolens illa Potentia* (that is France) would benefit the Protestant north, and they should not claim neutrality in the war in order to achieve commercial advantages.[48] We might say that for Pufendorf in his last years, the circumstances in which natural agents (that is, states) found themselves had changed, and the general requirement that they should sustain a decent social life amongst themselves now implied more mutual aggression than had seemed to be the case twenty years earlier.

So Pufendorf's final views, expressed in these historical and political works, were not in some ways so different from those of his more radical successors, which we shall consider in the next chapter. However, in the reissues of his juridical works in the course of the 1680s,[49] Pufendorf was content to maintain the ideas which he had put forward in the 1660s and 1670s, and it was this body of work which continued to influence many readers, particularly in Germany. A gap thus opened up among the heirs of Grotius: on the one hand were those (like Locke and Barbeyrac) who argued for an aggressive and interventionary foreign

[46] *Ipsi etiam me non movente, si mens non laeva est, intelligunt*. *De Habitu Religionis Christianae ad Vitam Civilem* (Bremen, 1687), 195. The English translation makes the hint explicit: they 'will, questionless without my Advice, take such measures, as may be most convenient for to secure themselves from so imminent a Danger' (p. 155).

[47] *The Divine Feudal Law: Or, Covenant with Mankind, Represented*, trans. T. Dorrington (London, 1703), 364. This is a translation of his *Jus Feciale Divinum sive De Consensu et Dissensu Protestantium Exercitatio Posthuma* (1695).

[48] This is from Ioannes Groningius, *Navigatio Libera, seu De Jure, quod Pacatis ad Belligerantium Commercia Competit* (Rostock, 1694), sig. D1. Groningius wrote in defence of the rights of neutrals, but sent an earlier version of his book to Pufendorf for comments, and printed Pufendorf's letter together with his own response to it. (I owe this reference to Dr T. Hochstrasser.)

[49] *De Jure Naturae et Gentium* was issued in a much enlarged second edn. at Frankfurt in 1684, and at Amsterdam in 1688. *De Officio Hominis et Civis* became a set text at Cambridge and was reissued repeatedly there or at London from 1682 onwards (earlier, the *Elementa* had been used as a set text there, being reprinted in 1672, presumably under the influence of Richard Cumberland).

policy, and on the other were those (like Christian Wolff and indeed Kant) who regarded such a thing as the immoral outcome of the competition between commercial nations. It was Pufendorf's great, and remarkably overlooked, contribution to this debate to have made the second view respectable among the theorists of natural jurisprudence, just as it was also his achievement to have transformed the weak notion of sociability in the Grotian tradition into a much stronger notion of human mutual aid. His *De Iure Naturali et Gentium* took its place alongside Grotius's *De Iure Belli ac Pacis* (particularly in Jean Barbeyrac's editions), the two together forming a two-volume encyclopaedia of contemporary political thought available in virtually every private or public library from the Urals to the Mississippi; much of these lectures has been written from my own copies of the English translations of Barbeyrac's editions. But, as we shall see in the next two chapters, Pufendorf's successors were left with the task of making sense out of the often conflicting messages which they received from the two volumes.

6

FROM LOCKE TO VATTEL[1]

As I said at the beginning of the previous chapter, the most popular response to Hobbes's view of the realm of international politics was to deny that it was a state of endemic war, and to draw the corollary that the state of nature for individuals was not one of war either. For Pufendorf, as we saw in that chapter, the rejection of Hobbes's theoretical foundations accompanied a rejection of many of the practical implications of Hobbes's theory, and in particular a rejection of many of the ideas about making war which Hobbes shared with Grotius and with the humanist tradition; indeed, as I argued there, the rejection of these practical implications may have been one of Pufendorf's principal motives in embarking on his philosophical project.

[1] When I gave this chapter as a lecture, I prefaced it with the following remarks. 'I must begin this lecture with a confession. For fifteen years, since we were graduate students together in Cambridge, James Tully and myself have been exchanging ideas about our work; indeed, for the past five years we have been writing together a general history of seventeenth-century political thought, with volume one (down to 1651) being my responsibility, and volume two (down to 1714) being Tully's. Despite this, the fact that we live at the moment on opposite sides of the Atlantic means that we see each other rather rarely, and can often go for some months without communication. I was therefore not only delighted but also astonished to discover towards the end of the Long Vacation last year that he was going to deliver to the Locke Conference at Christ Church (a conference I am sure some of you attended) a paper entitled 'Rediscovering America', which dealt with John Locke and the theoretical issues involved in American colonisation. I had already in the previous summer (unknown to him) written a paper outlining the Grotius–Pufendorf argument, with a brief excursus on Locke; when we exchanged the papers in September 1990, we found that we had independently come to the same conclusion, that the issues of America and international affairs were far closer to the centre of Locke's *Two Treatises of Government* than earlier scholars had ever been prepared to say. Accordingly, what I have to say in the first part of today's lecture is as much Jim Tully's work as it is my own; what I will do, however, is concentrate more than he did on the particular polemic against Pufendorf which I believe we can detect beneath the Second Treatise of Government.' Since then, of course, Tully has published his ideas on Locke and America in 'Rediscovering America: The *Two treatises* and Aboriginal Rights' in his collection of essays, *An Approach to Political Philosophy: Locke in Contexts* (Cambridge University Press, 1993), 137–78, and has enlarged upon his general theme in his Seeley Lectures for 1994, *Strange Multiplicity* (Cambridge University Press, 1995).

But other writers in the late seventeenth and eighteenth centuries were anxious to abandon Hobbes's account of the state of nature without sacrificing so much of the humanist or Grotian inheritance; in particular, they wished to preserve as much as possible of the humanist jurisprudence of war, with its emphasis on autonomous states, on the legitimacy (to an extent) of pre-emptive strikes, and on the right to seize uncultivated land. In some of them (notably, as we shall see, Locke), this concern came close to overwhelming their attempt to separate themselves from Hobbes or from the early Grotius—their hostility to the practical implications of Pufendorf's theory was so great that they were willing to flirt with Hobbes's ideas. The consequence, however, was very often a considerable confusion or lack of clarity in what they were arguing. From the perspective of Rousseau or Kant, as we shall see in the final chapter, this whole movement was as much of a failure as Pufendorf's enterprise; in their eyes, only Hobbes provided a coherent account of modern politics, however morally distasteful it might be. They would have seen all these other writers as inconsistent, and as pre-eminently the 'sorry comforters' of Kant's famous outburst in *Perpetual Peace*.

Locke as a Critic of Pufendorf

There has never been any doubt about Locke's interest in the European colonizing and exploring activity, and in the relations between European states. His library was filled with books on travel and international affairs, and in the 1660s he was involved in various diplomatic missions—in 1665–6 he was secretary to the emissary from England to the Great Elector about the Second Dutch War, and in 1666 he was offered secretaryships at the embassies in both Sweden and Spain. If it had not been for his developing acquaintance with Ashley Cooper during these years, it is probable that he would have found his career (like so many other humanists) in diplomacy. In addition, as is well known, from 1669 onward he was intimately involved in the development of Carolina, as Ashley Cooper began to capitalize on his interest as a proprietor of the colony under its charters of 1663 and 1665. Locke helped to draw up the Fundamental Constitutions of Carolina (March 1670); he was himself an investor in the Royal Africa Company and in the Bahamas Islands (which were given to Carolina in the early 1670s), and he became a Landgrave of Carolina. An island near Charleston, now called Edisto

Island, was originally named Locke Island. Nor has there ever been any doubt about the extent to which examples drawn from America fill the pages of Lockes's *Two Treatises*—there are in the region of twenty-five important references to America or the Indians in the course of the work, most of them being in the early theoretical chapters of the Second Treatise. But what has not been sufficiently recognized, I think, is the way in which the fundamental arguments of the Second Treatise develop point-by-point an answer to Pufendorf's critique of the ideology of the commercial nations.

We know that Locke had developed a particular interest in Pufendorf at about the time he wrote the *Two Treatises*. It remains unclear precisely when that was, and John Milton has recently pointed out sagely that the *Second Treatise* at least may well have been drafted and redrafted over a considerable length of time (as Locke's *Essay* undoubtedly was).[2] Locke was trying to buy the *De Iure Naturae et Gentium* and the *De Officio Hominis et Civis* in October 1677,[3] but he did not finally succeed until 1681.[4] I suspect that it was only at this stage that he fully engaged with Pufendorf's ideas, after he had already written the *First Treatise* as a critique of Filmer, in 1680–1.[5] Among the strong pieces of evidence for this, though neither Ashcraft nor Wootton has remarked on it, is the fact (particularly relevant to my present theme) that in the *First Treatise* (§§ 129–32) Locke discusses quite extensively the powers of life and death and of making war possessed by private individuals such as planters in the West Indies, but he nowhere implies that those powers might include the right to punish rather than retaliate—though it would have been very germane to his argument to have asserted this. In the *Second Treatise*, on the other hand, the natural private right to punish is a central element of the work. If what I have to say in this chapter is right, this is explicable by the fact that it was only

[2] J. R. Milton, 'Dating Locke's *Second Treatise*', *The History of Political Thought*, 16 (1995), 356–90.

[3] *Correspondence*, I, ed. E. De Beer (Oxford University Press, 1976), 518.

[4] Locke, *Essays on the Law of Nature*, ed. W. von Leyden (Oxford University Press, 1970), 39.

[5] Most people agree on this as the date for the *First Treatise*; disagreement has centred on the *Second*. My conjecture is broadly the same as the view of Richard Ashcraft, *Locke's Two Treatises of Government* (London, 1987), 286–95, replied to by Peter Laslett in his edn. of Locke's *Two Treatise of Government* (Cambridge University Press, 1988), 123–6. Despite my disagreement with him about the relationship between Locke and Tyrrell (see below, note 6), I also agree with Professor David Wootton about the dating of the *Two Treatises* (John Locke, *Political Writings*, ed. David Wootton (Penguin, 1993), 49–63).

in 1681 that Locke turned to address directly the issues raised by Pufendorf's critique of Grotius.[6]

Although von Leyden saw traces of the *Elementa* in Locke's early Christ Church lectures on moral philosophy, dating from 1664, I cannot say that there is anything in those lectures which unambiguously relates to the *Elementa*, and I would be surprised if Locke knew about the work so soon after its publication.[7] But the purchase of the texts in 1681 signalled the start of an intensive study of Pufendorf's ideas, the first fruits of which (in the form of an outline of the theory of property later found in the *Second Treatise*) were, as I suggested ten years ago, in fact incorporated at the very last minute into his friend James Tyrrell's *Patriarcha non Monarcha*, which appeared in that year.[8]

[6] Milton has also pointed out very convincingly that chapter V of the *Second Treatise* was written at a different time from the rest, as the biblical citations are in a different style—and one that Locke usually used later in his life (p. 374). However, Milton has shied away from drawing the obvious conclusion that chapter V was written later, as he wants to associate the American references in it with Locke's involvement in the Carolina settlement. But in the light of the critique of Pufendorf in chapter V (which Milton does not deal with), which belongs most naturally to 1681 or later, it is hard not to draw the obvious conclusion form the biblical citations. I give below a suggestion about an American context in these years also.

[7] Locke, *Essays on the Law of Nature*, ed. W. von Leyden (Oxford University Press, 1970), 38–9.

[8] See my *Natural Rights Theories* (Cambridge, 1979), 169–70. Professor David Wootton has recently suggested that the rewriting of Tyrrells's *Patriarcha non Monarcha* at the point at which a rather Lockean account of property is introduced was in fact a piece of self-censorship on Tyrrell's part, cutting out a discussion of Milton, and that the 'Lockean' theory was already present in the emended section (*Political Writings*, ed. David Wootton pp. 58–61). Tyrrell thus influenced Locke, and not vice versa. This would be remarkable, if true; but neither of the two pieces of evidence which Wootton adduces seem to me to be conclusive. The first piece of evidence is bibliographical, that the printed text of *Patriarcha non Monarcha* appears to have been shortened at the last minute rather than extended, and that remarks at the end of the preceding section imply that Tyrrell was planning to criticize Milton. On the face of it this tells us little, as even if Tyrrell's intention was to rewrite in order to eliminate a discussion of Milton, he might perfectly well have taken the opportunity to introduce a new treatment of property, given that the critique of Filmer on property occupied the same part of the book. The second piece of evidence is a letter from Tyrrell to Locke in August 1690, in which Tyrrell remarked to Locke about the recently published but anonymous *Two Treatises* that 'whoever had writ it . . . agreed perfectly with my conceptions in Patriarch non Mon:' (Locke, *Correspondence*, IV ed. E. De Beer, letter 1,312, p. 117). Wootton says of this letter, 'Had he read Locke on property before writing *Patriarcha non Monarcha*, or while it was in press, he might not have been so sure that it was he and not Locke who had influenced the author of the *Two Treatises*. He might have said, writing to Locke, "he agrees with us", or (if Locke had from the first concealed his own authorship) "he agrees with me and the author of that essay you showed me". But he was in no doubt that the ideas in *Patriarcha non Monarcha* were his own, and in no doubt, therefore, about which way the causal chain ran' (pp. 60–1). However, in this letter Tyrrell was reminding Locke

Locke may even have been responding to the fact that Tyrrell devoted the last part of the original version of his book to an enthusiastic summary and extensive translation of Pufendorf's remarks about sovereignty in the *De Iure Naturali et Gentium*—remarks about which, as we shall see presently, Locke was somewhat sceptical.

To see the way in which Locke's argument in the *Second Treatise* developed out of a critique of Pufendorf, we have only to go through the first five chapters of the work. Locke's account of the State of Nature in chapter I (and his clear and confident use of this term is itself, I think, a sign of the Pufendorfian influence—for apart from Hobbes and Pufendorf, most writers were still rather chary of using the expression)[9] has at its heart the celebrated claim that because men are obliged—as God's 'workmanship'—both to preserve themselves and to preserve 'the rest of Mankind'.

that all Men may be restrained from invading others Rights, and from doing hurt to one another, and the Law of Nature be observed, which willeth the Peace and *Preservation of all Mankind*, the *Execution* of the Law of Nature is in that State, put into every Mans hands, whereby every one has a right to

of a conversation they had had when the *Two Treatises* first appeared, in which he had deliberately tried to draw him out on the subject of the book's authorship; '. . . you may remember, that when I first waited of you at your Lodging as soon as I came to Towne, I fell purposely in talk of that book, and sayed that whoever had writ it, whether your self, or another, I thought him very much in the right in most things: and that he agreed perfectly with my conceptions in Patriarch non Mon; (which he had quoted) which I spoke on purpose that you might then take occasion to deny it if I were mistaken, which since I found you did not, but rather declined, [*sic*] the discourse, and turned it off to another subject; I must confesse I did then (as I doe still) entertaine some suspicions of your being the Author of it . . .'. To my mind, the fact that Tyrrell drew Locke's attention to the similarity between the *Two Treatises* and *Patriarch non Monarcha* in the course of this conversation suggests the opposite of what Wootton inferred: Tyrrell seems to have been presuming that Locke would understand that this similarity implied in some way that Locke might be the author of the *Two Treatises*, and this makes best sense if both Locke and Tyrrell knew that there had been some kind of Lockean input into *Patriarch non Monarcha*.

I should add that Wootton attributes to me the belief that the *Second Treatise* was already composed by June 1681, when *Patriarch non Monarcha* was published, and that he responds (reasonably, were it true), that Tyrrell should have remembered seeing it. Even in *Natural Rights Theories* I did not commit myself to such a claim, restricting myself to talk of 'Lockean material' and 'the basic material' of the *Two Treatises* being available to Tyrrell. If I am right now in supposing that a critique of Pufendorf underpins the *Second Treatise*, and that Locke had only begun such a critique in June 1681, then clearly there could be no question of Tyrrell seeing anything which would have resembled the finished version of the *Second Treatise*.

[9] Compare Locke's hesitancy about the term in his 1664 Oxford lectures on the law of nature: it appears only once, in the context of a summary of the Hobbesian position. *Essays on the Law of Nature*, p. 163.

punish the transgressors of that Law to such a Degree, as may hinder its Violation. (§7)

This is the claim that Locke referred to as something which 'will seem a very strange Doctrine to some Men', and whose strangeness has sometimes been taken for granted as a consequence (even by Laslett); but, in fact, Locke clearly had the long-standing argument about punishing non-Europeans for their breaches of the natural law, and was using the familiar Grotian argument against 'some Men', who must principally have included Pufendorf. As we saw in the previous chapter, a critique of Grotius on this matter was one of the central features of Pufendorf's work. Locke was even led to use an argument Grotius had put forward in the manuscript of *De Indis*, but which did not appear (at least in quite this form) in *De Iure Belli ac Pacis*, that the obviousness of this natural right to punish could be seen from the fact that a 'Prince or State' could 'put to death, or punish an Alien, for any crime be commits in their Country'; but the way he developed this point showed clearly enough what was on his mind.

'Tis certain their Laws by vertue of any Sanction they receive from the promulgated Will of the Legislative, reach not a Stranger. They speak not to him, nor if they did, is he bound to hearken to them. The Legislative Authority, by which they are in Force over the Subjects of that Common-wealth, hath no Power over him. Those who have the Supream Power of making Laws in *England*, *France* or *Holland*, are to an *Indian*, but like the rest of the World, Men without Authority: And therefore if by the Law of Nature, every Man hath not a Power to punish Offences against it, as he soberly judges the Case to require, I see not how the Magistrates of any Community, can *punish an Alien* of another Country. (§9)

From talking about the power of a magistrate over a visiting alien, Locke slipped insensibly into talking about the apparently wholly different case of punishment visited by European nations upon the inhabitants of America for sins against the natural law.

The same implicit polemic against Pufendorf can, I think, be detected in chapter IV, where Locke discussed slavery. Ostensibly, Locke's target here was of course 'Sir R. F.', and to refute him Locke restated more or less Grotius's view—that 'perfect' slavery, including an arbitrary right on the master's part to kill his slave, was only the result of taking captives in war; 'imperfect' slavery could be the result of voluntary cession of liberty, but would not then extend to the loss of rights to life—it was after all to preserve his life that the voluntary slave must have entered servitude in the first place. The former relationship had no contractual element in it, while the latter did. On neither view did patriarchal government have anything to do with it. But is should be stressed that Locke here, and in his legal drafts for Carolina, fully accepted 'an Absolute, Arbitrary, Despotical Power' possessed by a master over a slave taken in war, with 'the power to kill him, at any time' (§24). This should be stressed because Pufendorf was, once again, critical of Grotius on just this issue: in *De Iure Naturali* he argued that

> as, by the Right of War, an Enemy may fairly be killed; so the Conqueror may, if he pleaseth, give him his Life, upon his Promise of perpetual Service. In which Contract and Composition, the Good which the vanquished receives, is the Security of his Life, which, by the Right of War, might have been taken away; and the Good which he engages to bring to the Victor, is his Service and Obedience.[10]

Only if the slave was actually in chains, argued Pufendorf, was there no contractual element in the master–slave relationship, and hence an arbitrary power over the life of the slave—a position (as he acknowledged) in some ways closer to Hobbes than to Grotius or Locke. Those people who have occasionally said (like David Brion Davis) that Locke on slavery 'shows how remote abolitionism was from even the more liberal minds of the late seventeenth century',[11] ought to reckon with the fact that on his desk while he was writing the Second Treatise lay a much more liberal account of slavery, which he deliberately rejected.

But it is chapter V of the *Second Treatise*, the great chapter on property, in which Locke's strategy of defending Grotius against Pufendorf's criticisms is most clear (and which, as I suggested above, may have been written in its entirety after Locke embarked on his critique of Pufendorf). Let us remember what I said in the previous chapter about the way in which Pufendorf diverged from Grotius on the issue of property and colonization. In *De Iure Belli ac Pacis*, Grotius had argued that there was an absolute natural right, possessed by all

[10] *The Law of Nature and Nations*, trans. Basil Kennet (5th edn. London, 1,749), 613 (VI. 3. 6).

[11] David Brion Davis, *The Problem of Slavery in Western Culture* (Oxford University Press, New York, 1966), 121.

individuals, to occupy any portion of the earth's surface which was capable of cultivation but which was being left waste. A kind of political control, 'Jurisdiction', could be exercised over uncultivated territory—the armies of a local prince could roam over it and compel obedience, just as the fleets of a naval power could police the oceans. But such a prince could not forbid strangers from occupying the waste, provided they were willing to accept his jurisdiction; if he tried to prevent them, he would have broken the law of nature, and might be punished by any measures up to dispossession and death.

Pufendorf denied that this was so. There was strictly speaking no such thing as a 'natural' right to private property at all—even the right privately to consume some fruit of the earth was really a matter of human convention, the result of an agreement not to seize things from one another's mouths. Recognition of general human rights depended upon their being in some way functional to a 'cultured' and 'polished' life, and that might permit rights to occupy uncultivated or even uncultivatable territory (such as the ocean). As he said in the *Elementa*, in a striking image, a prince can be said to occupy an entire palace, even if he does not use every room in it—indeed, we might say the apogee of contemporary 'culture' and 'polish' was reached in a palace, at Versailles, where it was inconceivable that the prince could use every room. It followed that the native peoples of America had as good property rights in their ancestral forests as the Europeans had in their ancestral farmlands, and that the colonizing projects were morally highly dubious.

In chapter V of the *Second Treatise*, Locke went even further than Grotius had done in defence of the colonial enterprise as it had actually taken shape. He began, as is well known, with the claim that God has given the world to men in common, 'to make use of it to the best advantage of Life, and convenience' (§26). This is a claim that recurs throughout the *Two Treatises*, in different forms, and it was of course quite close to Pufendorf's initial assumptions about property. But Locke argued that because the world was thus given

> for the use of Men, there must of necessity be a means *to appropriate* them some way or other before they can be of any use, or at all beneficial to any particular Man. The Fruit, or Venison, which nourishes the wild Indian, who knows no Inclosure, and is still a Tenant in common, must be his, and so his, *i.e.* a part of

him, that another can no longer have any right to it, before it can do him any good for the support of his Life. (§26)

This must be directed against Pufendorf's idea that there is no natural right to consumption: Locke is arguing that God's gift was pointless unless there is property in the article we are about to consume, and therefore that on Pufendorf's own assumptions there must be such a right. Furthermore, Locke developed the so-called 'labour theory of impropriation' explicitly to deal with this problem, and thereby made more precise something which was essentially in Grotius's theory, but which Grotius had not himself been under any pressure to define.

He that is nourished by the Acorns he pickt up under an Oak, or the Apples he gathered from the Trees in the Wood, has certainly appropriated them to himself. No Body can deny but the nourishment is his. I ask then, When did they begin to be his? When he digested? Or when he eat? Or when he boiled? Or when he brought them home? Or when he pickt them up? And 'tis plain, if the first gathering made them not his, nothing else could. That *labour* put a distinction between them and common. (§28)

Locke used as his example of this principle, it comes as no surprise to find, the right to fish in 'the Ocean, that great and still remaining Common of Mankind' (§30).

The clear Grotian roots of this theory are further revealed, in a particularly striking way, by Locke's response to the objection that a natural right to consumption will lead to waste. As is again familiar, Locke argued that because God gave the world to mankind to enjoy, 'as much as any one can make use of to any advantage of life before it spoils; so much he may by his labour fix a Property in. Whatever is beyond this, is more than his share, and belongs to others' (§31). This is fairly clearly related to—or even derived from—a notable passage in Grotius's *De Veritate Religionis Christianae*, which I quoted in an earlier chapter:

our natural needs are satisfied with only a few things, which may be easily had without great labour or cost. As for what God has granted us in addition, we are commanded not to throw it into the sea (as some Philosophers foolishly asserted), nor to leave it unproductive [*inutile*], nor to waste it, but to use it to meet the needs [*inopiam*] of other men, either by giving it away, or by lending it to those who ask; as is appropriate for those who believe themselves to be not owners [*dominos*] of these things, but representatives or stewards [*procuratores ac dispensatores*] of God the Father.[12]

With these principles in place, Locke proceeded (in paragraphs 36 onwards) to make clearer than anyone had hitherto done the right to settle in the 'vacant places of America'. As he documented with great care, agriculture was far more productive of resources than hunting, and could therefore keep upwards (he alleged) of a hundred times more people alive and well fed—'for I aske whether in the wild woods and uncultivated wast of America left to Nature, without any improvement, tillage or husbandry, a thousand acres will yield the needy and wretched inhabitants as many conveniences of life as ten acres of equally fertile land does in Devonshire where they are well cultivated?' (§37). He also—and this, I believe, was a wholly original idea—argued that it was the absence of a general money, acceptable in a wide geographical area (as gold and silver were in the Old World) which had stopped the American Indians from developing proper agriculture. Interestingly, the commoner view (found among others in Pufendorf) was that money had come in 'after our Luxury had increased our Necessities, and we, not content with the Produce of our own Soil, had a mind to the Delicacies of other Nations' (V. I. II)—Locke was deliberately treating as a necessity something which other writers dismissed as a luxury.

So far, Locke might have been seen simply as a careful and thoughtful follower of Grotius, who had added little to his master's fundamental ideas. But in chapter VIII, *Of the Beginning of Political Societies*, he revealed his divergence from Grotius. Again, the basic argument is quite well known, though its significance in this context has never (I think) been realized. Locke argued that an individual consents to be part of a political community or commonwealth, 'and submits to the Community those Possessions, which he has, or shall acquire, that do not already belong to any other Government' (§120), and of course that he does so in order to protect all his property—both material possessions and his own person.

But since the Government has a direct Jurisdiction only over the Land, and reaches the Possessor of it, (before he has actually incorporated himself in the Society) only as he dwells upon, and enjoys that: *The Obligation* any one is

[12] Grotius, *Opera Omnia Theologica* (London, 1679), III, 43 (II. 14).

under, by Virtue of such Enjoyment, *to submit to the Government, begins and ends with the Enjoyment*. . . (§121)

The implication of this argument is that government follows the ownership of land: only if land has been brought into cultivation and thereby appropriated, can a government claim jurisdiction over it. Locke was fully aware (and indeed it is an important part of his argument at this point) that once a landowner had put his land under the jurisdiction of his political community or commonwealth, his descendants could not easily withdraw it from the commonwealth's control; but he was clear that a commonwealth could only claim jurisdiction over the territory under its control if that territory had been at some point brought into private ownership through cultivation. It followed that the kings of America could not claim jurisdiction over the waste lands (indeed, Locke was hesitant about whether they could claim to be full commonwealths at all—see his remarks at II §102), and that European settlers did not need to acknowledge their rights. The Dutch practice of buying land in order to indemnify themselves against the claims of the native rulers was thus, on Locke's account, illogical and unnecessary.

I could give many other examples of Locke's implicit criticisms of Pufendorf, but they would in most cases take me away from my main theme. One that is perhaps worth remarking on, however, is Locke's claim that absolute monarchy 'can be no Form of Civil Government at all' (II §90). As we saw earlier, Tyrrell had enthusiastically translated the sections of Pufendorf's *De Iure Naturali* which deal with sovereignty; Pufendorf said in these sections that 'a People who have given themselves under the Command of an absolute Sovereign, have no more a Right of regaining their Liberty by Force, than I have of recovering a Thing by Force, which I have already, upon Bargain, deliver'd to another Man' (VII. 8. 7). Pufendorf was prepared to qualify this somewhat; but Locke was determined to insist that no absolute Sovereign could count as the ruler of a true commonwealth. In this respect, of course, Locke was not putting himself forward as the defender of Grotius against Pufendorf, but was being equally critical of both the natural lawyers, as well as Filmer and (probably) Hobbes. On the other hand, in his famous view (II §149) that 'the *Community* may be said . . . to be *always the Supream Power*' whose agent any legal sovereign (legislative assembly or whatever) must be considered to be, Locke was close to the Grotian view that the *civitas* is itself the 'common subject' of sovereignty; and his denial that this was compatible with absolutism was strikingly similar to Grotius's original use of the argument in the *De Indis*.

In summary, we find in the *Second Treatise* a political theory which vindicates a private right of punishment against people or nations which break the law of nature; which allows arbitrary powers of life and death to the masters of slaves taken in war; and which allows settlers to occupy the lands of native peoples without consulting their wishes in any way. This theory is associated with an argument against the absolute powers of European rulers; but it might almost be said that one of the chief things which was wrong with such rulers, in Locke's eyes, was that they were behaving like wild Indians and claiming rights which sober agricultural settlers ought not to acknowledge. Indeed, Locke came quite close to saying this explicitly when he talked about the absolute prince being in a state of nature with regard to his subjects, and remarked that 'he that would have been insolent and injurious in the Woods of *America*, would not probably be much better in a Throne' (II §92),

This concentration on America and its problems needs some special explanation: it is not enough simply to treat it as a metaphor put to use in order to refute Sir Robert Filmer. The refutation of Filmer was the express object of the *First Treatise* or 'Book I', not of 'Book II'; moreover, much of what we have traced out as Locke's theory in the *Second Treatise* has very little real relevance to Filmer's case—Pufendorf, as Tyrrell perceived, was entirely adequate as a theorist to use against patriarchalism, and Locke's repeated dissociation of his views from those of Pufendorf must have been motivated by some other consideration than the need to score a polemical triumph over Filmer.

In part, the explanation is, as I have suggested, simply Locke's long-standing and independent interest in the colonizing projects. But his turning in 1681 to a defence of them in these terms was prompted, I suspect, by one event of great significance to the radical Whigs—the virtual defection from their cause of William Penn, and the foundation of Pennsylvania. A royal charter was given to Penn in March 1681 allowing him to found his colony: down to that time, Penn like many other leading Quakers had been a supporter of the radical Whig line on exclusion, and seems to have been a friend of Locke, but after the charter he steadily drifted away from the radicals. When the Duke of York finally came to the throne, Penn even acted as one of his more influential advisers. It is not unnatural to suppose (as many contemporaries, and some subsequent historians have done) that Penn's defection was in part connected with this massive grant to him.

Penn's attitude to the Indians in his colony has become legendary, but the legend is founded on fact: Penn undeniably sought to treat the native inhabitants as possessors of rights over the territory of Pennsylvania. As early as October 1681 he was writing to the Indian kings in the area assuring them 'that I am very sensible of the unkindness and injustice that has been too much exercised towards you by the people of these parts of the world', and in June 1682 he wrote to 'the Emperor of Canada' that 'The great God, that made thee and me and all the world, incline our hearts to love peace and justice that we may live friendly together as becomes the workmanship of the great God. The king of England, who is a great prince, has for divers reasons granted to me a large country in America which, however, I am willing to enjoy upon friendly terms with thee.'[13] The initial instructions he sent to his agents in 1681 ordered them 'to buy land of the true owners, which I think is the Susquehanna people' and 'to treat speedily with the Indians for land before they are furnished by others with things that please them'.[14] Penn's whole approach was diametrically opposite to that of Locke, and the founding of Pennsylvania represented a major challenge to the principles upon which the English colonies had so far been planted in America. Locke seems to have been suspicious not only of Penn's generosity to the Indians, but also of the absolutist tendencies displayed by Penn's 'frame of government' for the settlers—in 1686 he wrote an extensive critique of the constitution, attacking it for its 'dangerous' and 'unlimited' powers.[15] So Pennsylvania represented all the things which Locke was attacking in the *Second Treatise*.

If I am right in suggesting that much of the *Second Treatise* can be read as a defence of Grotius's conclusions against the attacks levelled at them by Pufendorf, then the natural question that arises is whether Locke was similarly concerned to defend Grotius's *premisses*. In other words, was Locke's conception of human sociability the narrow conception of Grotius, in which natural men did not harm one another, but did not provide each other with positive assistance, or was its

[13] Jean R. Soderlund, ed., *William Penn and the Founding of Pennsylvania, 1680–1684: A Documentary History* (University of Pennsylvania Press, 1983), 88 and 156.

[14] Ibid. 89.

[15] Bodleian, Locke MS, f. g, ff. 33–41.

Pufendorf's wider conception, in which human beings offered each other mutual aid? This is an extremely important question in the interpretation of Locke, but it should be said that it is remarkably difficult to answer. In his early lectures on natural law, Locke appears to have taken a broad view of the scope of natural law, treating (for example) the conferring of a benefit as falling within it.[16] 'Those precepts of the law of nature which are absolute and which embrace thefts, debaucheries, and slanders, and on the other hand religion, charity, fidelity and the rest, these I say, and others of that kind, are binding on all men in the world equally, kings as well as subjects [etc.].'[17] However, only three years later, in his *Essay Concerning Toleration*, he drew a firm distinction between the maintenance of the 'peace, safety or security' of a society, and the exercise of moral virtue more generously defined. He went so far as to write (though in a passage which he later struck out—an action which neatly reveals his uncertainty on just this issue) that

> even charity itself, which is certainly the great duty both of a man and a Christian, hath not yet in its full latitude an universal right to toleration, since there are some parts and instances of it which the magistrate hath absolutely forbidden, and that for ought I could ever hear without any offence to the tenderest consciences, for who doubts that to relieve with alms the poor, though beggars (if one sees them in want), is, if considered absolutely, a virtue and every man's particular duty, yet this is amongst us prohibited by a law, and the rigour of a penalty, and yet nobody in this case complains of the violation of his conscience, or the loss of his liberty.[18]

If charity can rightly be forbidden by a civil law, it is hard to see how it can be obliged by the natural law, at least in the same sense as justice is.

By the time of the *Second Treatise*, we have the famous proposition that the natural law 'teaches all Mankind, who will but consult it, that being all equal and independent, no one ought to harm another in his Life, Health, Liberty, or Possessions'. This is so because, all being God's workmanship,

> Every one as he is *bound to preserve himself*, and not to quit his Station wilfully; so by the like reason when his own Preservation comes not in competition, ought he, as much as he can, *to preserve the rest of Mankind*, and may not unless it be to do Justice on an Offender, take away, or impair the life, or what tends

[16] *Essays on the Law of Nature*, 213. At p. 157 Locke endorsed a precis of Grotius's words in the *Prolegomena* about human sociability, but we do not know precisely how he interpreted Grotius's theory at this time.

[17] Ibid. 197.

[18] *Political Writings*, ed. David Wootton, p. 196.

to the Preservation of the Life, the Liberty, Health, Limb or Goods of another. (§6)

Locke's exposition at this point did not use any idea of human sociability, whether of a Grotian or a Pufendorfian complexion. But we should remember how Grotius had distinguished between the obligations of natural law, and those of civil law: under civil law,

first, *Individual citizens should not only refrain from injuring other citizens, but should furthermore protect them, both as a whole and as individuals;* secondly, *Citizens should not only refrain from seizing one another's possessions, whether these be held privately or in common, but should furthermore contribute individually both that which is necessary to other individuals and that which is necessary to the whole.*[19]

Judged according to these criteria, a natural obligation to 'preserve the rest of Mankind' sounds more like the kind of obligation which Grotius had wished to restrict to civil society, and therefore more like Pufendorf's conception of the natural law.

This seems to be confirmed by Locke's remarks at II §128, where he summarized his view of the state of nature in the following terms.

In the State of Nature, to omit the liberty he has of innocent Delights, a Man has two Powers.

The first is to do whatsoever he thinks fit for the preservation of himself and others within the permission of the *Law of Nature*: by which Law common to them all, he and the rest of *Mankind are one Community*, make up one Society distinct from all other Creatures. And were it not for the corruption, and vitiousness of degenerate Men, there would be no need of any other; no necessity that Men should separate from this great and natural Community, and by positive agreements combine into smaller and divided associations.

The other power a Man has in the State of Nature, is the *power to punish the Crimes* committed against that Law. Both these he gives up, when he joyns in a private, if I may so call it, or particular Political Society, and incorporates into any Commonwealth, separate from the rest of Mankind.

However, Locke's marked refusal to talk in detail about human natural sociability, together with both the clear limits which he always put upon the extent of the natural obligation to preserve other men,[20]

[19] *De Jure Praedae Commentarius*, I trans. Gwladys L. Williams and Walter H. Zeydel (Oxford University Press, 1950) 21.

[20] See for a good example his remarks on exploitation in a foreign famine, in his essay *Venditio* (*Political Writings*, ed. David Wootton, p. 445).

and his insistence that the limits on our accumulation of property are intrinsic to the idea of property, rather than the effect of distributive justice (a term he scarcely mentions in his works), all served to qualify his acceptance of the Pufendorfian account. His evasiveness on this issue must be reckoned a major element in his argumentative strategy, for he was able to undercut Pufendorf's conclusions without obviously and unequivocally departing from his opponent's premisses; and that turned out to be a very popular strategy for writers in the next generation, many of whom specifically called Locke in aid for their project.

Commentators on Pufendorf

One of the best examples of this is Jean Barbeyrac, who first and most assiduously documented the conflict between Locke and Pufendorf, and who committed himnself firmly to Locke's side on one of its central issues. A French Protestant (whose uncle had known Locke), Barbeyrac was forced out of France as a boy by the Revocation of the Edict of Nantes in 1685, the practical consequence of which was, of course, the expulsion of the Protestants. He was brought up in Lausanne, tried briefly to make a career for himself in Prussia but failed because of his heterodox religious views, and then became a succesful professor, first of civil law and history at Lausanne and second of jurisprudence at Groningen in the United Provinces. In 1706 he produced a French translation and edition of Pufendorf's *De Iure Naturali*, heavily annotated, and in 1724 a companion edition of Grotius's *De Iure Belli*. Both editions were translated into English, and were widely circulated. Barbeyrac accepted the validity of Pufendorf's account of natural sociability, and also accepted Pufendorf's insinuation that it was a reasonable extension of Grotius's account; no doubt partly as a consequence, he also sympathized with Pufendorf's critique of Grotius on colonization, and distanced himself from Locke in this area. He commented on Grotius's argument in II. 2. 17 of *De Iure Belli ac Pacis* about the occupation of vacant land that

> I am not of our Author's Opinion in this Point; nor can I think the Reason here alledged solid. All the Land within the Compass of each respective Country is really occupied; tho' every Part of it is not cultivated, or assigned to any one in particular: It all belongs to the Body of the People.[21]

[21] *The Rights of War and Peace, in Three Books* (London, 1738), 156.

And he similarly dissented from Grotius on the question of *dominium maris*.[22] He was sympathetic to the views of the late seventeenth-century Dutch jurist Bynkershoek, who had argued that the seas could be owned by nations who could maintain an effective military presence over them (though in practice that usually meant only coastal waters)—the United Provinces had become much more interested in the possibility of *dominium maris* as English naval power had grown.[23]

But Barbeyrac was vehement in his opposition to Pufendorf's discussion of punishment, saying that Pufendorf

> here leaves Grotius, and in my Opinion, without any Necessity; tho' he is very much followed in that Respect, by those Authors who have lately written Treatises of the Law of Nature . . . However I will contradict them . . . with so much the more Confidence, since, besides the Advantage of defending Grotius, I shall only follow the Opinion of Mr. Locke.[24]

And he revealed his motive for this opposition when he remarked (in a note to VIII. 6. 3) that the Protestant princes might with a good conscience

> unite to destroy the Inquisition, and to oblige the Powers, who suffer it in their Dominions, to suppress this horrid Tribunal, under which Christianity has groaned so long. It would be a laudable Undertaking to destroy a Court, which, under a false Pretence of Zeal for the Glory of God, exercises the most detestable Tyranny, and the most contrary to the Good of human Society. Those who love to gain Glory by Arms could never find a more honourable, or lawful Occasion of signalizing [*sic*] their Courage; supposing they had Force enough to attempt such an Enterprize.[25]

The prospect of a general European war on behalf of Protestantism had also awakened the aged Locke's enthusiasm at the beginning of the War of the Spanish Succession.[26]

Even more of a Lockean gloss on Pufendorf was provided by the principal British commentator on Pufendorf, the Scot Gershom Carmichael. He produced a commentary on Pufendorf's *De Officio Hominis et Civis* in 1718 for the use of his students at Glasgow, in which Locke's theory of property was expressly defended against the views of Pufendorf, and in which he insisted that the Lockean rather than the

[22] *The Rights of War and Peace*, 147 n. 9.

[23] See Cornelis van Bynkershoek, *De Dominio Maris*, ed. James Bell Scott, trans. Ralp Van Deman Magoffin (Carnegie Endowment for International Peace, New York, 1923).

[24] *The Law of Nature and Nations*, trans. Basil Kennet, p. 762, n. 8.

[25] Ibid. 837. See also his remarks in his note to II. 5. 6, pp. 186–7.

[26] *Correspondence*, ed. E. De Beer (Oxford University Press, 1982) VII pp 291, 526.

Pufendorfian conditions should apply to the occupation of vacant land.[27] As James Moore and Michael Silverthorne have observed, Carmichael's use of Locke to elucidate Pufendorf in fact predated Barbeyrac's, as he was already praising the *Second Treatise* in his unpublished lectures on Pufendorf at Glasgow in 1702–3.[28] This tough-minded approach to problems of war and peace remained characteristic of British writers—thus Carmichael's successor at Glasgow, Francis Hutcheson, could argue that pre-emptive strikes against dangerously powerful nations were justifiable.

As among the members of a free state there may be potent reasons for preventing such immoderate acquisitions of a few, tho' made by innocent means, as may be dangerous to the whole body, there are the like reasons why neighbouring states should insist on proper securities from their safety from any one which is exceedingly increasing in power, or they may put a stop to its increase by force.[29]

Hutcheson also entirely accepted the Lockean account of acquisition of property, saying that

Mankind must not for ages be excluded from the earth *God* intended they should enjoy, to gratify the vain ambition of a few who would retain what they cannot use, while others are in inconvenient straits. Neighbouring states, upon offering a rateable share of the charges of the first discovery and occupation, have a right to obtain such lands as the first discoverers cannot cultivate.[30]

It is interesting that Hutcheson's English contemporary, the Regius Professor of Divinity at Cambridge, Thomas Rutherforth (to whose interest and importance Peter Miller has drawn our attention),[31] argued forcefully in his lectures on Grotius that Locke's account of property was in general quite mistaken—adding labour to something that was owned by someone else could not make it one's own, so how could it remove it from the common ownership of humanity?[32] All property rights were (as Pufendorf had alleged) conventional in character, and

[27] Samuel Puffendorf [*sic*], *De Officio Hominis et Civis* (Edinburgh, 1724), 212–16 and 221.

[28] James Moore and Michael Silverthorne, 'Gershoom Carmichael and the Natural Jurisprudence Tradition in Eighteenth-Century Scotland', in *Wealth and Virtue*, ed. Istvan Hont and Michael Ignatieff (Cambridge, 1983), 73–87.

[29] Francis Hutcheson, *A System of Moral Philosophy, in Three Books*, ed. Francis Hutcheson yr. (Glasgow, 1755), II, 350 (III. 10. 3).

[30] *A System of Moral Philosophy*, I, 328 (II. 7. 3).

[31] *Defining the Common Good: Empire, Religion and Philosophy in Eighteenth-Century Britain* (Cambridge University Press, 1994), 142–9.

[32] *Institutes of Natural Law. Being the Substance of a Course of Lectures on Grotius* De Jure Belli et [*sic*] Pacis *read in St. Johns College Cambridge* (Cambridge, 1754–6), I, 50–61.

consequently cultivation was irrelevant. Thus a nation might 'keep up' its claim to territory

> without any cultivation or use of the land, by including it from time to time, when the nation has made perambulations to ascertain the boundaries of its territories, or by setting up standing land-marks, or by notice to all persons, who have come thither for the purpose of setting upon it, to withdraw.[33]

This was an extremely rare example of a British writer repudiating Locke on colonization; but Rutherforth could not bring himself to abandon the general British hesitation about notions like natural sociability, and indeed he produced one of the most Hobbesian general moral theories available to the mid-eighteenth century, insisting in his lectures that the only societies are civil societies, and that 'all mankind are not one civil society'; prior to their entry into civil society, men were Hobbesian individuals with no objective moral rules to govern them.[34] It is not entirely clear how Rutherforth proposed to fit these two aspects of his theory together.[35]

MONTESQUIEU

Perhaps the most interesting attempt to give a theoretical expression to the conjunction of these two ideas—that the state of nature is one of human sociability and that quite extensive warfare is permitted in the international realm—was provided by Montesquieu. *The Spirit of the Laws* does not at first sight look like a contribution to the kind of literature which I have been discussing; in particular, it appears to be very far removed from the tradition of natural jurisprudence. But that appearance is to some extent deceptive: the work incorporates many of the *pensées* which Montesquieu had drafted while he was working on his projected *Traité des Devoirs*, and in them Montesquieu had explicitly

[33] *Institutes of Natural Law*. II, 481.

[34] When a man 'becomes a member of a civil society, the public or body politic claims a right of pointing out to him what is just and unjust, and of directing him likewise what good he is to do, and in what manner he is to do it. There is no way of making such a claim as this consistent with his natural right of thinking and chusing for himself; unless by his own consent, either express or tacit, he has waved this right, and has voluntarily agreed to be so guided and directed'. Ibid. II, 18; see II, 15 for the remark about mankind not being one civil society.

[35] The British seem in general to have been associated in the minds of continental writers with a moral casualness about war—e.g. Voltaire made the spokesman for cynical belligerence in his dialogue *Du Droit de la Guerre* into an Englishman. *Oeuvres Complètes*, ed. L. Moland (Paris, 1877–85), XXVI, 368–75.

engaged with the texts of natural jurisprudence such as Hobbes and Grotius.[36] The second chapter of *The Spirit of the Laws* itself still took the form of a critique of Hobbes, which (as we shall see) was enormously influential on Rousseau—though Rousseau dissented from it in an instructive fashion.

Montesquieu's central idea in this critique, and his solution to the problem I have diagnosed, was to propose that the state of nature, understood as a state in which *individuals* might find themselves, is indeed a state of sociability, but understood as a state in which *nations* find themselves, it is a state of war. The full passage in *The Spirit of the Laws* reads:

A man in the state of nature . . . would at first feel only his weakness; his timidity would be extreme: and as for evidence, if it is needed on this point, savages have been found in forests; everything makes them tremble, everything makes them flee.

In this state, each feels himself inferior; he scarcely feels himself an equal. Such men would not seek to attack one another, and peace would be the first natural law.

Hobbes gives men first the desire to subjugate one another, but this is not reasonable. The idea of empire and domination is so complex and depends on so many other ideas, that it would not be the one they would first have.

Hobbes asks, *If men are not naturally in a state of war, why do they always carry arms and why do they have keys to lock their doors?* But one feels that what can happen to men only after the establishment of societies, which induced them to find motives for attacking others and for defending themselves, is attributed to them before that establishment.

Man would add the feeling of his needs to the feeling of his weakness. Thus another natural law would be the one inspiring him to seek nourishment.

I have said that fear would lead men to flee one another, but the marks of mutual fear would soon persuade them to approach one another. They would also be so inclined by the pleasure one animal feels at the approach of an animal of its own kind. In addition, the charm that the two sexes inspire in each other by their difference would increase this pleasure, and the natural entreaty they always make to one another would be a third law.

Besides feelings, which belong the outset, they also succeed in gaining knowledge; thus they have a second bond, which other animals do not have.

[36] See his *Pensées. Le Spicilège*, ed. Louis Desgraves (Paris Robert Laffont, 1991), 422–6 (*pensées* 1266 and 1267). See also his remark on pp. 494 and 573 (*pensées* 1537 and 1863): 'Je rends grâce à Messieurs Grotius et Puffendorf d'avoir si bien exécuté ce qu'une partie de cet ouvrage demandait de moi, avec cette hauteur de génie, à laquelle je n'aurais pu atteindre.'

Therefore, they have another motive for uniting, and the desire to live in society is a fourth natural law . . .

As soon as men are in society, they lose their feeling of weakness; the equality that was among them ceases, and the state of war begins.

Each particular society comes to feel its strength, producing a state of war among nations. The individuals within each society begin to feel their strength; they seek to turn to their favor the principal advantages of this society, which brings about a state of war among them . . .[37]

The state of war between nations, Montesquieu argued, was one in which quite far-reaching rights of war were permitted, including (notably) a right to make pre-emptive strikes out of fear.

The life of states is like that of men. Men have the right to kill in the case of natural defense; states have the right to wage war for their own preservation. In the case of natural defense, I have the right to kill, because my life is mine, as the life of the one who attacks me is his; likewise a state wages war because its preservation is just, as is any other preservation. Among citizens, the right to natural defense does not carry with it a necessity to attack. Instead of attacking they have the recourse of the tribunals. Therefore, they can exercise that right of defense only in cases that occur so suddenly that one would be lost if one waited for the aid of laws. But among societies, the right of natural defense sometimes carries with it a necessity to attack, when one people sees that a longer peace would put another people in a position to destroy it and that an attack at this moment is the only way to prevent such destruction. Hence small societies more frequently have the right to wage wars than large ones, because they are more frequently in a position to fear being destroyed.[38]

Montesquieu's idea was a characteristically subtle one. He was not denying the force of the analogy between the international arena and the state of natural individuals: similar principles governed each of them. But, one might say, the *balance* of the principles was different: states would be governed much more by fear and much less by human sociability, partly because they are not sexual beings and therefore will not be pulled by their sexual feelings into relationships of attachment. As a result, Montesquieu's theory was less liable to tip over into Hobbesianism on close examination than that of most of his predeces-

[37] *The Spirit of the Laws*, ed. Anne M. Cohler, Basia Carolyn Miller, and Harold Samuel Stone (Cambridge University Press, 1989), 6–7. This passage was based on the fragment of his projected *Traité des Devoirs*, *pensée* 1266.

[38] *The Spirit of the Laws*, I. 10. 2, p. 138.

sors in this tradition. But, of course, by the same token it was much less a theory of *individual autonomy* than they had usually wanted—and far less than Rousseau and Kant were to desire.

Wolff

These attempts in the first half of the eighteenth century to restate the ideology of the commercial powers disturbed those who were still loyal to the practical conclusions of Pufendorf, though they found it surprisingly difficult to reassert the original character of Pufendorf's work. The best example of someone who tried to do so was the Prussian theorist Christian Wolff. Wolff is best known, probably, for his role as an extender and systematizer of Leibniz's ideas, and for his tempestuous relationship with the Prussian government—dismissed by Frederick William I from his post at the University of Halle in 1723 for religious heterodoxy, his reinstatement in 1740 was a famous gesture by Frederick the Great to the world of the *philosophes*, by which the new king symbolized his dissociation from the policies of his father. During the 1740s Wolff published a vast work on natural law, dedicated to Frederick, the last volume of which (1749) was devoted to the law of nations. I do not want here to discuss Wolff's philosophical underpinnings to his theory; but it is worth drawing attention to the way in which his account of the *content* of the law of nations followed Pufendorf, though starting from a rather different basis.

Wolff first accepted that a state of nature, whether of individuals or nations, is sociable in character: 'Nature herself has established society among all nations and binds them to preserve society. For nature herself has established society among men and binds them to preserve it.'[39] The essence of this sociableness was, as in Pufendorf, the desire for mutual aid—'the purpose of natural society, and consequently of that society which nature herself has established among men, is to give mutual assistance in perfecting itself and its condition . . . consequently the promotion of the common good by its combined powers' (§8).

But he differed from Pufendorf in arguing that this commonality could not be promoted unless nations formed some kind of global political entity: particular states promoted the principles of general

[39] Christian Wolff, *Jus Gentium Methodo Scientifica Pertractatum*, ed. Otfried Nippold, trans. Joseph H. Drake and Francis J. Hemelt (Carnegie Endowment for International Peace, Oxford University Press, 1934), II, 11(§7).

human society through civic institutions, and what he called the 'supreme state' consisting of individual nations would do the same.

All nations are understood to have come together into a state, whose separate members are separate nations, or individual states. For nature herself has established society among all nations and compels them to preserve it, for the purpose of promoting the common good by their combined powers. Therefore since a society of men united for the purpose of promoting the common good by their combined powers, is a state, nature herself has combined nations into a state. (§9)

This 'supreme state' was established for 'common security' (see, for example, §652); it is a democracy of equal nations (§19), in which the will of the majority should prevail, and which possesses 'some sovereignty' over the individual nations (§15). But since

all the nations scattered throughout the whole world cannot assemble together, as is self-evident, that must be taken to be the will of all nations which they are bound to agree upon, if following the leadership of nature they use right reason. Hence it is plain, because it has to be admitted, that what has been approved by the more civilized nations is the law of nations. (§20)

The supreme state can even be thought of as having a ruler, though Wolff was at pains to stress that this was a 'fiction': 'he can be considered the ruler of the supreme state who, following the leadership of nature, defines by the right use of reason what nations ought to consider as law among themselves' (§21).

We can understand the relationship between natural sociability and the supreme state in Wolff as follows. In a state of nature, individuals display the basic characteristics of sociability, including the desire for mutual assistance. Particular states are expressions of this desire, or functionally related to it—they are effective mechanisms for the practical implications of the principles of sociability. By the same token, the supreme state is also an effective mechanism for *individuals* to secure their desires: although Wolff did freely use analogies between individuals and states, his account in fact presupposed that the relations between states were designed to fulfil the desires of their individual citizens. He expressed this thought most clearly in a note to §7:

If we should consider that great society, which nature herself has established among men, to be done away with by particular societies, which men enter, when they unite into a state, states would be established contrary to the law of nature, in as much as the universal obligation of all toward all would be terminated; which assuredly is absurd. Just as in the human body individual organs do not cease to be organs of the whole human body, because certain ones taken together constitute one organ; so likewise individual men do not cease to be members of that great society which is made up of the whole human race, because several have formed together a particular society. And in so far as these act together as associates, just as if they were all of one mind and one will; even so are the members of that society united, which nature has established among men. After the human race was divided into nations, that society which before was between individuals continues between nations.

Like Pufendorf, therefore, Wolff had in effect elided the state of nature with civil society—natural men were sociable, and civil institutions were a straightforward expression of this. International law could then be seen as genuinely *law*, promulgated by a kind of organization whose object was to implement the requirements of natural sociability. And also like Pufendorf, Wolff used his theory in order to limit rather than to expand the range of moral possibilities in international affairs. Although many contemporaries were troubled by the idea of a supreme state, seeing it as a potential justification for universal monarchy of the Spanish or French type, in fact Wolff was at pains to emphasize its limitations. As he said about the sovereignty of the supreme state over its members, 'that sovereignty will seem paradoxical to some. But . . . it will be evident in its own place that nothing at all results from this, except those things which all willingly recognise as in accordance with the law of nations . . .' (§15). In particular, though one might suppose that a supreme state would claim the right to police the conduct of its members in a fashion similar to that of an ordinary civil society, Wolff stressed that Pufendorf was quite correct in assailing Grotius's theory of international punishment.

Since a punitive war is not legal except for one who has received irreparable injury from another, a punitive war is not allowed against a nation for the reason that it is very wicked, or violates dreadfully the law of nature, or offends against God . . . Grotius declares there is a just cause of war against those who are without reverence for parents, who eat human flesh, who practise piracy. But he confuses those things which are united with wrong to others with those by which no wrong is done to others. (§637)

And Wolff went even further than Pufendorf: he expressed extreme opposition to any intervention by one state in another's affairs on behalf of an oppressed or tyrannized group: 'if the ruler of a state should burden his subjects too heavily or treat them too harshly, the ruler of another state may not resist that by force' (§258); 'the decision does not rest with foreign nations as to matters arising between subjects and ruler of any state, inasmuch as they ought not to intrude themselves in the affairs of others' (§1011). Indeed, it is far from clear that Wolff regarded any form of practical resistance by citizens as legitimate (see his remarks in §§1011–12). He was also clear that 'the increasing power of a neighbouring nation and fear of the neighbour's power is not a just cause of war' (§640).

The one form of international punishment which Wolff clearly sanctioned was, as in Pufendorf, against a people who delighted in war *as such*, and who were not influenced by considerations either of justice or of utility as commonly understood (for example, reasons of state)—considerations which Wolff termed 'justifying' and 'persuasive' reasone (§621).

> Since the war of those who, influenced neither by justifying nor persuasive reasons, are carried into wars, transgress the law of humanity, if follows that belligerents of that sort, whom war as such delights, do not hesitate to injure any nations simply for self-gratification, evidently despising the natural obligation by which they are bound to other nations; and since the right belongs to nations as a whole to coerce the individual nations, if they are unwilling to satisfy their obligations, a right of war belongs to all nations in general against those who, in their eagerness for wars as such, are carried into wars for reasone neither justifying nor persuasive. (§627)

It is notable, however, that later in the book Wolff argued that a just war against 'a disturber of the public peace . . . who harasses other nations in reckless and unjust war' ought to be conducted only on the basis of formal treaties with the victim of his attacks (§§965–8).

Wolff displayed a similar unhappiness about the Grotian principles of war when he came to discuss the question of native peoples. Here, he argued (§310) that families 'which have no settled abode but wander through uncultivated wilds' will have what he termed a 'mixed community-holding' in the land.

> Since lands subject to private use or to the use of individuals in that territory in which separate families wander hither and thither are subject to the mixed community-holding of those families, and consequently, since those who are not in the number of those families are excluded from the ownership which

they have in those lands, those lands can be occupied by no one coming into the territory inhabited by these families, even if at the time those who inhabit the territory are not using those lands. Ownership is not lost by non-user [*sic*]. And if separate families wander through uncultivated places, they intend a use of the places in alternation, a thing which is readily evident, if only you turn your attention to the reason which impels them to wander through uncultivated places. (§312)

(It is worth remembering that Wolff's dismissal for heterodoxy at Halle was for the excessive praise he had lavished on the Chinese—he seems to have had a general and unusual sympathy for non-Europeans.) His view about ownership of the sea was also, as one might expect, along broadly the same lines—namely that a nation can occupy the sea in so far as there is some point to it, such as protection, though it cannot legitimately deny access to other nations for fishing and navigation (§§121–8).

Vattel

Though Wolff's work was widely praised, its implicit criticisms of the international behaviour of the commercial empires did not go unnoticed, or unanswered. The importance of Emmerich de Vattel, the last of Kant's 'sorry comforters', is that he sought to reinstate as the guiding principle of international relations what one might term the Lockean interpretation of Pufendorf—the tradition of Locke, Carmichael and Barbeyrac. Moreover, he did so as a critic both of Wolff and—though to a lesser extent—of the new way of thinking about the state of nature represented by Rousseau, which will be the subject of my next chapter. Though Vattel was born a subject of the King of Prussia, it was in the distant and anomalous territory of Neuchâtel, and he was really far more Swiss than Prussian. He failed to get permanent employment in Berlin, and from 1746 onwards worked as a diplomat and political adviser to the Elector of Saxony, one of the leaders of the opposition to Prussia in European affairs. In August 1755 he published a critical review of Rousseau's *Discourse on the Origin of Inequality* in the *Journal Helvétique*, and two years later he produced *Le Droit des Gens*. This was a year after Frederick II of Prussia had invaded Saxony and precipitated the Seven Years War; Vattel was appointed a Privy Councillor to the Elector in the course of the war.

Superficially, *Le Droit des Gens* was intended simply to be the means of conveying to 'a wider circle of readers' the ideas contained in the work of Wolff, 'this great philosopher'.[40] But, in fact, Vattel took many of Wolff's arguments and derived quite different conclusions from them. In particular, he explicitly registered his dissent from the idea of a supreme state, and insisted on the original analogy between the actual modern states system and a state of nature.

I find the fiction of such a republic neither reasonable nor well enough founded to deduce therefrom the rules of a Law of Nations at once universal in character, and necessarily accepted by sovereign States. I recognize no other natural society among Nations than that which nature has set up among men in general. It is essential to every civil society (*Civitas*) that each member should yield certain of his rights to the general body, and that there should be some authority capable of giving commands, prescribing laws, and compelling those who refuse to obey. Such an idea is not to be thought of as between Nations. Each independent state claims to be, and actually is, independent of all the others. (p. 9a)

Natural human society, for Vattel, was broadly the same as it had been for Pufendorf.

The end of the natural society established among men in general is that they should mutually assist one another to advance their own perfection and that of their conditions; and Nations, too, since they may be regarded as so many free persons living together in a state of nature, are bound mutually to advance this human society. Hence the end of the great society established by nature among all nations is likewise that of mutual assistance in order to perfect themselves and their condition. (*Introduction*, §12, p. 6)

This was also the chief point on which he had reproved Rousseau:

I do not yet see on what basis M. ROUSSEAU pretends that man is isolated in the pure state of Nature. He denies the principle of sociability, from which GROTIUS and other great Authors have deduced the whole of the Natural Law. But why should not Nature have made man apt to live in Society, as she has destined Beavers, Bees, Ants and other animals?[41]

But Vattel was aware that the practical conclusions he wished to draw did not sit very easily with a premiss of this kind, and when he

[40] Emmerich de Vattel, *Le Droit des Gens*, ed. Albert de Lapradelle, trans. Charles G. Fenwick and G. D. Gregory (Carnegie Endowment for International Peace, Washington, 1916), III, 6a–7a.

[41] Emmerich de Vattel, 'Reflexions sur le Discours de M. Rousseau touchant l'origine de l'inégalité parmi les hommes', in his *Mélanges de Littérature, de Morale et de Politique* (Neuchâtel, 1760), 82–3.

turned to discuss in detail the mutual duties of nations he observed (only half ironically) that

since one Nation owes, in its way, to another Nation the duties that one man owes to another, we may boldly lay down this general principle: Each State owes to every other State all that it owes to itself, as far as the other is in actual need of its help and such help can be given without the State neglecting its duties towards itself. Such is the eternal and immutable law of Nature. Those who may find it completely subversive of wise statesmanship will be reassured by the two following considerations.

(1) Sovereign States, or the political bodies of which society is composed, are much more self-sufficient than individual men, and mutual assistance is not so necessary among them, nor its practice so frequent. Now, in all matters which a Nations can manage for itself, no help is due it from others.

(2) The duties of a Nation to itself, and especially the care of its own safety, call for much more circumspection and reserve than an individual need exercise in giving assistance to others. (II. 1. 3, p. 114)

Having introduced these two qualifications, Vattel proceeded to restate in quite a pure form the ideas of Grotius or Locke on international relations.

For example, he took Wolff's remarks about the right to make war on states which delight in war *as such*, and proceeded to draw a conclusion which Wolff himself had expressly rejected, that war might legitimately be made against a prospectively hegemonic power:

if there should be found a restless and unprincipled Nation, ever ready to do harm to others, to thwart their purposes, and to stir up civil strife among their citizens, there is no doubt that all the others would have the right to unite together to subdue such a Nation, to discipline it, and even to disable it from doing further harm . . . The designs of Philip II of Spain were such as to make all Europe unite against him, and Henry the Great with good reason formed the plan of breaking down a power whose strength was so great and whose policy so destructive. (II. 4. 53, p. 130; see also p. 135, and the long discussion on pp. 248–52)

Vattel gave a further defence of this argument when he asserted that although there was no general supreme international state, modern Europe did form

a political system in which the Nations inhabiting this part of the world are bound together by their relations and various interests into a single body. It is no longer, as in former times, a confused heap of detached parts, each of which had but little concern for the lot of the others, and rarely troubled itself over what did not immediately affect it. The constant attention of sovereigns to all that goes on, the custom of resident ministers, the continual negotiations that take place, make of modern Europe a sort of Republic, whose members—each independent, but all bound together by a common interest—unite for the maintenance of order and the preservation of liberty. This is what has given rise to the well-known principle of the balance of power. (III. 3. 46, p. 251)

The most effective means of maintaining peace and freedom in such a republic was precisely though constantly shifting alliances against prospectively dominant powers, whereas devices such as confederations would simply lead to princes becoming 'the instruments of a power which will one day swallow up either themselves or their successors'.

In the same way, Vattel asserted first that 'it clearly follows from the liberty and independence of Nations that each has the right to govern itself as it thinks proper, and that no one of them has the least right to interfere in the government of another', but then continued

But if a prince, by violating the fundamental laws, gives his subjects a lawful cause for resisting him; if, by his insupportable tyranny, he brings on a national revolt against him, any foreign power may rightfully give assistance to an oppressed people who ask for its aid. The English justly complained of James II. The nobility and the patriotic leaders resolved to put a check upon his policy, which clearly tended to overthrow the Constitution and to destroy the liberties and the religion of the people, and they obtained the help of the United Provinces . . . To give help to a brave people who are defending their liberties against and oppressor by force of arms is only the part of justice and generosity. (II. 3. 56, p. 131; see also p. 340)

On the other hand, he was unequivocal in his agreement with Wolff that penal wars of the fully Grotian type were illegitimate, remarking

It is surprising to hear the learned and judicious Grotius tell us that a sovereign can justly take up arms to punish Nations which are guilty of grievous crimes against the natural law, which 'treat their parents in an inhuman manner, like the Sogdians, which eat human flesh, like the ancient Gauls', etc . . . Did not Grotius perceive that in spite of all the precautions added in the following paragraphs, his view opens the door to all the passions of zealots and fanatics, and gives to ambitious men pretexts without number? Mahomet and his successors laid waste to and subdued Asia to avenge the disbelief in the unity of God; and all those whom they regarded as *associateurs*, or idolaters, were victims of their fanaticism. (II. 1. 7, p. 116)

But perhaps the most revealing issue on which he separated from Wolff was the question of colonization. Again, he ostensibly agreed with Wolff that 'when a country is occupied by wandering families, like those of pastoral tribes, which move from place to place according to their needs, it is possessed by them in common. They hold it to the exclusion of other peoples'. But he promptly continued, 'But let us repeat again here . . . that the savage tribes of North America had no right to keep to themselves the whole of that vast continent' (II. 7. 97, p. 143). He had earlier justified this view in the following terms:

> The cultivation of the soil . . . is . . . an obligation imposed upon man by nature. The whole earth is designed to furnish sustenance for its inhabitants; but it can not do this unless it be cultivated. Every Nation is therefore bound by the natural law to cultivate the land which has fallen to its share . . . Those peoples, such as the ancient Germans and certain modern Tartars, who, though dwelling in fertile countries, disdain the cultivation of the soil and prefer to live by plunder, fail in their duty to themselves, injure their neighbours, and deserve to be exterminated like wild beasts of prey . . . Thus, while the conquest of the civilized Empires of Peru and Mexico was a notorious usurpation, the establishment of various colonies upon the continent of North America might, if done within just limits, have been entirely lawful. The peoples of those vast tracts of land rather roamed over them than inhabited them. (I. 7. 81, pp. 37–8; see also pp. 85–6)

In *Le Droit des Gens*, then, we have a more or less faithful version of the Grotian arguments, as developed by Locke, and we can see how the themes which we have been tracing throughout this study were still vividly alive in the middle of the eighteenth century. It was still the case that a clutch of what had originally been humanist arguments—such as the defence of colonization in these terms, or a respect for balance-of-power arguments—had great force for the *littérateurs* and politicians of eigthteenth-century Europe, and it was also still the case that an international state system describable in these terms was a model for fundamental human moral relations. Liberal politics, of the kind that both Vattel and Locke amply subscribed to, went along in their work with a willingness to envisage international adventurism and exploitation, and this was no accident: for the model of the independent moral agent upon which their liberalism was based was precisely the belligerent post-Renaissance state. On the other hand, the Prussian tradition, as represented by Pufendorf and Wolff, was wedded to a much more pacific model of human and state interaction, in which the self-protective entities of the Grotian tradition operated within a very tightly circumscribed moral framework, and there was a general respect for the autonomy of all other agents; but at the same time, that was not a tradition which put much stress on traditional liberal values *within* civil society. There is a kind of violence within liberalism of the Lockean type which goes back to its origins in the violent politics of the Renaissance, in which liberty and warfare (both civil war and international conflict) were bound together.

7

ROUSSEAU AND KANT

The Hobbesianism of Rousseau I

Sociability

As we saw in the previous chapter, even as Vattel was putting together his *Le Droit des Gens* he had become aware of the challenge to his ideas presented by a fellow Swiss, Jean-Jacques Rousseau. As we also saw, his reply to Rousseau's *Discourse on the Origin of Inequality* was very feeble, and no doubt unavoidably so: for Rousseau saw more deeply than any of his contemporaries how the natural jurisprudential tradition stemming from Pufendorf had failed. Rousseau's response was not, however, the flippant denunciation of the tradition which we find (for example) in Voltaire,[1] but a profound reconsideration of its origins, in which (in many ways) the original insights of both Grotius and Hobbes were restated in a new form. Rousseau and Kant, it can be said, were the eighteenth century's two most perceptive and interesting readers of Hobbes, both of them able to see past the vulgar denunciations of his views found in most modern writers and willing to incorporate important elements of his theories in their own.

In particular, both of them put forward ideas which were extremely close to Hobbes's, if the interpretation of Hobbes which I advanced in Chapter 4 is correct. In the case of Kant, this may have been intentional, since his view of Hobbes may have been broadly along those lines;[2] in the case of Rousseau, it is more difficult to say, for while at times he could endorse the conventional view of his age (saying, for example,

[1] One could say of Voltaire what he said of Grotius and Pufendorf, that his arguments on the subject were 'profoundly frivolous' (*Oeuvres Complètes*, ed. L. Moland (Paris, 1877–85), X, 193). He was fond of denouncing both modern warfare and the jurists of war (see also *Oeuvres Complètes*, XIX, pp. 318–22; XXVII, pp. 368–75), but he did not engage with the issues at any deep level—his response to arguments such as those of Montesquieu was simply that one should never make war out of fear. 'If that is the spirit of the laws, it is the spirit of the laws of the Borgias and Machiavelli' (XIX, p. 322).

[2] See below p. 208.

that Hobbes had concluded 'that because man has no idea of goodness, he must be naturally wicked; that he is vicious because he does not know virtue . . .),[3] he could also produce astonishingly insightful and original remarks, such as his observation in *Emile* that

True political theory [*Le droit politique*] is yet to appear, and it is to be presumed that it never will. Grotius, the master of all the *savants* in this subject, is but a child; and, what is worse, a dishonest child [*enfant de mauvaise foi*]. When I hear Grotius praised to the skies and Hobbes covered with execration, I see how far sensible men read or understand these two authors. The truth is that their principles are exactly the same: they only differ in their expression. They also differ in their method. Hobbes relies on sophisms, and Grotius on the poets; all the rest is the same.[4]

It is also worth noting that some of the very early readers of Rousseau (such as the Bernese writer Isaak Iselin in his *Patriotic Dreams*, which appeared at the same time as the Second Discourse and which was informed by a personal knowledge of Rousseau) explicitly linked his views to those of Hobbes.[5]

One of the difficulties about assessing Rousseau's considered thoughts is that his way of working was to draft paragraphs or short 'chapters' containg his thoughts on various topics, and to draw on these *pensées* (as they should be thought of) for his printed works; many of the most interesting *pensées* remained in manuscript until quite recent times. One consequence of this is that (as is always true of authors of *pensées*) it is hard to extract an entirely straightforward and consistent theory from his works; the reputation which Rousseau enjoyed among contemporaries or near-contemporaries (such as the Jacobins) is a particularly misleading guide to what he actually thought, since his *oeuvre* was one of the most contestable of any major political theorist.

The central statement of Rousseau's view about human sociability, in the *Discourse on the Origin of Inequality*, could stand as a perfectly accurate summary of the views of both Grotius and Hobbes.

[3] *Oeuvres Politiques*, ed. Jean Roussel (Paris: Classiques Garnier, 1989), 42; 'A Discourse on the Origin of Inequality', in *The Social Contract and Discourses*, trans. and ed. G. D. H. Cole, rev, J. H. Brumfitt and John C. Hall (London: Everyman's Library, 1973), 65.

[4] Rousseau, *Political Writings*, ed. C. E. Vaughan (Cambridge University Press, 1915), II, 147.

[5] I owe this most important and interesting information to an unpublished paper by Béla Kapossy of the University of Lausanne. Professor Kapossy suggests that this became a familiar German-language account of Rousseau, to be found in Mendelssohn, Lessing, and Herder.

Contemplating the first and most simple operations of the human soul, I think I can perceive in it two principles prior to reason, one of them deeply interesting us in our welfare and preservation, and the other exciting a natural repugnance at seeing any other sensible being, and particularly any of our own species, suffer pain or death. It is from the agreement and combination which the understanding is in a position to establish between these two principles, without its being necessary to introduce that of sociability, that all the rules of natural right appear to me to be derived.[6]

Rousseau seems to have been aware that a theory of this kind could be attributed to Hobbes, for, after saying that Hobbes 'had seen clearly the defects of all the modern definitions of natural right', he continued

but the consequences which he deduces from his own show that he understands it in an equally false sense. In reasoning on the principles he lays down, he ought to have said that the state of nature, being that in which the care for our own preservation is the least prejudicial to that of others, was consequently the best calculated to promote peace, and the most suitable for mankind. He does say the exact opposite, in consequence of having improperly admitted, as part of savage man's care for self-preservation, the gratification of a multitude of passions which are the work of society, and have made laws necessary.[7]

But, of course, Rousseau's natural man was by definition in a state with which Hobbes had not been particularly concerned, for he was in a state in which there was effectively *no* interaction with other men. As we have seen, Hobbes himself thought that the 'multitude of passions' which led to conflict were the consequence of men measuring themselves against one another. It is true that this was not 'society' for Hobbes, since for him a 'society' had to be well ordered and intentionally created; but Hobbes never supposed that in his state of nature men would be as isolated as they were in Rousseau's. Had he been asked how one would describe the character of men entirely cut off from one another, his answer would presumably have been very like Rousseau's, since such men would not yet have developed the passions which sprang from their 'imagination' of one another's power.

So it is not surprising that the account which Rousseau proceeded to give in the *Discourse* of the growth of conflict once men began to have any dealings with one another, was in effect a conflation of Grotius and Hobbes. The narrative of the gradual growth of private property was

[6] *Oeuvres Politiques*, p. 20; *The Social Contract and Discourses*, p. 41.

[7] *Oeuvres Politiques*, p. 42; *The Social Contract and Discourses*, p. 65.

Grotius's (and signalled as such),[8] and included Grotius's thought that conflicts over property in the state of nature were one of the reasons for the emergence of civil society. But the much wider account of the potential for human conflict, in which it was the passions for comparison and emulation between men, growing out of the need for self-preservation, which led to a state of war, reads very like the interpretation of Hobbes which I have suggested. Like Hobbes, he was extremely wary of explaining warfare as conflict over scarce resources: indeed, in one striking passage in which he recapitulated the central notion of his earlier *Discourse on the Arts and Sciences*, he asserted that it was artistic rivalry and not economic necessity which led to the state of war. Once men

> accustomed themselves to assemble before their huts round a large tree; singing and dancing, the true offspring of love and leisure, became the amusement, or rather the occupation, of men and women thus assembled together with nothing else to do. Each one began to consider the rest, and to wish to be considered in turn; and thus a value came to be attached to public esteem. Whoever sang or danced best, whoever was the handsomest, the strongest, the most dexterous, or the most eloquent, came to be of most consideration; and this was the first step towards inequality, and at the same time towards vice. From these first distinctions arose on the one side vanity and contempt and on the other shame and envy: and the fermentation caused by these new leavens ended by producing combinations fatal to innocence and happiness.[9]

Rousseau's concentration here on aesthetic values rather than fundamental needs as the source of conflict would have appealed to Hobbes.

The Hobbesianism of Rousseau II

The State

The kinship between Rousseau and Hobbes is revealed in the very areas where there were important differences between them. The first and most obvious difference (though, I think, ultimately the less interesting) was over the question of what constituted the well-founded commonwealth which might put an end to this state of war. Rousseau caricatured Hobbes's idea of the Leviathan state in his remarks in the *Discourse on the Origin of Inequality* about the way in which, from amidst the conflicts and struggles of social life,

[8] *Oeuvres Politiques*, p. 60; *The Social Contract and Discourses*, p. 85.
[9] *Oeuvres Politiques*, p. 57; *The Social Contract and Discourses*, p. 81.

despotism, gradually raising up its hideous head and devouring everything that remained sound and untainted in any part of the State, would at length trample on both the laws and the people, and establish itself on the ruins of the republic. The times which immediately preceded this last change would be times of trouble and calamity; but at length the monster would swallow up everything, and the people would no longer have either chiefs or laws, but only tyrants. From this moment there would be no question of virtue or morality; for despotism (*cui ex honesto nulla est spes*), wherever it prevails, admits no other master; it no sooner speaks than probity and duty lose their weight and blind obedience is the only virtue which slaves can still practise.

This is the last term of inequality, the extreme point that closes the circle, and meets that from which we set out. Here all private persons return to their first equality, because they are nothing; and, subjects having no law but the will of their master, and their master no restraint but his passions, all notions of good and all principles of equity again vanish[10]

This image of despotism 'raising its head' may even be a reference (conscious or unconscious) to the famous frontispiece of *Leviathan*, and certainly the description of the despotic state in the *Discourse* is close to Hobbes's picture of civil society, in which the sovereign is the exclusive moral arbiter of the commonwealth. It should be said that Rousseau had no scruples in principle about according the civil sovereign such a role—in *Économie Politique*, which depicts (on the whole) a well-founded state, Rousseau remarked that the *corps politique* is

a corporate being possessed of a will; and this general will, which tends always to the preservation and welfare of the whole and every part, and is the source of the laws, constitutes for all the members of the State, in their relations to one another and to it, the rule of what is just or unjust: a truth which shows, by the way, how idly some writers have treated as theft the subtlety prescribed to children at Sparta for obtaining their frugal repasts, as if everything ordained by the law were not lawful.[11]

His rupture with Hobbes came instead over the question of the way in which the sovereign *represented* the people. For Hobbes, the sovereign represented his citizens simply by virtue of being the agreed moral authority for the commonwealth, and this agreement could be expressed (or, as in the case of conquest, exacted) in a variety of ways. For Rousseau, certainly by the time he composed the final version of *Du*

[10] *Oeuvres Politiques*, pp. 76–7; *The Social Contract and Discourses*, pp. 102–3.

[11] *Oeuvres Politiques*, p. 122; *The Social Contract and Discourses*, pp. 120–1. The remark about the Spartans is precisely the same as Hobbes's in *De Cive*, VI. 16.

Contrat Social, representation had to be a more active process, in which the citizens actually voted for the measures which the *corps politique* pronounced as morally binding upon them; while his remarks on the need to eliminate partial associations from the state in *Economie Politique* suggest that already at that stage he was envisaging something like the state of *Du Contrat Social*. The evils of the first interactions between men were therefore to be overcome, Rousseau believed, by a transition to a genuinely democratic republic.

But even in this area it would be a mistake to overemphasize the gulf between Rousseau and Hobbes: Hobbes, too, in all his works, regarded democratic voting as the most natural way of generating sovereignty, and his own use of the term 'representation' to describe the role of the sovereign inevitably had overtones of electoral politics. Moreover, Rousseau and Hobbes were absolutely at one with regard to partial association: both felt that it was the greatest threat to the well-founded commonwealth, and would obscure what ought to be the direct relationship between citizen and sovereign. They also agreed about the deficiencies of actual democratic societies—as Rousseau said in *Économie Politique*, in an entirely Hobbesian passage, what he had to say was not contradicted by examples such as Athenian politics, for 'Athens was not in fact a Democracy, but a very tyrannical Aristocracy, governed by philosophers and orators.'[12] It should also not be forgotten that in the final version of *Du Contrat Social* Rousseau tracked Hobbes into the most daring of all his speculations, the idea of a civil religion, and did so entirely knowingly.[13]

The Hobbesianism of Rousseau III

The State of War

Rousseau's most subtle criticism of Hobbes was not in fact over the question of representation, but over the question of whether any civil state at all could bring an end to the state of war. The remarkable essay *The State of War* composed (probably) shortly after the *Discourse on the*

[12] *Oeuvres Politiques*, p. 124; *The Social Contract and Discourses*, p. 122. See Hobbes, *De Cive*, X. 5–15 for similar sentiments.

[13] 'It is not so much what is false and terrible in his political theory, as what is just and true, that has drawn down hatred on it.' *Oeuvres Politiques*, pp. 351–2; *The Social Contract and Discourses*, p. 271. For the similar ambitions of Hobbes and Rousseau in this area, see my 'The Civil Religion of Thomas Hobbes', in *Political Discourse in Early Modern Britain*, ed. Nicholas Phillipson and Quentin Skinner (Cambridge University Press, 1993), 120–38.

Origin of Inequality, explores further a thought which had come to him in the *Discourse*, that the consequence of 'bodies politic' remaining in the state of nature *vis-à-vis* one another was widespread international conflict, with more murders 'than were committed in the state of nature during whole ages over the whole earth'. At the heart of the modern tragedy, he now suggested in this essay, was the fact that

> as man with man, we live in the civil state and subject to laws; as people with people, each one enjoys natural liberty: and our situation is far worse than if these distinctions were unknown. For living at the same time in the social order and in the state of nature, we are subject to the inconveniences of both, without finding the security of either.[14]

To analyse this plight Rousseau initially followed Hobbes extremely closely, insisting first (in his account of the general character of a state of war) that

> The constitution of this universe does not permit all the rational beings [*êtres sensibles*] who compose it to agree at the same time on their mutual welfare, but the well-being of one being the evil of another, each one according to the law of nature gives preference to himself and works for his own advantage and the disadvantage of another . . . Eventually, when things are such that a rational being [*un être doué de raison*] is convinced that the need for his own preservation is incompatible not only with the well-being of another but even with his existence, then he arms himself against the other's life and seeks to destroy him with the same ardour with which he seeks to preserve himself, and for the same reason.[15]

As a consequence, the true state of war is, exactly as Hobbes had said, a state of continual threat even when not manifested in actual

[14] This essay has still not been properly edited. It survives in the form of three sheets in the Bibliothèque de la Ville in Neuchâtel, and a fourth in the Bibliothèque publique et universitaire in Geneva. The Neuchâtel sheets have been printed on a number of occasions since their first discovery in 1896, though the modern editions all rely on the work of C. E. Vaughan (Rousseau, *Political Writings*, I, 281–307). The Geneva sheet has been printed twice, first by its discoverer Bernard Gagnebin, in 'Un inedit de Rousseau sur l'état de guerre', in *De Ronsard a Breton: Hommages à Marcel Raymond* (Paris: Librairie Jose Corti, 1967), 103–9, and then in Rousseau's *Oeuvres Complètes*, II ed. Jean Fabre and Michel Launay (Paris: Editions du Seuil, 1971), 379–81. Grace Roosevelt has recently suggested a most persuasive reconstruction of the order in which the sheets should be read, and has provided a translation of them, but the original text has still to be sought in Vaughan and Gagnebin. Grace G. Roosevelt, *Reading Rousseau in the Nuclear Age* (Philadelphia: Temple University Press, 1990), 15–17 (introduction) and 185–98 (text). See also her 'A Reconstruction of Rousseau's Fragments on the State of War', *History of Political Thought*, 8 (1987), 225–44. This quotation is from the Neuchâtel MS, Vaughan, I p. 304, Roosevelt, *Reading Rousseau*, p. 186.

[15] Gagnebin, 'Un inedit', p. 108; Roosevelt, *Reading Rousseau*, pp. 194–5.

belligerence; it will be marked by 'preparations, the stockpiling of weapons and of *materiel* for sieges'.[16]

But as Rousseau eloquently emphasized, this state was not eliminated by the formation of civil societies, for those societies were themselves Hobbesian 'rational beings', and indeed displayed in the purest form possible the attributes of the Hobbesian agent, far exceeding natural individuals in their competitive belligerence.

Man, fundamentally, has no need of any connection with his kin [*semblables*]: he can exist perfectly easily without their help. He does not need the aid of men as much as he needs the fruits of the earth; and the earth produces more than is necessary to feed all its inhabitants. Add that a man has a limit fixed by nature to his energy and size, and that he cannot pass it. Whichever way he looks, he finds his abilities limited. His life is short, his years are numbered. His stomach does not expand along with his wealth; there is no point in his passions developing, for his pleasures are their measure; his heart has its bounds, like everything else; his capacity for pleasure is always the same. He might well have the idea of growing, but he always remains small.

The State, on the other hand, being an artificial body, has no determined limit; its proper size is indefinite; it can always extend itself; it thinks itself feeble as long as there are others stronger than it. Its security, its preservation, require that it make itself more powerful than all its neighbours . . . The inequality of men has bounds imposed by the hands of nature, but that of societies can increase incessantly, until one alone absorbs all the rest.

Thus, the size of the *corps politique* is purely relative, for it is forced to compare itself with others in order to know itself . . .

It seems that we are bent on reversing all the true ideas of things. Everything leads the natural man to rest; eating and sleeping are the only needs he recognises, and only hunger draws him from laziness . . . [While] a thousand writers have dared to say that the *corps politique* is passionless, and that the only reason of state is reason itself, none of them have seen that, on the contrary, the essence of a society consists in the activity of its members, and that a State without motion would be merely a dead body . . . It is necessary for the State to survive that the vivacity of its passions provides it with motion and that its will gives its life up to the point at which its power weakens. This is the law of self-preservation which nature herself has established between species, and which maintains them all, despite their inequality.[17]

The rationality of this corporate agent then dragged its members into wars which were far bloodier than they would in general have found

[16] Gagnebin, 196.
[17] Vaughan, I, pp. 298, 299; Roosevelt, *Reading Rousseau*, pp. 191–2.

themselves in outside civil society— 'it is only after he has formed a society with some one else, that a man decides to attack another man: he only becomes a soldier after he has become a citizen'.[18]

This theory, of course, was based originally on Montesquieu's critique of Hobbes in *The Spirit of the Laws*; but Rousseau modified Montesquieu in such a way that the theory became much less critical of Hobbes. In the critique, which I quoted *in extenso* in the previous chapter, Montesquieu had also made the point that the state of war began with the formation of human societies: 'as soon as men are in society, they lose their feeling of weakness; the equality that was among them ceases, and the state of war begins'. But unlike Rousseau, he had also insisted that before these civil societies were created, men were fundamentally sociable beings.

> I have said that fear would lead men to flee one another, but the marks of mutual fear would soon persuade them to approach one another. They would also be so inclined by the pleasure one animal feels at the approach of an animal of its own kind. In addition, the charm that the two sexes inspire in each other by their difference would increase this pleasure, and the natural entreaty they always make to one another would be a third law.
>
> Besides feelings, which belong to men from the outset, they also succeed in gaining knowledge; thus they have a second bond, which other animals do not have. Therefore, they have another motive for uniting, and the desire to live in society is a fourth natural law.[19]

There can be no doubt that in his discussion of these matters, Rousseau deliberately drew a distinction between himself and Montesquieu: much of what Rousseau wished to argue could have been supported simply by Montesquieu's point about the state of war being a product of civil society, but instead of resting content with this, Rousseau emphatically insisted that by nature men are *not* sociable— the claim which all contemporary readers associated with Hobbes. His reason for so doing, as I have suggested, is that fundamentally he shared Hobbes's vision of stand-offish and unsociable humanity, and that he wished to use the wars of modern states to make a deep point about the life of autonomous individuals, once they had any interactions whatsoever with one another.

Rousseau offered little hope of an end to this state of war between

[18] Vaughan, I, p. 294; Roosevelt, *Reading Rousseau*, pp. 188–9.

[19] *The Spirit of the Laws*, ed. Anne M. Cohler, Basia Carolyn Miller, and Harold Samuel Stone (Cambridge University Press, 1989), 6–7.

modern states. It is true that he gave some considerable thought to the question which was posed (as we have seen) particularly by Saint-Pierre, namely, if the civil sovereign is the solution to the problems of the state of nature, should not a continental sovereign be the solution to the problems of continental war? Indeed, it may have been his deep reflection on Saint-Pierre, induced by a commission from the Saint-Pierre family to edit his works, which led him to his thoughts on Hobbes.[20] But his considered response to Saint-Pierre was a pessimistic one:

> even with the good will that princes and their ministers never display, it would not be easy to find a favourable moment to execute such a scheme; for it would be necessary that the sum of particular interests did not overcome the common interest, and that each person thought that he saw in the good of all, the best which he could aspire to for himself.

Saint-Pierre's scheme was 'too good to be adopted'.[21]

Rousseau did sketch his own alternative scheme, but the essay which included it was apparently destroyed,[22] so we are largely thrown back on the summary of it in *Émile*. Here, he said (in words which echo *The State of War*) that

> we shall ask ourselves whether, in the foundation of societies, men have not done either too much or too little; whether the submission of the individual to the authority of the Law and of other men, while at the same time the several communities remain as regards each other in the state of nature, does not leave him exposed to all the evils of both conditions, without the advantages of either; whether, in fine, it would not be better to have no civil society than to have several . . . Is it not this partial and incomplete association which is the cause of tyranny and war? And are not tyranny and war the two worst scourges of mankind?
>
> We shall examine finally the kind of remedy that men have sought against these evils in Leagues and Federations, which, leaving each State master in its own house, arm it against all unjust aggression from without. We shall enquire what are the means of establishing a good form of federal association, what can give it permanence, and how far we can extend the rights of the Federation without trenching on those of Sovereignty.[23]

[20] In 1754 Rousseau had arranged with the de Saint-Pierre family to edit the works of the Abbé. Only his *Extrait* from the *Paix Perpetuelle* was published in Rousseau's lifetime (in 1761), but the rest of his work on Saint-Pierre, including his *Jugement*, was published in the posthumous edn. of his works in 1782, and so was available to Kant (unlike the essay, the *State of War*).

[21] *Oeuvres Politiques*, pp. 188, 192 (from the *Jugement sur la Paix Perpetuelle*).

[22] Vaughan, II, pp. 135–6.

[23] Vaughan, I, p. 96.

But we are in the dark about these remedies, and it is probable that Rousseau in the end felt himself unable to provide them.

In the essay on *The State of War*, Rousseau hinted at quite another solution to the problem. War between *corps politiques*, like war between any beings, would end in the death of the defeated; but, as he pointed out, the death of an artificial body was encompassed by the destruction of its 'soul', the social contract which had created and sustained it. This destruction could even take place through the deliberate moral corruption of the enemy citizens, without anyone being killed—though he acknowledged that an attack on the social contract would normally involve a physical attack on the members of the society. Rousseau also observed that princes make war more freely because they are not themselves at risk, and hinted that if they were ruled 'by the laws of the State' and if their lives thereby 'belonged to the State' they might be less ready to go to war. But this is merely a hint, and there is no suggestion even in this essay that democracies might make war significantly less often or less brutally than monarchies.

We are left with the conclusion that Rousseau had, in effect, given a sceptical twist to Hobbes's theory, just as Hobbes himself had done to Grotius's: if there cannot be international peace, then the formation of Hobbesian states cannot protect their citizens from the ravages of the state of nature, since on Hobbes's own account the state is itself an agent in a state of nature. But Hobbes's theory of state formation was the most plausible on offer, and Rousseau could provide no solution to his own problem.

The Hobbesianism of Kant I

The State of Nature

A very similar relationship to Hobbes can be detected in Kant's work. In all his mature political writings, Kant stressed that Hobbes was right in his characterization of the state of nature, and that as a consequence the fundamental moral duty men are under is to leave the state of nature and enter civil society. Repeatedly, he described the state of nature in the most accurately Hobbesian terms, most strikingly (perhaps) in section 44 of 'The Doctrine of Right' in *The Metaphysics of Morals*:

> It is not experience from which we learn of men's maxim of violence and of their malevolent tendency to attack one another before external legislation endowed with power appears. It is therefore not some fact that makes coercion

through public law necessary. On the contrary, however well disposed and law-abiding men might be, it still lies a priori in the rational Idea of such a condition (one that is not rightful) that before a public lawful condition is established, individual men, peoples, and states can never be secure against violence from one another, since each has its own right to do *what seems right and good to it* and not to be dependent upon another's opinion about this. So, unless it wants to renounce any concepts of Right, the first thing it has to resolve upon is the principle that it must leave the state of nature, in which each follows its own judgement, unite itself with all others (with which it cannot help interacting), subject itself to a public lawful external coercion, and so enter into a condition in which what is to be recognized as belonging to it is determined *by law* and is allotted to it by adequte *power* (not its own but an external power).[24]

The first part of this passage was of course an extremely sensitive reading of Hobbes, fully alive to the fact that Hobbes did not suppose that men in the state of nature were inherently aggressive, and to the fact that it was conflict of judgement which constituted the Hobbesian problem; that it was consciously a reading of Hobbes is illustrated by a remark in his lectures on natural jurisprudence where he made a similar point, and then observed that 'Hobbes and Rousseau really have the same idea about this'.[25] It is also illustrated by a passage in *Religion within the Limits of Reason Alone* in which he summarized his theory of the state of nature, and appended the following note:

Hobbes' statement, *status hominum naturalis est* bellum *omnium in omnes*, is correct except that it should read, *est* status *belli*, etc. For even if one does not concede that actual *hostilities* are continually in progess between men who stand under external and public laws, yet the *state* (*status juridicus*) is the same; *i.e.*, the relationship in and through which men are fitted for the acquisition and maintenance of rights—a state in which each wants to be the judge of what shall be his rights against others, but for which rights he has no security against others, and gives others no security: each has only his private strength. This is a state of war in which everyone must be perpetually armed against everyone else. Hobbes's second statement, *exeundum esse e statu naturali*, follows from the first; for this state is a continual infringement upon the rights of all others through man's arrogant insistence on being a judge in his own affairs and

[24] *The Metaphysics of Morals*, ed. Mary Gregor (Cambridge University Press, 1991), 124.

[25] 'Hobbes und Rousseau haben schon davon einige Begriffe'. Kant, *Gesammelte Schriften* XVII. 2. 2, p. 1337. See also his remark about Hobbes's state of nature in *Religion within the Limits of Reason Alone*, ed. and trans. by Theodore M. Greene and Hoyt H. Hudson (New York, 1960), 89.

giving men no other security in their affairs save his own arbitrary will [*Willkür*].[26]

Both in these passages about the state of nature among individuals, and in the comparable passages (again, scattered throughout these works) about the state of nature among states, Kant was entirely unmoved by the claims of the German natural law writers that there was a general society of mankind.[27] His views are well summarised by 'The Doctrine of Right' section 54 of *The Metaphysics of Morals*:

(1) States, considered in external relation to one another, are (like lawless savages) by nature in a nonrightful condition. (2) This nonrightful condition is a *condition* of war (of the rights of the stronger), even if it is not a condition of actual war and actual attacks being constantly made (hostilities). Although no state is wronged by another in this condition (insofar as neither wants anything better), this condition is in itself still wrong in the highest degree, and states neighbouring upon one another are under obligation to leave it.[28]

It was no doubt his firm conviction that in this respect, also, Hobbes had been right, that led him to express his contempt for the other jurists of international law, in the famous passage of *Perpetual Peace* in which he poured scorn on 'the sorry comforters' Grotius, Pufendorf, and Vattel, whose 'philosophically or diplomatically formulated codes do not and cannot have the slightest *legal* force, since states as such are not subject to a common external constraint'.[29]

Jeremy Waldron has recently emphasized the surprise one should feel about this view, and in particular about the passage in 'The Doctrine of Right' section 44 of *The Metaphysics of Morals*.[30] He has pointed out that a conventional interpretation of Kant's theory would rule out a genuine clash of sincere belief: surely, if we all think according to the categorical imperative, no conflict can, by definition, result? This has certainly been the view of some twentieth-century commentators on Kant, such as Robert Paul Wolff.[31] But it was not Kant's view,

[26] *Religion within the Limits of Reason Alone*, p. 89.

[27] Achenwall, like the others, had made such a claim: see his *Ius Naturale*, II. 1. 1, in Kant, *Gesammelte Schriften*, XIX, 333.

[28] *The Metaphysics of Morals*, p. 151.

[29] *Political Writings*, p. 103. Kant was accepting here the conventional account in Germany of Grotius's theory. It is worth remarking that in his lectures he recommended Vattel as the best book on international law (*Gesammelte Schriften*, XVII. 2. 2, 1392).

[30] In his recent Seeley Lectures, *The Dignity of Legislation*, forthcoming from Cambridge University Press.

[31] See e.g. his *The Autonomy of Reason* (New York: Harper & Row, 1973), 223–6.

and the very structure of *The Metaphysics of Morals* shows what his view in fact was. The book is divided into the Doctrine of Right, which deals with *external* law, and the Doctrine of Virtue, which deals with *internal* law.[32] The principles of both ultimately rest on the categorical imperative, but only in the domain of right can someone's action be coerced by an external authority—that is to say, be brought into line with the collective wishes of an actual group of people, manifested through some sovereign. In the domain of ethics, we can pursue our own moral ends and live a life of virtue in accordance with the categorical imperative, and this life will include external actions such as acts of charity; but our actions based on the principles of ethics must give way when they encounter the rule of right. A state can, for example, regulate the provision of charity, and can even forbid it altogether without the citizens being entitled to disregard its commands.

This is what Kant means in 'The Doctrine of Right', section 44: when it comes to the actions of many people who must live together, the pursuit of ethics can lead to conflict, since it denies anyone else a say in how we should live. Many circumstances in the material world require that we submit our will to other people's, and this cannot be the task of ethical reflection, since such reflection cannot determine which will is to be dominant—there is, for example, an inherent arbitrariness in the decisions of a legislative assembly. The distinction between right and ethics is neatly expressed by Kant in a remark in the Introduction to the Doctrine of Virtue:

> The concept of duty stands in immediate relation to a *law* (even if I abstract from all ends, as the matter of law). The formal principle of duty, in the categorical imperative, 'So act that the maxim of your action could become a universal *law*,' already indicates this. Ethics adds only that this principle is to be thought as the law of *your* own will, and not of will in general, which could also be the will of others; in the latter case the law would provide a duty of Right, which lies outside the sphere of ethics. (p. 193)

The important difference between Hobbes and Kant, in this area, was that (as we have seen) Hobbes treated the pronouncements of the sovereign as canonical for the individual in the sphere of ethics as well as right, whereas Kant always insisted that there remained scope for private judgement in a state. The interesting disagreement between

[32] See in particular the remarks in section III of the Introduction, pp. 45–7 of the Gregor edn.

them was not over the sphere of ethics—since Hobbes was not concerned with a wholly private ethics (or, more properly, since he took the genuinely inner life to be wholly inscrutable to an external observer); and since Kant accepted that as far as external matters were concerned, the sovereign's command *was* to decide matters, the practical divergence between their views was rather slight. But Kant also insisted, explicitly against Hobbes, that it was possible for subjects to make private judgements in the sphere of *right*.

However, the presentation of this case, in the section entitled 'Against Hobbes' in *On the Common Saying: 'This May be True in Theory, but it does not Apply in Practice'* (1793), is often misunderstood. The first part of that section is in fact a fairly faithful reconstruction of Hobbes's theory of sovereignty: Kant's 'republican' account of the construction of a sovereign is much closer to Hobbes than Rousseau's had been, though this too is often misunderstood (as, for example, by Hans Reiss in his edition). Kant made clear in this section that the legislative sovereign was the entire body of the people agreeing *unanimously* on its measures (p. 78). As a consequence, it could in general only pass in its own person the foundational enactment of the society, and thereafter it would have to be *represented* by the supreme legislator, whatever that might be—and it could of course be a monarch. At this stage in his life, Kant did not make any distinction between a legislative and an executive power, and even when he did do so (notably in *The Metaphysics of Morals*) the distinction was far from being like a Montesquieuian or Madisonian separation of powers. As 'The Doctrine of Right' section 51 makes clear, it was a *conceptual* distinction, with a single-person legislator being quite possible and even desirable on the grounds of simplicity.

Hobbes was not expressly criticized in 'Against Hobbes' until Kant turned to the question of whether it follows from this theory that everything the sovereign does has to count as *just* for the citizen; and the interesting feature of Kant's argument at this point is that he presents it as a natural extension of Hobbes's fundamental presuppositions, rather than a refutation of them. He proposed that the same test which Hobbes had suggested (in effect) for the legitimacy of the *sovereign*, that he should be thought of as the outcome of a general will, should be used also for testing the legitimacy of the sovereign's particular *enactments*. That is, the things which the sovereign does have to be the sorts of things which a being of that kind *would* do, otherwise the sovereign was not being properly conceived by the citizens—we could say in Hobbes's terminology that it would be an internally contradictory 'fiction'. As he said, 'if the law is such that a whole people could not *possibly* agree to it (for example, if it stated that a certain class of *subjects* must be privileged as a hereditary ruling class), it is unjust; but if it is at least *possible* that a people could agree to it, it is our duty to consider the law as just, even if the people is at present in such a position or attitude of mind that it would probably refuse its consent if it were consulted.' (p. 79).

Kant thus allowed the possibility which Hobbes had ruled out, of a meaningful description of a law as unjust; though since he also of course forbade resistance to an unjust law, the practical difference was again rather slight. If the sovereign sought (for example) to limit freedom of religious expression, 'in all cases . . . where the supreme legislation did nevertheless adopt such measures, it would be permissible to pass general and public judgements upon them, but never to offer any verbal or active resistance' (p. 85). It might also be remarked that Hobbes had also always allowed it to be logically possible to say of the sovereign that he would break the law of nature, if what he did was not sincerely intended to protect himself and his citizens, even though such an action could never be described as 'unjust'; so Hobbes himself had supposed that the acts of a sovereign ought in some way to match the conception of a sovereign, without it being the case that the citizens could resist those acts which did not.

An interesting parallel to these discussions in *The Metaphysics of Morals* and *Theory and Practice* is provided by the passage in which Kant first discussed Hobbes's state of nature, in the *Critique of Pure Reason*. This illuminates the kind of relationship which Kant envisaged between the disparate opinions of the state of nature and the uniform conduct of citizens. His central claim in the *Critique* was that the arguments among 'dogmatic' philosophers over the basic metaphysical issues—in particular, the existence of a God, the character of time and space, the infinite divisibility of matter, and the freedom of the will—were not to be ended with victory for one side or the other. Instead, a 'critical' philosophy would show that each view belonged to a particular and ineluctable view of the world—so that (for example) a human being seen as an element in a natural world governed by causal laws could not be free, but the same human being seen from his own perspective as a deliberative agent could not be determined. Neither viewpoint was *mistaken*, and the job of the critical philosopher was to be entirely clear about which viewpoint was being employed at any one time, and thereby to end futile disputes.

To explain this, Kant turned to the image of Hobbes's state of nature:

The critique of pure reason can be regarded as the true tribunal for all disputes of pure reason; for it is not involved in these disputes—disputes which are immediately concerned with objects—but is directed to the determining and estimating of the rights of reason in general, in accordance with the principles of their first institution.

In the absence of this critique reason is, as it were, in the state of nature, and can establish and secure its assertions and claims only through *war*. The critique, on the other hand, arriving at all its decisions in the light of fundamental principles of its own institution, the authority of which no one can question, secures to us the peace of a legal order, in which our disputes have to be conducted solely by the recognised methods of *legal action*. In the former state, the disputes are ended by a victory to which both sideas lay claim, and which is generally followed by a merely temporary armistice, arranged by some mediating authority; in the latter, by a *judicial sentence* which, as it strikes at the very root of the conflicts, effectively secures an eternal peace. The endless disputes of a merely dogmatic reason thus finally constrain us to seek relief in some critique of reason itself, and in legislation based upon such criticism. As Hobbes maintains, the state of nature is a state of injustice and violence, and we have no option save to abandon it and submit ourselves to the constraint of law, which limits our freedom solely in order that it may be consistent with the freedom of others and with the common good of all.

This freedom will carry with it the right to submit openly for discussion the thoughts and doubts with which we find ourselves unable to deal, and to do so without being decried as troublesome and dangerous citizens. This is one of the original rights of human reason, which recognises no other judge than that universal human reason in which everyone has his say. And since all improvement of which our state is capable must be obtained from this source, such a right is sacred and must not be curtailed. (A752/B780)[33]

As the last paragraph illustrates, this was rather more than merely a metaphor in the *Critique of Pure Reason*: Kant's picture of a well-founded human society was one in which no victory would go to one of the warring dogmatic parties, so that (for example) the sincere and troubled atheist must be tolerated alongside the mistakenly confident naive theist (and this argument for the desirability of intellectual

[33] *Critique of Pure Reason*, trans. Norman Kemp Smith (London: Macmillan, 1933), 601–2.

toleration went, of course, through all Kant's works). The second of the two sections into which the *Critique of Pure Reason* is divided, entitled 'Transcendental Doctrine of Method', is the place where Kant works out the implications of his idea that the war of dogmatisms is to be reconciled by critical philosophy, and he makes it clear in that section, first, that the conflicts of reason were in some sense necessary to their eventual resolution—a critical philosophy could, after all, not emerge unless there were positions for it to criticize—and second, that the kinds of beliefs which pure reason sought to establish conclusively would *continue* to be a feature of any world in which the critique acted as a tribunal.

What would disappear would be the claims of these beliefs to victory and exclusivity: the theist would disavow any ability to overcome the theist by argument. Not only were the dogmatic philosophers thus precisely analogous to the men in Hobbes's state of nature (as Hobbes himself implied in *De Cive*, I. 5);[34] Kant's solution itself had at least a family resemblance to Hobbes's solution, in which the public tribunal would ideally permit the free expression of religious belief, provided that no sect claimed superiority over the others.[35] But one must always remember, in both Hobbes and Kant, that this was an *ideal*, and could not be imposed on a sovereign by his citizens.

The Hobbesianism of Kant II

The Right of Nations[36]

Kant's ideas about international relations have this same complex connection with Hobbes's ideas. Like Rousseau, Kant saw very clearly that

[34] See also the remarkable letter from François Peleau to Hobbes: Hobbes, *Correspondence*, ed. Noel Malcolm (Oxford University Press, 1994), 424.

[35] See the eloquent passage in *Leviathan* in which Hobbes praised the 'Independency of the Primitive Christians to follow Paul, or Cephas, or Apollos, every man as he liketh best: Which, if it be without contention, and without measuring the Doctrine of Christ, by our affection to the Person of his Minister, (the fault which the Apostle reprehended in the Corinthians,) is perhaps the best: First, because there ought to be no Power over the Consciences of men, but of the Word it selfe, working Faith in every one, not alwayes according to the purpose of them that Plant and Water, but of God himself, that giveth the Increase: and secondly, because it is unreasonable in them, who teach there is such danger in every little Errour, to require of a man endued with Reason of his own, to follow the Reason of any other man, or of the most voices of many other men; Which is little better, then to venture his Salvation at crosse and pile.' (*Leviathan*, ed. R. Tuck (Cambridge, 1996), 479–80).

[36] The account of Kant's theory of perpetual peace here is broadly similar to the view found in Hinsley's classic book (see F. H. Hinsley, *Power and the Pursuit of Peace*

the Hobbesian theory entailed no end to the state of war, for modern states are inextricably involved in a continuous and destructive warfare; in the section on 'The Right of Nations' in *The Metaphysics of Morals*, he gave an extremely Hobbesian account of the international state of nature, even down to ascribing to states the right to commit pre-emptive strikes against one another ('The Doctrine of Right' section 56). Rights in a state of nature, for both individuals and states, were for Kant 'provisional' in character—that is, they must 'leave open the possibility of leaving the state of nature . . . and entering a rightful condition' ('The Doctrine of Right' section 57, see also section 9). But on Hobbes's argument, all the rights which he ascribed to men in a state of nature *were* of this kind, and Kant seems to have questioned this much less than one might have expected.

Thus on pre-emptive strikes in a state of nature, he diverged markedly from the German orthodoxy of his time. Achenwall's *Ius Naturale*, the textbook in his lectures, had declared that the growing power of a neighbouring state could be grounds for aggressive war only 'if it is linked to an immediate attack', and that there could be no general right to maintain a balance of power;[37] Kant however said that 'in addition to active violations' a state

> may be *threatened*. This includes another state's being the first to undertake *preparations*, upon which is based the right of *prevention* (*ius praeventionis*), or even just the *menacing* increase in another state's *power* (by its acquisition of territory) (*potentia tremenda*). This is a wrong to the lesser power merely by the *condition* of the *superior power*, before any deed on its part, and in the state of nature an attack by the lesser power is indeed legitimate. Accordingly, this is also the basis of the right to a balance of power among all states that are contiguous and could act on one another. ('The Doctrine of Right' section 56)

The only area where he unequivocally aligned himself with Pufendorf's account of the state of nature between nations was the issue of punitive war: here, Kant firmly rejected the idea that in nature there could be such a thing, on the grounds that 'punishment occurs only in the relation of a superior to those subject to him, and states do not stand in that relation to each other' ('The Doctrine of Right' section 57). But these grounds were of course as much Hobbesian as Pufendorfian.

(Cambridge University Press, 1963) 62–80), though Hinsley did not recognize the extent to which Kant was attempting to mediate between Hobbes and Pufendorf (neither of whom, oddly, play much of a role in his book).

[37] Achenwall, *Ius Naturale*, II. 265, in Kant, *Gesammelte Schriften*, XIX, 436.

We can see the same features in Kant's discussion of the other central issue for contemporary international jurisprudence, the question of the natural right of acquisition. The fundamental condition for acquiring property of a provisional kind in nature, Kant argued, is *priority of occupation* ('The Doctrine of Right' section 14), but Kant described the principle of occupation in remarkably Hobbesian terms.

The question arises, how far does authorization to take possession of a piece of land extend? As far as the capacity for controlling it extends, that is, as far as whoever wants to appropriate it can defend it—as if the land were to say, if you cannot protect me you cannot command me. This is how the dispute over whether the sea is *free* or *closed* also has to be decided; for example, as far as a cannon shot can reach no one may fish, haul up amber from the ocean floor, and so forth, along the coast of a territory that already belongs to a certain state. Moreover, in order to acquire land is it necessary to develop it (build on it, cultivate it, drain it, and so on)? No . . . When first acquisition is in question, developing land is nothing more than an external sign of taking possession, for which many other signs that cost less effort can be substituted. ('The Doctrine of Right' section 15)

He did not enlarge on the notion of control, nor did he deal directly with the obvious problem that people's capacity to defend territory changes over time, and that (for example) the Europeans could control and defend territory far more effectively than the aboriginals of America. It is striking that the passage at this point in *The Metaphysics of Morals* ('The Doctrine of Right' section 15) where Kant tentatively dealt with this question is far from straightforward. He asked whether Europeans should have been authorized to acquire the lands of

the American Indians, the Hottentots, and the inhabitants of New Holland . . . especially since nature utself (which abhors a vacuum) seems to demand it, and great expanses of land in other parts of the world, which are now splendidly populated, would have otherwise remained uninhabited by civilized people or, indeed, would have to remain forever uninhabited, so that the end of creation would have been frustrated?

He answered that 'such a way of acquiring land is . . . to be repudiated'; indeed, throughout this discussion he was quite clear that a Lockean defence of colonization on the grounds of agriculture was illegitimate, for he had seen the link in Locke and his successors between this defence and the idea of natural sociability. But he immediately added, 'the indeterminacy, with respect to quantity as well as quality, of the external object that can be acquired makes this problem (of the sole, original external acquisition) the hardest of all to solve'—he was not prepared to clarify the implications of the account of property as (in origin) 'mechanical ability' to control material objects.

These Hobbesian sentiments about pre-emptive strikes and acquisition belong, it should be stressed again, to Kant's exposition of the state of nature and provisional rights; they do not belong to his exposition of international right in the sense of the laws of an international association, nor to his exposition of what he termed 'cosmopolitan' right. In both these areas, Kant sought to provide what Rousseau had failed to deliver, namely a proper account of the principles which might govern a society of nations formed out of the state of nature.

However, the first thing to say about these systems of non-provisional international right is that in his mature philosophy, Kant was not as pessimistic as Rousseau about the consequences of their *non*-appearance. On the eve of the *Critique*, in his lectures on ethics, he was condemning modern warfare in relatively conventional terms: 'if we look at the most enlightened portion of the world, we see the various States armed to the teeth, sharpening their weapons in time of peace the one against the other. This consequences of this are such that they block our approach to the universal end of perfection . . . '. Given that Saint-Pierre's suggestions, which Kant praised, are nevertheless naive, 'how then is perfection to be sought? Wherein lies our hope? In education, and in nothing else.'[38] But in *Conjectures on the Beginning of Human History*, published in 1786, two years after the *Idea for a Universal History* which began his post-critical thinking about politics, he wrote:

> We have to admit that the greatest evils which oppress civilised nations are the result of *war*—not so much of actual wars in the past or present as of the unremitting, indeed ever-increasing *preparation* for war in the future . . . But if this constant fear of war did not compel even heads of state to show this *respect for humanity*, would we still encounter the same culture, or that close association of social classes within the commonwealth which promotes the well-being of all? Would we still encounter the same population, or even that degree of freedom which is still present in spite of highly restrictive laws? We need only look at *China*, whose position may expose it to occasional unforeseen incursions but not to attack by a powerful enemy, and we shall find that, for this very reason, it has been stripped of every vestige of freedom. So long as human

[38] See *Lectures on Ethics*, trans. Louis Infield, ed. Lewis White Beck (New York, Harper & Row, 1963), 252–3.

culture remains at its present stage, war is therefore an indispensable means of advancing it further; and only when culture has reached its full development—and only God knows when that will be—will perpetual peace become possible and of benefit to us.[39]

Precisely the same sentiment is expressed in the *Critique of Judgement* (1790),[40] and a rather similar one is found in *Religion within the Limits of Reason Alone* (1791–3).[41]

These thoughts, which emphasized the benefits to culture of the actual practice of warfare, went alongside the more familiar argument in the works from these years, that military antagonism itself was the spur to international co-operation. This idea seems to have appeared for the first time in his *Idea for a Universal History* of 1784, which was clearly a spin-off from the work on the *Critique*,[42] in the form of the famous idea of 'unsocial sociability'.

The means which nature employs to bring about the development of innate capacities is that of antagonism within society, in so far as this antagonism becomes in the long run the cause of a law-governed social order. By antagonism, I mean in this context the *unsocial sociability* of men, that is, their tendency to come together in society, coupled, however, with a continual resistance which constantly threatens to break this society up.[43]

The impossibility of coping with these antagonisms would eventually lead people to create a social order in which they could be subsumed, just as the conflicts of the philosophers were subsumed by criticism. Similarly, in the field of international relations, the conflicts between states would eventually persuade people that they could only enjoy the kind of security for which their wars were fought by creating a system of international agreements between states 'which, like a civil commonwealth, can maintain itself *automatically*'.[44] The introduction of this system would be greatly facilitated by the spread of free civil institutions within each country, which would force governments to recognize the damage which war did to the interests of the individual citizens, particularly their commercial interests; Kant was notably more

[39] *Political Writings*, ed. Hans Reiss (Cambridge University Press, 1991), 232.

[40] *The Critique of Judgement*, trans. James Creed Meredith (Oxford University Press, 1952), II, 96.

[41] *Political Writings*, pp. 29–30.

[42] See e.g. the first sentence, which firmly links it to the discussion of the free will in the *Critique* (p. 41).

[43] *Political Writings*, p. 44.

[44] Ibid. 48.

optimistic than Rousseau about the propensity of republics to live in peace with one another. These associated states would then be governed by the principles of non-provisional international law, and Kant gave a full account of what those principles would be in his famous essay on *Perpetual Peace* of 1795 (he refers only briefly to them in his *Metaphysics of Morals* ('The Doctrine of Right' section 61), where however he clearly links them to the notion of 'perpetual peace'; giving a full account of them may have been the chief purpose of *Perpetual Peace*).

In it, he argued that if a loose confederacy of sovereign nations were to be formed (its looseness a guarantee that the dangers of a Chinese peace would not prevail), then the effective way of ensuring that each pursued a course of justice was to insist on the principle that a state's actions must have a publically avowable character, just as an individual citizen's actions must have in a well-constituted republic. It followed from this principle that (for example) a right to make pre-emptive strikes had to disappear in the state of international right:

> 'If a neighbouring power which has grown to a formidable size (*potentia tremenda*) gives cause for anxiety, can one assume that it will *wish* to oppress other states because it *is able* to do so, and does this give the less powerful party a right to mount a concerted attack upon it, even if no offence has been offered?' If a state were to *let it be known* that it affirmed this maxim, it would merely bring about more surely and more quickly the very evil it feared. For the greater power would anticipate the lesser ones, and the possibility that they might unite would be but a feeble reed against one who knew how to use the tactics of *divide et impera*. Thus this maxim of political expediency, if acknowledged publicly, necessarily defeats its own purpose and is consequently unjust.[45]

And, indeed, in general the account Kant gave of the rules governing an association of this kind was broadly modelled on the German orthodox theory of the sociable *state of nature*—he had simply restricted the scope of this theory to international *society*, properly so-called.

The Hobbesianism of Kant III

Cosmopolitanism

This is an important point to stress, since the ambition of Kant in *Perpetual Peace* is often misunderstood. The rules governing the

[45] Ibid. 128.

federation which he envisaged as covering Europe were the rules which Pufendorf and his followers had proposed as general laws of nature which would govern the affairs of the sovereign and discrete states of their time. When Kant denounced the 'sorry comforters', his complaint (as we have seen) was that their 'philosophically or diplomatically formulated codes do not and cannot have the slightest *legal* force, since states as such are not subject to a common external constraint'.[46] In his account of international right, he was giving those same codes an adequate legal force, but he was not questioning their substance; his ingenious idea was that the textbooks of natural jurisprudence could be seen by a Hobbesian as the lawbooks of an international Leviathan.

We find the same thing in his admittedly sparse remarks about 'cosmopolitan right'—that is, the principles which one would believe to apply if one came to think of all human societies as in some way partaking in associative relations. This world community could not even be governed by the rules which would govern a pan-European association, let alone be a genuine world state.[47] Instead, its principles would be those which Pufendorf prescribed for the dealings of European nations with the rest of the world, being principally concerned with trade, commerce, and colonization. Kant was clear that under a regime of cosmopolitan right, the kind of European settlements which had taken place in the rest of the world would be condemned as acts of injustice. Strangers should not be turned away inhospitably; but

> if we compare with this ultimate end the *inhospitable* conduct of the civilised states of our continent, especially the commercial states, the injustice which they display in *visiting* foreign countries and people (which in their case is the same as *conquering* them) seems appallingly great. America, the negro countries, the Spice Islands, the Cape, etc. were looked upon at the time of their discovery as ownerless territories; for the native inhabitants were counted as nothing. (*Perpetual Peace*)[48]

But though this cosmopolitanism was desirable, Kant was never willing to say that it was necessary, nor to deny the continued moral

[46] *Political Writings*, 103. Kant was accepting here the conventional account in Germany of Grotius's theory. It is worth remarking that in his lectures, he recommended Vattel as the best book on international law (*Gesammelte Schriften*, XVII. 2. 2, 1392).

[47] See his remarks in 'Theory and Practice', two years earlier, in *Political Writings*, p. 90. Contrast with what he had to say in 'Perpetual Peace', ibid. 108.

[48] *Political Writings*, p. 106. See also *The Metaphysics of Morals*, §I. 62, pp. 158–9.

possibility of a more Hobbesian understanding of international affairs. Even in *Perpetual Peace* he still insisted that

> while natural right allows us to say of men living in a lawless condition that they ought to abandon it, the right of nations does not allow us to say the same of states. For as states, they already have a lawful internal constitution, and have thus outgrown the coercive right of others to subject them to a wider legal constitution in accordance with their conception of right.[49]

If states did not voluntarily recognize the principles of international and cosmopolitan right, there was nothing which other states could do to compel them, nor could the other states treat them *as if* they had acceded to the principles. In the absence of their consent, international relations would have to be conducted on Hobbesian and not Pufendorfian lines. (Although Kant does not make this clear, being, as I have said, scarcely interested in the subject, presumably this implies that cosmopolitan right does not apply unless the non-European nations in some way also acknowledge its force.) We should understand the contrast here with Pufendorf, for the essence of a Pufendorfian approach is that we are obliged to act on the basis of his laws of nations, as they are identical to the laws of nature whose obligatory power is felt by all beings in a state of nature.

I have stressed that Kant's intention was to show that a genuinely Hobbesian account of modern international relations was possible, and that Rousseau's pessimism on this score was unfounded: it was not the case that one was caught between the Scylla of a world state and the Charybdis of perpetual war. The central aspect of this claim was that the rules governing the relationship of modern states would be minimal in character, thicker (on Kant's account) than those of a Hobbesian state of nature, but much thinner than those of a civil society. That this is a plausible account of Kant's intentions is confirmed by the fact that this was very much how he was read by his first readers, especially in France.

It is well known that in *Perpetual Peace* Kant depicted himself as in some sense an enthusiast for the French revolutionary war. In it, Kant asserted that

> this idea of *federalism*, extending gradually to encompass all states and thus leading to perpetual peace, is practicable and has objective reality. For if by

[49] *Political Writings*, p. 104.

good fortune one powerful and enlightened nation can form a republic (which is by its nature inclined to seek perpetual peace), this will provide a focal point for federal association among other states. These will join up with the first one, thus securing the freedom of each state in accordance with the idea of international right, and the whole will gradually spread further and further by a series of alliances of this kind.[50]

Clearly, this 'powerful and enlightened nation' is France, and it has usually and reasonably been supposed that it was the Treaty of Basle in 1795 which is being referred to here—the treaty between Prussia and France which left the French free to annex much of the Rhineland, and which proposed the calling of a pan-European peace conference.[51]

But it has also often been supposed that *Perpetual Peace* should therefore be aligned with other works of revolutionary cosmopolitanism, defending the progress of the revolutionary armies in terms of the moral unity of mankind. However, we should be historically cautious here. It is true (as Alain Ruiz has observed) that it was *Perpetual Peace* which first caught the eye of the French revolutionaries and which led them to think that Kant was their great ally in Germany.[52] But it is important to note that while Ruiz describes this as the 'Jacobin legend', in fact much of the admiration for and interest in Kant was on the part of what one might term the 'Sieyèsians', whom the best modern scholarship wants sharply to distinguish from the Jacobins.[53] In particular, Istvan Hont has argued compellingly that one of the major divisions between Sieyèsian and Jacobin was precisely over the issue of nationalism, with the Sieyèsians holding to a Hobbesian picture of the nation state and the Jacobins expressing (at least in the years I and II)[54] a form of cosmopolitanism (pp. 206–9); the Sieyèsians, we can say, welcomed *Perpetual Peace* precisely because it was *not*

[50] *Political Writings*, 104.

[51] *Perpetual Peace* was offered to its publisher in August 1795, and Kant can therefore have taken into account all the developments in France down to that date. See *Political Writings*, p. 276.

[52] Alain Ruiz, 'Aux Origines de la Légende Jacobine de Kant en France: Le Traité vers la Paix Perpétuelle traduit et commenté dans la Presse Parisienne en 1796', *Cahiers d'Histoire Littéraire Comparée Publiés par l'Université de Metz*, 8/9 (1985), 205–22.

[53] See in particular Istvan Hont, 'The Permanent Crisis of a Divided Mankind: Contemporary Crisis of the Nation State in Historical Perspective', in John Dunn ed., *Contemporary Crisis of the Nation State?* (Oxford: Blackwell, 1995), 166–231.

[54] The Revolutionary Calendar began on 22 September 1792, when the Republic was proclaimed. L'an I was 1792–3; l'an II 1793–4. *Perpetual Peace* was published at the end of year III.

'cosmopolitan' or 'philanthropic' in the conventional eighteenth-century sense.[55]

We can see this clearly in one of the earliest Parisian responses to the work, by Adrien de Lezay-Marnesia (himself a German, and destined to be Napoleon's Prefect in Koblenz), published in Pierre-Louis Roederer's *Journal d'èconomie publique, de morale et de politique* in 1796. Roederer was a loyal follower of Sieyès, as well as being himself a keen student, and translator, of Hobbes.[56] Lezay was very clear about the essential features of the book, emphasizing that Kant founded his argument not on 'philanthropy', but on a vision of the state of nature as the state of war. Picking up on Kant's remark about the powerful and enlightened nation, he remarked (with ironic modesty) that 'I would nominate France, if she were as enlightened as she is powerful'.[57]

To see what Lezay had in mind when he contrasted Kant's Hobbesianism with philanthropy, we merely have to look at the writings of another francophile German, the notorious Anacharsis Cloots. Although most modern historians have dismissed Cloots as 'ridiculous' or 'absurd', he was taken seriously by his fellow Jacobins (and indeed fell a victim to the Terror when it began to consume its own progenitors in the year II). Cloots was the most extreme 'philanthropist' possible, famous for presenting himself at the head of a delegation from the human race to the Assembly in 1790, and he defended the war in terms

[55] Sieyès's own political theory was highly Hobbesian—see Murray Forsyth, *Reason and Revolution: The Political Thought of the Abbé Sieyès* (Leicester University Press, 1987) 66; and Hont, 'The Permanent Crisis of a Divided Mankind', p. 203. He was also sympathetic to the anti-naturalism of Rousseau; but he famously diverged from Rousseau, and from the Jacobins, over the question of representation, expressing great hostility to the idea of direct democracy. However, it is not at all clear which of these two groups was in fact the true heirs of Rousseau—the Jacobins hijacked him in the service of their cause, but on fundamental matters the Sieyèsians were often much closer to him. The question of Rousseau in the Revolution—one of the oldest topics in the modern history of political thought—still warrants further reflection in the light of the distinctions which Hont has suggested. It might also be noted that Sieyès's foreign policy in the years III–V was aimed at constructing supportive leagues of neighbouring republics, and he was later consistently associated with the attempt to construct a Franco-Prussian axis against England. See Glyndon G. van Deusen, *Sieyès: His Life and His Nationalism* (New York: Columbia University Studies in History, Economics Etc. 362, 1932), 106–29.

[56] See Hont, 'The Permanent Crisis of a Divided Mankind', p. 203, n. 79.

[57] 'Observations d'Adrien Lezay, sur le Projet de Paix Perpétuelle d'Emmanuel Kant', in Pierre-Louis Roederer, ed., *Journal d'économie publique, de morale et de politique*, I. 5, 20 vendémiaire an V, 232–44. His observation about the state of war is pp. 234–5, and about France p. 241.

of a literal cosmopolitanism. His *L'orateur du genre-humain* of 1791 advocated a genuine world state, observing that 'it is easier for a large state to be just, than a small one', and proclaimed Paris as the centre of a new world state. 'Rome was the world metropolis through warfare; Paris will be the world metropolis through peace.'[58] But, revealingly, it also contained a long footnote attacking Rousseau for his hostility to natural sociability, and expressing the author's preference for Voltaire[59]—a reminder that Voltaire, as much as or more than Rousseau, could be seen as an inspiration for the Terror.

Lezay and the other French readers seem to have thought that Kant was envisaging the kind of relationship between France and other republican states which had seemed imminent when the Revolution spilt across the Rhine—the kind of arrangement which the revolutionary 'Clubists' of Mainz (who included another admirer of Kant, Georg Forster, in their leadership) had wanted in the heady days of 1792–3 when they ran their city under the protection of French bayonets, in the first test of the Revolution in a German state.[60] Although by 1795 the Mainz experiment had failed, with the defeat of the French by the Austrians and Prussians, the Treaty of Basle (and this may be its relevance) made it clear that the Revolution would again advance to the Rhine, and allowed the Parisians in 1796 to interpret *Perpetual Peace* in the light of this advance. This seems also to have been Sieyès's view when in 1795 he suggested a new federation in Germany, 'constituted more soundly and vigorously than that erected by chance in the Gothic ages, and guaranteed by the Republic'.[61] I do not see why we should not assume that Kant intended to be read along these lines, for he must have known how the remark about a powerful and enlightened nation would be interpreted in the Europe of the year III.[62]

Although it is often supposed that Kant marked a major break with the international jurisprudence of previous generations, if his theory is read carefully one can see that, on the contrary, it represents in many

[58] Anacharsis Cloots, *L'orateur du genre-humain* (Paris, 1791), 136, 141.

[59] Ibid. 33.

[60] Ruiz draws attention to the relationship between Kant and the Clubists—'Aux origines', p. 208. See also the classic study by Jacques Droz, *L'Allemagne et la Révolution Française* (Paris, 1949).

[61] Sydney Seymour Biro, *The German Policy of Revolutionary France* (Harvard University Press, 1957), 379.

[62] It might be worth observing that Kant himself arranged for a French translation of *Perpetual Peace* to appear in 1796 from his usual publisher in Königsberg—Ruiz, 'Aux origines', p. 212 and n. 44.

ways the vindication of the ideas of Hobbes and Rousseau against their critics, and the perpetuation of those ideas into the new diplomatic world of the nineteenth century. Sieyès presided (albeit with later regret) over the *coup d'état* of General Bonaparte, and Bonapartism owed a great deal to the ideas put forward by the early French admirers of Kant; one might even say that the Bonapartist state was profoundly Hobbesian in character. It is more than a coincidence that these two heroes of the Revolution, Rousseau and Kant, were also the two most accurate and interesting Hobbesian writers of the late eighteenth century.

CONCLUSION

At the heart of this book has been the question of *autonomy*, and what the real character of an autonomous agent might be. One answer, and the answer which I have tried to explore, is suggested by the history of the word *autonomy* itself: in Greek, αὐτονομία meant literally 'having one's own laws', and it was almost always used to describe the independence of a political community—the pages of Thucydides are thick with struggles over the 'autonomy' of city states. Only rarely was it used in a wider sense—one striking case is in Sophocles' *Antigone*, when the chorus addresses Antigone: αὐτόνομος you alone of mortals while yet alive descend to Hades' (l. 821). Here, the image is human independence from the kingdom of Hades, and 'autonomy' is still a living and poetic metaphor in which a person can momentarily be depicted as a city. As I have argued in the preceding chapters, the history of autonomy is essentially a history of this metaphor being taken increasingly seriously, until in the seventeenth century a host of enormous and densely argued books appeared tracing the implications of the metaphor in copious detail. Kant's untroubled use of the term to mean moral independence (and he seems to have been one of the first people to use it extensively) was made possible by the previous one hundred and fifty years in which the parallels between states and individuals had been explored.

However, as I suggested in the first two chapters, this would not have been sufficient to give rise to the distinctive notion of the sovereign and autonomous agent which we find in the seventeenth- and eighteenth-century writers. A view of the international arena in which states had an array of thickly described obligations to one another—in which there was a genuine 'international community' resembling other human communities—would not have produced the vision of autonomous agents which actually gripped European writers four hundred years ago. That vision grew out of a sense of the world as populated by autarchic and sovereign states warily constructing temporary alliances of convenience between themselves. In Chapter 1, I argued that this was indeed what had happened by 1600, as humanist jurists explored the implications of the authentically Roman idea of international relations which they had imbibed along with the rest of Roman culture.

The roots of this story are very deep: it seems clear that the Romans did have a picture of their state which closely resembled the Renaissance version, while the Greeks were always more hesitant about it. More precisely, Greek *philosophers* were always more hesitant—as I suggested, the antithesis in this context between Greece and Rome is better thought of as an antithesis between philosophy and rhetoric. Rhetoricians by their trade were committed to taking the interests of their city as the starting point of their arguments, for they were appealing to political bodies (juries or assemblies, or princes' courts) whose *raison d'être* was the welfare of their particular community. Philosophers were equally committed to a wider view, and to addressing people in non-political contexts, as were their Christian successors. Throughout the Middle Ages, both attitudes persisted: it is a profound historical mistake to suppose that the Renaissance rediscovered the Roman literature, or even that it rediscovered its practical relevance—orators and historians had been expressing Roman ideas in the context of medieval politics for generations. What marked out the fifteenth and sixteenth centuries in Italy as special was simply that the orators no longer thought of their activity as *subsidiary* and limited to the exigencies of particular circumstances, such as the struggle for independence by a subject nation. The Roman themes could now be broadened and generalized to form a systematic alternative to the arguments of the Christian theologians.

In the case of international relations, the antithesis between humanist and theologian is captured in the antithesis between Gentili and Molina which I explored in the first two chapters. The critical difference between them, from which much else derived, was over the question of the limits on state action: for Gentili, the survival of a state was of such overriding importance that many conventional moral constraints (notably, the requirement not to strike pre-emptively on the basis of fear) did not apply to it. For Molina, on the other hand, the state had to be seen as involved from the beginning in a network of moral obligations given by a rich account of natural law, in which pre-emptive strikes were no more permitted to a state than they were to an individual. Gentili's state was already in effect the autonomous agent of the great seventeenth-century writers, governed by an extremely thin set of moral requirements—and in particular, his state was already Hobbes's man, acting on the basis of fear and striking at whatever seemed to be a threat, whether it had manifested itself as such or not.

Seen in this light, the transition from Gentili to Hobbes was straightforward: it merely needed the single extraordinary idea of Hugo Grotius, that there was no reason why an individual should not be thought of as morally identical to a state. As I argued in Chapter 3, though this is a simple idea, it required one major change in moral thinking, for it had been all but universally assumed that a state possessed one right which no individual could possibly possess: the right to sit in judgement upon and execute criminals. If the *ius gladii* could only be possessed by a properly constituted magistrate, then the way that magistrate used his sword in war could not be a meaningful analogy for a private individual. Grotius destroyed this assumption with an argument which John Locke seventy years later could still describe as a 'strange Doctrine' unacceptable to many of his contemporaries, and in the process created the characteristic form of a seventeenth- or eighteenth-century political theory, with a state of nature inhabited by jurally minimalist creatures who were to a greater or lesser extent at war with one another.

For Grotius himself, and for Locke, it was a lesser extent: the war between natural individuals had something of the pre-emptive strike about it, but mostly it was an attempt to enforce respect for each other's rights upon recalcitrant men. But for Hobbes, of course, it was a much greater extent, for Hobbes took absolutely seriously the picture of war in the humanist writers. His state of nature was peopled by agents preoccupied with their own protection, and willing to use any violence necessary in order to ensure their survival. As an account of the actual condition of international relations, particularly when qualified by Hobbes's famous observation that 'as the nature of Foule weather, lyeth not in a showre or two of rain; but in an inclination thereto of many dayes together: So the nature of War, consisteth not in actual fighting; but in the known disposition thereto',[1] this was more plausible than Grotius's—or at least, more plausible than one interpretation of Grotius (as we saw in Chapter 3, it is hard to give a definitive characterization of Grotius's ideas—in particular, the early *De Indis* is

[1] *Leviathan*, ed. Richard Tuck (Cambridge University Press, 1996) 88–9 (p. 62 of the original edn.).

much more 'Hobbesian' than *De Iure Belli ac Pacis*, and 'Hobbesian' elements lurk even in the later work, to be spotted by sharp-eyed readers such as Rousseau). But because of this plausibility, Hobbes bequeathed a critical problem to his successors, and it is part of the general argument of this book that none of them successfully solved it.

The problem arises from the conjunction of the following three propositions. The first is that there is something about the picture of the world in the humanist writers and in Hobbes which we *value*: people for many hundreds of years have been emotionally and imaginatively gripped by the sight of countries fighting for their independence from their rivals, and from larger entities which would incorporate them. The original Roman literature, populated by noble and courageous citizens sacrificing themselves in war to protect their *respublica*, was not read by generations of schoolboys for nothing (though it may be relevant that it was read by school*boys* rather than their sisters). The value people have put on this world of self-protective and independent states is evidenced by the fact that for five hundred years it has been very difficult for any serious political thinker to propose a world government: suspicion of 'universal empire' runs very deep in modern Western thinking. The second proposition is that in so far as we can have any clear sense of what a world of autonomous agents is going to be like, it will resemble this world of autonomous states protecting their independence, though in a suitably qualified and nuanced way. The third one is that domestic political regimes—structures of government—are justified as the deliberate creations of autonomous agents seeking to protect their autonomy.

The obvious implication of this last proposition is that world government should also be desirable to protect the autonomy of the agents at that level, the states: but this seems to be a deeply distasteful idea which would normally be seen as imperilling precisely the autonomy which it is supposed to protect. Why is government at the domestic level (and not just government, but the whole repertory of obligations and commitments which constitute our developed social life) not seen immediately as a similar peril to autonomous agents? How far is a conviction that we can both value autonomy and respect the richness of real social life an act of bad faith? The international arena has been the laboratory for testing liberal political ideas since their invention, and what happens in it seems to suggest that the government of real political entities is incompatible with a clear notion of human autonomy; at least one

Kantian (Robert Paul Wolff) has duly drawn the conclusion that the only genuinely Kantian political theory is anarchism, though few modern liberals have followed his lead.

As I tried to show in Chapter 7, this problem is present in both Rousseau and Kant. In Rousseau, it takes the form of a most brilliant and pessimistic critique of Hobbes. Rousseau (I argued) accepted the basic premisses of Hobbes, despite the ostensible distance between them; that is, he accepted that men are essentially self-protective and stand-offish, and that when they encounter one another their self-protective instincts will lead to emulation and conflict. But he realized that Hobbes's solution could not work, precisely because of the analogy between the state of nature and the international arena: men who sought to avoid death by creating Leviathan states would find themselves at far greater risk of death than they had faced in nature, as their states confronted each other in the circumstances of modern warfare. In his essay 'The State of War', Rousseau dazzlingly showed how the analogy between state and individual was at the imaginative as well as the theoretical heart of Hobbes, and how the Hobbesian 'man' was *really* a state all along, displaying characteristics that were usually encountered only in states, such as a constant and unforgiving striving for power.

Rousseau, as I said, was pessimistic: no solution could be expected to these problems, since neither a return to the solipsism of early man nor a global Leviathan was possible. Men would have to continue to occupy the middle ground, with its continued threat of war and destruction. But—though this is a less familiar view—in a sense Kant was a pessimist too. As I argued in Chapter 7, Kant was much more Hobbesian, and explicitly so, than has usually been recognized. Like Hobbes, he accepted that genuine human autonomy implied moral conflicts, and like Hobbes he understood that real moral conflict could only be settled by an authority which did not suppose that any party in the conflict had right on its side; a neutral government above the arena of moral debate was therefore much more central to Kant's actual ethical theory than has often been supposed, even by people who do not wish to go all the way down Robert Paul Wolff's path. As a consequence, he remained hemmed in by the Hobbesian dilemma about international relations, for (despite his popular reputation) he was as wary about a global Leviathan as any of his predecessors. No non-Hobbesian international regime was *required* on Kant's account of the matter,[2] though a minimal set of international rules might be seen by enlightened states as both desirable and compatible with their continued autonomy.

The real alternative to Hobbes present in the eighteenth century, I suggested, were the ideas found in Pufendorf and his followers. They did try very seriously to preserve some of the insights of the first generation of liberal writers without committing themselves to the account of international relations found in their predecessors. Their distinctive achievement has (ironically) been overshadowed by the success of one of their strategies, for it was an important element in their programme to establish that Grotius had not been as alarming as he seemed. By expanding the theory of natural sociability found in Grotius's *De Iure Belli ac Pacis*, they were able to recruit him to their own 'socialist' cause, so that their own originality was lessened. But as I have said, access to Grotius's manuscripts from the nineteenth century onwards has allowed us to see that in fact Grotius was closer to Hobbes than to Pufendorf. As a result, we have to treat Pufendorf as a theorist in his own right, and ask whether he succeeded in squaring this particular liberal circle.

As I suggested in Chapter 5, the best answer to this question is that he did not: Pufendorf had in effect to abandon the basic notion of individual autonomy in order to produce what we would nowadays regard as a 'liberal' approach to foreign affairs, in which states have very little basis for aggressive conduct towards one another (less, in fact, than they have on many modern views—for example, a Pufendorfian would not have sanctioned the Allied defence of Kuwait against Iraq). Pufendorf had more belief in the possibility of a rich moral life lived outside civil society than either Grotius and Hobbes, or Rousseau and Kant; but correspondingly, he had lost the sense of autonomous agents constructing their ethical environment which we find in the other writers. His work illustrates the paradox (confirmed by Locke's critique of Pufendorf) that a liberal attitude to the rules of civil society—that they are constructed by free agents and may be changed by them—is both conceptually and historically associated with international

[2] 'While natural right allows us to say of men living in a lawless condition that they ought to abandon it, the right of nations does not allow us to say the same of states. For as states, they already have a lawful internal constitution, and have thus outgrown the coercive right of others to subject them to a wider legal constitution in accordance with their conception of right.' *Political Writings*, ed. Hans Reiss (Cambridge University Press, 1991), 104. See the discussion of this passage above p. 221.

aggression, and that the more morally authoritarian views of the early eighteenth-century Germans were associated with (at least in theory) a great mildness in international relations, and a dislike of the freewheeling commercial nations which were carving up the world between them.

This contrast between Pufendorf and Hobbes, or even Locke, shows that certain practical issues have been at the heart of this story. Two in particular have dominated the account which I have been giving, both arising out of the European encounter with non-European peoples. The first, which was principally an issue in the European incursions into the highly developed trading economies of the Far East, was the question of free navigation; as we saw in Chapter 2, this was a question with a long history, for European nations had always had to sort out the juridical issues raised by navigation and trade, first among themselves and secondly with the technologically similar societies of the Far East. Although relations with the very culturally distinct peoples of the New World have caught the eye of most historians, and were indeed strange and dramatic, it is probably true to say that it was the relations with the Asiatic economies which were of greater historical importance (as Montesquieu observed, and as modern scholarship has confirmed, it was the use of American products in the Far East which rendered the first European colonies in the New World financially viable).[3] It should not therefore be surprising that it was in a book dealing with the theoretical issues thrown up by Far Eastern trade, Grotius's astonishing *De Indis*, or *De Iure Praedae*, that (I have argued) the first truly modern political theory is to be found.

But the second practical issue, the question of how to legitimate the Western agricultural colonies, *was* of great interest; and in the writings we have surveyed, we can see a distinctively modern approach to the colonies emerging as part of the new political theory. As I have emphasized throughout the book, the characteristic justification of European colonial activity in America put forward by the 'liberal' writers was the claim found most famously in Locke, but present in Grotius, Hobbes, Hutcheson, Vattel, and many others (though *not* Pufendorf), that farmers have rights in land which hunter–gatherers do not. The aboriginal peoples of North America (who were supposed not to be farmers) then turned out to be guilty of a moral crime against the European settlers

[3] See the ch. on 'The Discovery of Two New Worlds', in *The Spirit of the Laws*, Bk 21, ch. 21.

if they tried to prevent them from occupying their hunting grounds. This was of course a bizarre reversal of common-sense morality, but it would be a mistake to suppose that it was simply a cynical ploy to justify expropriation.

Governor Cotton spoke from the heart when he said in his debate with Roger Williams that 'we did not conceive that it is a just Title to so vast a Continent, to make no other improvement of millions of Acres in it, but onely to burne it up for pastime'.[4] The first settlers came from societies which lived constantly on the edge of famine and demographic collapse, and it was only with hindsight that (for example) the English colonists could have known that the famine of 1623 was the last true famine which England was ever to experience;[5] indeed, it is perfectly possible that it was the growth of the colonies which helped to eliminate famine. The idea that it was *necessary* to seize the underdeveloped temperate lands of North America—that it was literally a matter of life or death for Europeans, but was not (apparently) for the aboriginals—echoed the passage in Tacitus which Gentili and, later, Grotius cited in defence of their unusual claim: 'looking up to the Sun and Stars as if present, and within hearing, they asked them, whether they could bear to look on those uninhabited lands, and whether they would not rather pour in the Sea upon those who hindered other to settle on them'.[6]

The moral failure of the Europeans lay not so much in their adherence to this idea, as in their indifference to the facts about the North Americans—facts such as the actual prevalence of a form of agriculture among them (screened from view, often, by the circumstance that it was *women* who tilled the fields, and that their activity was promptly labelled gardening), the acute danger to the aboriginals posed by European diseases, and the inability of hunting societies to adapt to the loss of their hunting grounds. The attempt to save the lives of Europeans resulted in the mass slaughter of aboriginals on a scale far beyond even the great famines of the fourteenth century in Europe.

These issues of life and death around the world remind us that the liberal theories we have been looking at were born in a period of astonishing violence and political transformation, comparable to anything seen in the twentieth century. Their deepest subject-matter is

[4] Roger Williams, *The Complete Writings* (New York, 1963), 47.

[5] See Keith Wrightson, *English Society 1580–1680* (London: Hutchinson, 1982), 144–6.

[6] See above pp. 47 and 105.

violence, of individual against individual and state against state. But we live now in a more policed world: in international affairs it is reasonable to suppose that since the foundation of the League of Nations, and even more since the foundation of the United Nations, states no longer possess their old autonomy. In a sense, Kant has been vindicated: we can now think of international relations in precisely the same way as we think of civil society, since the international order is itself a constructed one. Indeed, public opinion has run well ahead of the juridical facts—for example, the so-called 'world community' has been pleaded in justification of many actions in recent years which it would be hard to defend on a close reading of the actual rules of the United Nations, including, most spectacularly, intervention in the internal affairs of member states.

At the same time, and in obvious association with this development, there has been a much greater willingness on the part both of philosophers and the general public to accept the existence of a wide range of moral constraints on the principles which can govern a civil society—the idea of sovereignty is unpopular both in politics and in ethics, and the dangers of the unpoliced international realm are seen as mirroring the dangers of the unpoliced civil society. So, is the long tradition of political thought which has been the subject of this book of any relevance to us any more?

The answer to this is what I suggested at the end of the Introduction, after quoting Weber's profound and gloomy observation about the link between overseas expansion and the growth of liberalism and democracy. This tradition is the richest tradition we have for thinking about human freedom. It was historically contingent, and it is as a consequence precarious—it presupposes a kind of agent whom we would not now much like to encounter. But it is important that we are clear about what autonomy meant in the days when it became the central virtue, so that we can also be clear about what we may be losing in our own time.

INDEX

Milton Keynes UK
Ingram Content Group UK Ltd.
UKHW021930181024
449751UK00016B/309

9 780199 248148